VIVA MODERN CRITICAL INTERPRETATIONS

T.S. Eliot's *The Waste Land*

Updated Edition

Edited and with an Introduction by

HAROLD BLOOM
Sterling Professor of the Humanities
Yale University

Viva Books
New Delhi | Mumbai | Chennai | Kolkata | Bengaluru | Hyderabad | Kochi | Guwahati

First Indian Edition 2008
Reprinted 2010

VIVA BOOKS PRIVATE LIMITED

- 4737/23 Ansari Road, Daryaganj, New Delhi 110 002
  E-mail: vivadelhi@vivagroupindia.net, Tel. 42242200
- 76, Service Industries, Shirvane, Sector 1, Nerul, Navi Mumbai 400 706
  E-mail: vivamumbai@vivagroupindia.net, Tel. 27721273, 27721274
- Jamals Fazal Chambers, 26 Greams Road, Chennai 600 006
  E-mail: vivachennai@vivagroupindia.net, Tel. 28290304, 28294241
- B-103, Jindal Towers, 21/1A/3 Darga Road, Kolkata 700 017
  E-mail: vivakolkata@vivagroupindia.net, Tel. 22836381, 22816713
- 7, Sovereign Park Apartments, 56-58, K. R. Road, Basavanagudi, Bangalore 560 004
  E-mail: vivabangalore@vivagroupindia.net, Tel. 26607409, 26607410
- 101-102 Mughal Marc Apartments, 3-4-637 to 641, Narayanguda, Hyderabad 500 029
  E-mail: vivahyderabad@vivagroupindia.net, Tel. 27564481, 27564482
- Beevi Towers, First Floor, SRM Road, Kaloor, Kochi 682 018, Kerala
  E-mail: vivakochi@vivagroupindia.net, Tel: 0484-2403055, 2403056
- 232, GNB Road, Beside UCO Bank, Silpukhuri, Guwahati 781 003
  E-mail: vivaguwahati@vivagroupindia.net, Tel: 0361-2666386

www.vivagroupindia.com

Published by arrangement with

Facts on File, Inc.
132 West 31st Street
New York 10001
USA

ISBN : 978-81-309-0468-9

Published by Vinod Vasishtha for Viva Books Private Limited, 4737/23, Ansari Road, Daryaganj, New Delhi-110 002. Printed and bound by Anand Sons, Delhi - 110092.

L0000

Contents

Editor's Note

My introduction amiably locates the authentic precursor of *The Waste Land* in the greatest and most American of all our poets, Walt Whitman.

Hugh Kenner, high priest of what now should be termed antiquarian Modernism, sees Eliot's brief epic as lamenting the Death of Europe, which to me seems part of the original insight of Whitman.

In a brilliant essay, Eleanor Cook maps *The Waste Land* as the junction of London, the Roman Mediterranean, and India, since Eliot combines all these in his cultural vision.

Something of the inevitable (though slow to develop) realization that *The Waste Land* was Whitmanian, in its own despite, is glimpsed by James E. Miller, after which Gregory S. Jay gives a general sense of Eliot's proto-Catholic version of his precursors.

Intricately, Cleo McNelly Kearns unweaves the Whitmanian and Hindu threads in the poem.

A belated Modernist defender of Eliot, Louis Menand, shrewdly sees the poet as having created his own work through a fruitful misunderstanding of French (supposed) models, after which James Longenbach subtly wonders whether the quite Paterian *Waste Land* might after all have been the last Modernist poem.

Wayne Koestenbaum, with ironically authentic charm, sees Ezra Pound as having revised Eliot's "feminine" poem into masculinity, while Eric W. Sigg detects *The Waste Land*'s pattern of making its interpreter into a voyager.

In this volume's final essay Jo Ellen Green Kaiser considers the importance of Eliot's notes.

HAROLD BLOOM

Introduction

In his essay, "The *Pensées* of Pascal" (1931), Eliot remarked upon Pascal's adversarial relation to his true precursor, Montaigne:

> One cannot destroy Pascal, certainly; but of all authors Montaigne is one of the least destructible. You could as well dissipate a fog by flinging hand-grenades into it. For Montaigne is a fog, a gas, a fluid, insidious element. He does not reason, he insinuates, charms, and influences.

Walt Whitman, too, is "a fluid, insidious element," a poet who "insinuates, charms, and influences." And he is the darkest of poets, despite his brazen self-advertisements, and his passionate hopes for his nation. *Song of Myself*, for all its joyous epiphanies, chants also of the waste places:

> Of the turbid pool that lies in the autumn forest,
> Of the moon that descends the steeps of the
> soughing twilight,
> Toss, sparkles of day and dusk—toss on the
> black stems that decay in the muck,
> Toss to the moaning gibberish of the dry limbs.

No deep reader of Whitman could forget the vision of total self-rejection that is the short poem, "A Hand-Mirror":

Hold it up sternly—see this it sends back, (who is
it? is it you?)
Outside fair costume, within ashes and filth,
No more a flashing eye, no more a sonorous voice
or springy step,
Now some slave's eye, voice, hands, step,
A drunkard's breath, unwholesome eater's face,
venerealee's flesh,
Lungs rotting away piecemeal, stomach sour and
cankerous,
Joints rheumatic, bowels clogged with abomination,
Blood circulating dark and poisonous streams,
Words babble, hearing and touch callous,
No brain, no heart left, no magnetism of sex;
Such from one look in this looking-glass ere you go
hence,
Such a result so soon—and from such a beginning!

Rather than multiply images of despair in Whitman, I turn to the most rugged of his self-accusations, in the astonishing "Crossing Brooklyn Ferry":

It is not upon you alone the dark patches fall,
The dark threw its patches down upon me also,
The best I had done seem'd to me blank and suspicious,
My great thoughts as I supposed them, were they not
in reality meagre?
Nor is it you alone who know what it is to be evil,
I am he who knew what it was to be evil,
I too knotted the old knot of contrariety,
Blabb'd, blush'd, resented, lied, stole, grudg'd,
Had guile, anger, lust, hot wishes I dared not speak,
Was wayward, vain, greedy, shallow, sly, cowardly,
malignant,
The wolf, the snake, the hog, not wanting in me,
The cheating look, the frivolous word, the adulterous
wish, not wanting,
Refusals, hates, postponements, meanness, laziness,
none of these wanting,
Was one with the rest, the days and haps of the rest,
Was call'd by my nighest name by clear loud voices of young
men as they saw me approaching or passing,

Felt their arms on my neck as I stood, or the negligent
leaning of their flesh against me as I sat,
Saw many I loved in the street or ferry-boat or public
assembly, yet never told them a word,
Lived the same life with the rest, the same old
laughing, gnawing, sleeping,
Play'd the part that still looks back on the actor or
actress,
The same old role, the role that is what we make it, as
great as we like,
Or as small as we like, or both great and small.

The barely concealed allusions to Milton's Satan and to *King Lear* strengthen Whitman's catalog of vices and evasions, preparing the poet and his readers for the darker intensities of the great *Sea-Drift* elegies and "Lilacs," poems that are echoed everywhere in Eliot's verse, but particularly in "The Death of Saint Narcissus," *The Waste Land*, and "The Dry Salvages." Many critics have charted these allusions, but I would turn consideration of Eliot's agon with Whitman to the question: "Why Whitman?" It is poetically unwise to go down to the waterline, or go to the headland with Walt Whitman, for then the struggle takes place in an arena where the poet who found his identifying trope in the sea-drift cannot lose.

An answer must be that the belated poet does not choose his trial by landscape or seascape. It is chosen for him by his precursor. Browning's quester in "Childe Roland to the Dark Tower Came" is as overdetermined by Shelley as Eliot is overdetermined by Whitman in *The Waste Land*, which is indeed Eliot's version of "Childe Roland," as it is Eliot's version of Percivale's quest in Tennyson's "The Holy Grail," a poem haunted by Keats in the image of Galahad. "Lilacs" is everywhere in *The Waste Land*: in the very lilacs bred out of the dead land, in the song of the hermit thrush in the pine trees, and most remarkably in the transumption of Whitman walking down to where the hermit thrush sings, accompanied by two companions walking beside him, the thought of death and the knowledge of death:

Then with the knowledge of death as walking one
side of me,
And the thought of death close-walking the other
side of me,
And I in the middle as with companions, and as
holding the hands of companions,

I fled forth to the hiding receiving night that talks
not,
Down to the shores of the water, the path by the
swamp in the dimness,
To the solemn shadowy cedars and ghostly pines so
still.

The "crape-veil'd women" singing their dirges through the night for Lincoln are hardly to be distinguished from Eliot's "murmur of maternal lamentation," and Whitman's "tolling tolling bells' perpetual clang" goes on tolling reminiscent bells in *The Waste Land* as it does in "The Dry Salvages." Yet all this is only a first-level working of the influence process, of interest mostly as a return of the repressed. Deeper, almost beyond analytical modes as yet available to criticism, is Eliot's troubled introjection of his nation's greatest and inescapable elegiac poet. "Lilacs" has little to do with the death of Lincoln but everything to do with Whitman's ultimate poetic crisis, beyond which his strongest poetry will cease. *The Waste Land* has little to do with neo-Christian polemics concerning the decline of Western culture, and everything to do with a poetic crisis that Eliot could not quite surmount, in my judgment, since I do not believe that time will confirm the estimate that most contemporary critics have made of *Four Quartets*.

The decisive moment or negative epiphany of Whitman's elegy centers upon his giving up of the tally, the sprig of lilac that is the synecdoche for his image of poetic voice, which he yields up to death and to the hermit thrush's song of death. Eliot's parallel surrender in "What the Thunder Said" is to ask "what have we given?," where the implicit answer is "a moment's surrender," a negative moment in which the image of poetic voice is achieved only as one of Whitman's "retrievements out of the night."

In his essay on Pascal, Eliot says of Montaigne, a little resentfully but with full accuracy, that "he succeeded in giving expression to the skepticism of *every* human being," presumably including Pascal, and Shakespeare, and even T. S. Eliot. What did Whitman succeed in expressing with equal universality? Division between "myself" and "the real me" is surely the answer. Walt Whitman, one of the roughs, an American, is hardly identical with "the Me myself" who:

Looks with its sidecurved head curious what will come
next,
Both in and out of the game, and watching and
wondering at it.

Thomas Stearns Eliot, looking with side-curved head, both in and out of the game, has little in common with Walt Whitman, one of the roughs, an American, yet almost can be identified with that American "Me myself."

The line of descent from Shelley and Keats through Browning and Tennyson to Pound and Eliot would be direct, were it not for the intervention of the genius of the shores of America, the poet of *Leaves of Grass*. Whitman enforces upon Pound and Eliot the American difference, which he had inherited from Emerson, the fountain of our eloquence and of our pragmatism. Most reductively defined, the American poetic difference ensues from a sense of acute isolation, both from an overwhelming space of natural reality, and from an oppressive temporal conviction of belatedness, of having arrived after the event. The inevitable defense against nature is the Gnostic conviction that one is no part of the creation, that one's freedom is invested in the primal abyss. Against belatedness, defense involves an immersion in allusiveness, hardly for its own sake, but in order to reverse the priority of the cultural, pre-American past. American poets from Whitman and Dickinson onwards are more like Milton than Milton is, and so necessarily they are more profoundly Miltonic than even Keats or Tennyson was compelled to be.

What has wasted the land of Eliot's elegiac poem is neither the malady of the Fisher King nor the decline of Christianity, and Eliot's own psychosexual sorrows are not very relevant either. The precursors' strength is the illness of *The Waste Land*; Eliot after all can promise to show us "fear in a handful of dust" only because the monologist of Tennyson's *Maud* already has cried out: "Dead, long dead, / Long dead! / And my heart is a handful of dust." Even more poignantly, Eliot is able to sum up all of Whitman's extraordinary "As I Ebb'd with the Ocean of Life" in the single line: "These fragments I have shored against my ruins," where the fragments are not only the verse paragraphs that constitute the text of *The Waste Land*, but crucially are also Whitman's floating sea-drift:

> Me and mine, loose windrows, little corpses,
> Froth, snowy white, and bubbles,
> (See, from my dead lips the ooze exuding at last,
> See, the prismatic colors glistening and rolling,)
> Tufts of straw, sands, fragments,
> Buoy'd hither from many moods, one contradicting
>   another.
> From the storm, the long calm, the darkness, the swell,

Musing, pondering, a breath, a briny tear, a dab of
 liquid or soil,
Up just as much out of fathomless workings fermented
 and thrown,
A limp blossom or two, torn, just as much over waves
 floating, drifted at random,
Just as much for us that sobbing dirge of Nature,
Just as much whence we come that blare of the cloud—
 trumpets,
We, capricious, brought hither we know not whence,
 spread out before you,
You up there walking or sitting,
Whoever you are, we too lie in drifts at your feet.

"Tufts of straw, sands, fragments" are literally "shored" against Whitman's ruins, as he wends "the shores I know," the shores of America to which, Whitman said, Emerson had led all of us, Eliot included. Emerson's essays, Eliot pugnaciously remarked, "are already an encumbrance," and so they were, and are, and evermore must be for an American writer, but inescapable encumbrances are also stimuli, as Pascal learned in regard to the overwhelming Montaigne.

HUGH KENNER

The Waste Land

This dust will not settle in our time.
—Samuel Beckett

i

The Waste Land was drafted during a rest cure at Margate ("I can connect Nothing with nothing") and Lausanne ("In this decayed hole among the mountains") during the autumn of 1921 by a convalescent preoccupied partly with the ruin of post-war Europe, partly with his own health and the conditions of his servitude to a bank in London, partly with a hardly exorable apprehension that two thousand years of European continuity had for the first time run dry. It had for epigraph a phrase from Conrad's *Heart of Darkness* ("The horror! The horror!"); embedded in the text were a glimpse, borrowed from Conrad's opening page, of the red sails of barges drifting in the Thames Estuary, and a contrasting reference to "the heart of light." "Nothing is easier," Conrad had written, "... than to evoke the great spirit of the past upon the lower reaches of the Thames."

In Paris that winter, Ezra Pound has recalled, "*The Waste Land* was placed before me as a series of poems. I advised him what to leave out." Eliot, from about the same distance of time, recalls showing Pound "a sprawling chaotic poem ... which left his hands, reduced to about half its size, in the

---

form in which it appears in print." Since "the form in which it appears in print," with its many sudden transitions and its implication, inhering in tone and cross-references and reinforced by notes, of a center of gravity nowhere explicitly located, remained for many years the most sensational aspect of *The Waste Land*, this transaction requires looking into. The manuscript with the Conrad epigraph and Pound's blue-pencilling has been lost sight of; John Quinn appears to have made a private bestowal of it before his collection was dispersed in 1924. From surviving clues—chiefly three letters that passed between Pound and Eliot in the winter of 1921–1922—one may hazard guesses concerning the nature of the original series.

The letters, though they were exchanged after the major operation on the poem had been performed, disclose Eliot still in the act of agonizing not only about residual verbal details but about the desirability of adding or suppressing whole sections. "There were long passages in different metres, with short lyrics sandwiched in between," he has since recalled. The long passages included "a rather poor pastiche of Pope," which was presumably the occasion of Pound's dictum, elsewhere recorded, that pastiche is only justified if it is better than the original; "another passage about a fashionable lady having breakfast in bed, and another long passage about a shipwreck, which was obviously inspired by the Ulysses episode in the *Inferno*." This would have led up to the "death by water" of the "drowned Phoenician sailor"; Victor Bérard's speculations concerning the possible origin of the *Odyssey* in Phoenician *periploi* had been in print for twenty years and had occupied the attention of James Joyce. The deletion of these passages was apparently accepted without protest. The lyrics, on the other hand, contained elements Eliot struggled to preserve. After they have been removed from the body of *The Waste Land* he proposes putting them at the end, and is again dissuaded: "The thing now runs from 'April ...' to 'shantih' without a break. That is 19 pages, and let us say the longest poem in the English langwidge. Don't try to bust all records by prolonging it three pages further." One of the lyrics contained a "sweats with tears" passage which Eliot, after deletion from its original context, proposed working into the "nerves monologue: only place where it can go." Pound vetoed it again: "I dare say the sweats with tears will wait." It didn't wait long; we find it in a poem contributed pseudonymously to Wyndham Lewis' *Tyro* a little before the publication of *The Waste Land*, and later revised for publication in a triad of *Dream Songs*, all three of which may have descended from the *ur-Waste Land*.[1] Pound also dissuaded Eliot from installing *Gerontion* as a prelude to the sequence, forebade him to delete "Phlebas the Phoenician," and nagged about the Conrad epigraph until a better one was discovered in Petronius.

These events are worth reconstructing because they clarify a number of things about the scope and intention of the poem. It was conceived as a somewhat loose medley, as the relief of more diffuse impulses than those to which its present compacted form corresponds. The separate preservation of the *Dream Songs* and the incorporation of some of their motifs, after much trial and error, into what is now *The Hollow Men*, testifies to Eliot's stubborn conviction that there was virtue in some of the omitted elements, whether or not their presence could be justified within the wholeness, not at first foreseen by the author, which the greater part of *The Waste Land* at length assumed. That wholeness, since it never did incorporate everything the author wanted it to, was to some extent a compromise, gotten by permu ing with another's assistance materials he no longer had it in him to rethink; and finally, after Pound, by simply eliminating everything not of the first intensity, had revealed an unexpected corporate substantiality in what survived, Eliot's impulse was to "explain" the poem as "thoughts of a dry brain in a dry season" by prefixing *Gerontion.*

That is to say, the first quality of *The Waste Land* to catch a newcomer's attention, its self-sufficient juxtaposition without copulae of themes and passages in a dense mosaic, had at first a novelty which troubled even the author. It was a quality arrived at by Pound's cutting; it didn't trouble Pound, who had already begun work on *The Cantos*. But Eliot, preoccupied as always with the seventeenth-century drama and no doubt tacitly encouraged by the example of Browning, naturally conceived a long poem as somebody's spoken or unspoken monologue, its shifts of direction and transition from theme to theme psychologically justified by the workings of the speaker's brain. *Prufrock* and *Gerontion* elucidate not only a phase of civilization but a perceiving—for the purpose of the poem, a presiding—consciousness. For anyone who has undergone immersion in the delicate phenomenology of Francis Herbert Bradley, in fact, it is meaningless to conceive of a presentation that cannot be resolved into an experienced content and a "finite center" which experiences. The perceiver is describable only as the zone of consciousness where that which he perceives can coexist; but the perceived, conversely, can't be accorded independent status; it is, precisely, all that can coexist in this particular zone of consciousness. In a loose sequence of poems these considerations need give no trouble; the pervading zone of consciousness is that of the author: as we intuit Herrick in *Hesperides*, or Herbert in *The Temple*. But a five-parted work of 434 lines entitled *The Waste Land*, with sudden wrenching juxtapositions, thematic links between section and section, fragments quoted from several languages with no one present to whose mind they can occur: this dense textural unity, as queer as *Le Sacre du Printemps*, must have seemed to Eliot a little factitious until he had gotten used to the poem in its final form; which, as everyone who has encountered it knows, must take some time. So we discover him endeavoring to square the artistic fact with his pervasive intuition of fitness by the note on Tiresias, which offers to supply the poem with a nameable point of view:

> Tiresias, although a mere spectator and not indeed a "character," is yet the most important personage in the poem, uniting all the rest. Just as the one-eyed merchant, seller of currants, melts into the Phoenician Sailor, and the latter is not wholly distinct from Ferdinand Prince of Naples, so all the women are one woman, and the two sexes meet in Tiresias. What Tiresias sees, in fact, is the substance of the poem.

If we take this note as an afterthought, a token placation, say, of the ghost of Bradley, rather than as elucidative of the assumption under which the writing was originally done, our approach to *The Waste Land* will be facilitated. In fact we shall do well to discard the notes as much as possible; they have bedeviled discussion for decades.

The writing of the notes was a last complication in the fractious history of the poem's composition; it is doubtful whether any other acknowledged masterpiece has been so heavily marked, with the author's consent, by forces outside his control. The notes got added to *The Waste Land* as a consequence of the technological fact that books are printed in multiples of thirty-two pages.

The poem, which had appeared without any annotation whatever in *The Criterion* and in the *Dial* (October and November, 1922, respectively), was in book form too long for thirty-two pages of decent-sized print and a good deal too short for sixty-four. So Eliot (at length disinclined, fortunately, to insert *Gerontion* as a preface or to append the cancelled lyrics) set to work to expand a few notes in which he had identified the quotations, "with a view to spiking the guns of critics of my earlier poems who had accused me of plagiarism."[2] He dilated on the Tarot Pack, copied out nineteen lines from Ovid and thirty-three words from Chapman's *Handbook of Birds of Eastern North America*, recorded his evaluation of the interior of the Church of St. Magnus Martyr, saluted the late Henry Clarke Warren as one of the great pioneers of Buddhist studies in the Occident, directed the reader's attention to a hallucination recorded on one of the Antarctic expeditions ("I forget which, but I think one of Shackleton's"), and eventually, with the aid of quotations from Froude, Bradley, and Hermann Hesse's *Blick ins Chaos*, succeeded in padding the thing out to a suitable length. The keying of these items to specific passages by the academic device of numbering lines—hence

Eliot's pleasantry, twenty-four years later, about "bogus scholarship"—may be surmised to have been done in haste: early in *What the Thunder Said* a line was missed in the counting. "I have sometimes thought," Eliot has said, "of getting rid of these notes; but now they can never be unstuck. They have had almost greater popularity than the poem itself.... It was just, no doubt, that I should pay my tribute to the work of Miss Jessie Weston; but I regret having sent so many enquirers off on a wild goose chase after Tarot cards and the Holy Grail." We have license therefore to ignore them, and instead "endeavour to grasp what the poetry is aiming to be ... to grasp its entelechy."

That the entelechy is graspable without source-hunting, and without even appeal to any but the most elementary knowledge of one or two myths and a few Shakespearean tags, is a statement requiring temerity to sustain in the face of all the scholarship that has been expended during a third of a century on these 434 lines. It inheres, however, in Dr. Leavis' admirably tactful account of the poem in *New Bearings*, and in Pound's still earlier testimony. In 1924 Pound rebutted a piece of reviewer's acrimony with the flat statement that the poem's obscurities were reducible to four Sanskrit words, three of which are

> so implied in the surrounding text that one can pass them by ... without losing the general tone or the main emotion of the passage. They are so obviously the words of some ritual or other.

[One does need to be told that "shantih" means peace."]

> For the rest, I saw the poem in typescript, and I did not see the notes till 6 or 8 months afterward; and they have not increased my enjoyment of the poem one atom. The poem seems to me an emotional unit....
>
> I have not read Miss Weston's *Ritual to Romance*, and do not at present intend to. As to the citations, I do not think it matters a damn which is from Day, which from Milton, Middleton, Webster, or Augustine. I mean so far as the functioning of the poem is concerned. One's incult pleasure in reading *The Waste Land* would be the same if Webster had written "Women Before Woman" and Marvell the *Metamorphoses*.

His parting shot deserves preservation:

> This demand for clarity in every particular of a work, whether essential or not, reminds me of the Pre-Raphaelite painter who

was doing a twilight scene but rowed across the river in day time to see the shape of the leaves on the further bank, which he then drew in with full detail.

ii

A Game of Chess is a convenient place to start our investigations. Chess is played with Queens and Pawns: the set of pieces mimics a social hierarchy, running from "The Chair she sat in, like a burnished throne," to "Goonight Bill. Goonight Lou. Goonight May. Goonight." It is a silent unnerving warfare

(“Speak to me. Why do you never speak. Speak.
“What are you thinking of? What thinking? What?
“I never know what you are thinking. Think.”)

in which everything hinges on the welfare of the King, the weakest piece on the board, and in this section of the poem invisible (though a "barbarous king" once forced Philomel.) Our attention is focused on the Queen.

The Chair she sat in, like a burnished throne,
Glowed on the marble, where the glass
Held up by standards wrought with fruited vines
From which a golden Cupidon peeped out
(Another hid his eyes behind his wing)
Doubled the flames of sevenbranched candelabra
Reflecting light upon the table as
The glitter of her jewels rose to meet it,
From satin cases poured in rich profusion....

This isn't a Miltonic sentence, brilliantly contorted; it lacks nerve, forgetting after ten words its confident opening ("The Chair she sat in") to dissipate itself among glowing and smouldering sensations, like a progression of Wagner's. Cleopatra "o'erpicturing that Venus where we see / The fancy outwork nature") sat outdoors; this Venusberg interior partakes of "an atmosphere of Juliet's tomb," and the human inhabitant appears once, in a perfunctory subordinate clause. Pope's Belinda conducted "the sacred rites of pride"—

This casket India's glowing gems unlocks,
And all Arabia breathes from yonder box.

The woman at the dressing-table in *The Waste Land*, implied but never named or attended to, is not like Belinda the moral center of an innocent dislocation of values, but simply the implied sensibility in which these multifarious effects dissolve and find congruence. All things deny nature; the fruited vines are carved, the Cupidons golden, the light not of the sun, the perfumes synthetic, the candelabra (seven-branched, as for an altar) devoted to no rite, the very color of the fire-light perverted by sodium and copper salts. The dolphin is carved, and swims in a "sad light," not, like Antony's delights, "showing his back above the element he lives in."

No will to exploit new sensations is present; the will has long ago died; this opulent ambience is neither chosen nor questioned. The "sylvan scene" is not Eden nor a window but a painting, and a painting of an unnatural event:

> The change of Philomel, by the barbarous king
> So rudely forced; yet there the nightingale
> Filled all the desert with inviolable voice
> And still she cried, and still the world pursues,
> "Jug Jug" to dirty ears.

Her voice alone, like the voice that modulates the thick fluid of this sentence, is "inviolable"; like Tiresias in Thebes, she is prevented from identifying the criminal whom only she can name. John Lyly wrote down her song more than two centuries before Keats (who wasn't interested in what she was saying):

> What bird so sings yet so dos wayle?
> O 'Tis the ravishd Nightingale.
> Jug, Jug, Jug, tereu, shee cryes,
> And still her woes at Midnight rise.
> Brave prick song! ...

Lyly, not being committed to the idea that the bird was pouring forth its soul abroad, noted that it stuck to its script ("prick song") and himself attempted a transcription. Lyly of course is perfectly aware of what she is trying to say: "tereu" comes very close to "Tereus." It remained for the nineteenth century to dissolve her plight into a symbol of diffuse *Angst*, indeed to impute "ecstasy" amid human desolation, "here, where men sit and hear each other groan"; and for the twentieth century to hang up a painting of the event on a dressing-room wall, as pungent sauce to appetites jaded with the narrative clarity of mythologies, but responsive to the visceral thrill and the pressures of "significant form." The picture, a "withered stump of time," hangs there, one item in a collection that manages to be not edifying but sinister:

> staring forms
> Leaned out, leaning, hushing the room enclosed.

Then the visitor, as always in Eliot, mounts a stairway—

> Footsteps shuffled on the stair.

—and we get human conversation at last:

> "What is that noise?"
> The wind under the door.
> "What is that noise now? What is the wind doing?"
> Nothing again nothing.
> "Do
> "You know nothing? Do you see nothing? Do you remember
> "Nothing?"
> I remember
> Those are pearls that were his eyes.

"My experience falls within my own circle, a circle closed on the outside; and, with all its elements alike, every sphere is opaque to the others which surround it." What is there to say but "nothing"? He remembers a quotation, faintly apposite; in this room the European past, effects and *objets d'art* gathered from many centuries, has suffered a sea-change, into something rich and strange, and stifling. Sensibility here is the very inhibition of life; and activity is reduced to the manic capering of "that Shakespeherian Rag," the past imposing no austerity, existing simply to be used.

> "What shall we do tomorrow?
> "What shall we ever do?"
> The hot water at ten.
> And if it rains, a closed car at four.
> And we shall play a game of chess,
> Pressing lidless eyes and waiting for a knock upon the door.

If we move from the queens to the pawns, we find low life no more free or natural, equally obsessed with the denial of nature, artificial teeth, chemically procured abortions, the speaker and her interlocutor battening fascinated at second-hand on the life of Lil and her Albert, Lil and Albert interested only in spurious ideal images of one another

(He'll want to know what you done with that money he gave you
To get yourself some teeth....
He said, I swear, I can't bear to look at you.)

And this point—nature everywhere denied, its ceremonies simplified to the brutal abstractions of a chess-game

(He's been in the army four years, he wants a good time,
And if you don't give it him, there's others will, I said.
Oh is there, she said. Something o' that, I said.
Then I'll know who to thank, she said, and give me a straight look.)

—this point is made implicitly by a device carried over from *Whispers of Immortality*, the juxtaposition without comment or copula of two levels of sensibility: the world of one who reads Webster with the world of one who knows Grishkin, the world of the inquiring wind and the sense drowned in odors with the world of ivory teeth and hot gammon. In Lil and Albert's milieu there is fertility, in the milieu where golden Cupidons peep out there is not; but Lil and Albert's breeding betokens not a harmony of wills but only Albert's improvident refusal to leave Lil alone. The chemist with commercial impartiality supplies one woman with "strange synthetic perfumes" and the other with "them pills I took, to bring it off," aphrodisiacs and abortifacients; he is the tutelary deity, uniting the offices of Cupid and Hymen, of a world which is under a universal curse.

From this vantage-point we can survey the methods of the first section, which opens with a denial of Chaucer:

Whan that Aprille with his shoures soote
The droughte of March hath perced to the roote
And bathed every veyne in swich licour
Of which vertu engendred is the flour....
Thanne longen folk to goon on pilgrimages.

In the twentieth-century version we have a prayer-book heading, *The Burial of the Dead*, with its implied ceremonial of dust thrown and of souls reborn; and the poem begins,

April is the cruellest month, breeding
Lilacs out of the dead land, mixing
Memory and desire, stirring
Dull roots with spring rain.

No "vertu" is engendered amid this apprehensive reaching forward of participles, and instead of pilgrimages we have European tours:

> we stopped in the colonnade,
> And went on in sunlight, into the Hofgarten,
> And drank coffee, and talked for an hour.

Up out of the incantation breaks a woman's voice, giving tongue to the ethnological confusions of the new Europe, the subservience of *patria* to the whim of statesmen, the interplay of immutable fact and national pride:

> Bin gar keine Russin, stamm' aus Litauen, echt deutsch.

—a mixing of memory and desire. Another voice evokes the vanished Austro-Hungarian Empire, the inbred malaise of Mayerling, regressive thrills, objectless travels:

> And when we were children, staying at the archduke's,
> My cousin's, he took me out on a sled,
> And I was frightened. He said, Marie,
> Marie, hold on tight. And down we went.
> In the mountains, there you feel free.
> I read, much of the night, and go south in the winter.

"In the mountains, there you feel free." We have only to delete "there" to observe the collapse of more than a rhythm: to observe how the line's exact mimicry of a fatigue which supposes it has reached some ultimate perception can telescope spiritual bankruptcy, deracinated ardor, and an illusion of liberty which is no more than impatience with human society and relief at a temporary change. It was a restless, pointless world that collapsed during the war, agitated out of habit but tired beyond coherence, on the move to avoid itself. The memories in lines 8 to 18 seem spacious and precious now; then, the events punctuated a terrible continuum of boredom.

The plight of the Sibyl in the epigraph rhymes with that of Marie; the terrible thing is to be compelled to stay alive. "For I with these my own eyes have seen the Cumaean Sibyl hanging in a jar; and when the boys said, 'What do you want, Sibyl?' she answered, 'I want to die.' The sentence is in a macaronic Latin, posterior to the best age, pungently sauced with Greek; Cato would have contemplated with unblinking severity Petronius' readers' jazz-age craving for the cosmopolitan. The Sibyl in her better days answered questions by flinging from her cave handfuls of leaves bearing letters which the postulant was required to arrange in a suitable order; the wind commonly blew half of them away. Like Tiresias, like Philomel, like the modern poet, she divulged forbidden knowledge only in riddles, fitfully. (Tiresias wouldn't answer Oedipus at all; and he put off Odysseus with a puzzle about an oar mistaken for a winnowing-fan.) *The Waste Land* is suffused with a functional obscurity, sibylline fragments so disposed as to yield the utmost in connotative power, embracing the fragmented present and reaching back to "that vanished mind of which our mind is a continuation." As for the Sibyl's present exhaustion, she had foolishly asked Apollo for as many years as the grains of sand in her hand; which is one layer in the multi-layered line, "I will show you fear in a handful of dust." She is the prophetic power, no longer consulted by heroes but tormented by curious boys, still answering because she must; she is Madame Sosostris, consulted by dear Mrs. Equitone and harried by police ("One must be so careful these days"); she is the image of the late phase of Roman civilization, now vanished; she is also "the mind of Europe," a mind more important than one's own private mind, a mind which changes but abandons nothing en route, not superannuating either Shakespeare, or Homer, or the rock drawing of the Magdalenian draughtsmen; but now very nearly exhausted by the effort to stay interested in its own contents.

Which brings us to the "heap of broken images": not only desert ruins of some past from which life was withdrawn with the failure of the water supply, like the Roman cities in North Africa, or Augustine's Carthage, but also the manner in which Shakespeare, Homer, and the drawings of Michelangelo, Raphael, and the Magdalenian draughtsmen coexist in the contemporary cultivated consciousness: fragments, familiar quotations: *poluphloisboio thalasse*, to be or not to be, undo this button, one touch of nature, etc., God creating the Sun and Moon, those are pearls that were his eyes. For one man who knows *The Tempest* intimately there are a thousand who can identify the lines about the cloud-capp'd towers; painting is a miscellany of reproductions, literature a potpourri of quotations, history a chaos of theories and postures (Nelson's telescope, Washington crossing the Delaware, government of, for and by the people, the Colosseum, the guillotine). A desert wind has blown half the leaves away; disuse and vandals have broken the monuments—

> What are the roots that clutch, what branches grow
> Out of this stony rubbish? Son of man,
> You cannot say, or guess, for you know only
> A heap of broken images, where the sun beats,
> And the dead tree gives no shelter, the cricket no relief,
> And the dry stone no sound of water....

Cities are built out of the ruins of previous cities, as *The Waste Land* is built out of the remains of older poems. But at this stage no building is yet in question; the "Son of man" (a portentously generalizing phrase) is moving tirelessly eastward, when the speaker accosts him with a sinister "Come in under the shadow of this red rock," and offers to show him not merely horror and desolation but something older and deeper: fear.

Hence the hyacinth girl, who speaks with urgent hurt simplicity, like the mad Ophelia:

"You gave me hyacinths first a year ago;
They called me the hyacinth girl."

They are childlike words, self-pitying, spoken perhaps in memory, perhaps by a ghost, perhaps by a wistful woman now out of her mind. The response exposes many contradictory layers of feeling:

—Yet when we came back, late, from the Hyacinth garden,
Your arms full, and your hair wet, I could not
Speak, and my eyes failed, I was neither
Living nor dead, and I knew nothing,
Looking into the heart of light, the silence.

The context is erotic, the language that of mystical experience: plainly a tainted mysticism. "The Hyacinth garden" sounds queerly like a lost cult's sacred grove, and her arms were no doubt full of flowers; what rite was there enacted or evaded we can have no means of knowing.

But another level of meaning is less ambiguous: perhaps in fantasy, the girl has been drowned. Five pages later *A Game of Chess* ends with Ophelia's words before her death; Ophelia gathered flowers before she tumbled into the stream, then lay and chanted snatches of old tunes—

Frisch weht der Wind
Der Heimat zu...

while her clothes and hair spread out on the waters. *The Burial of the Dead* ends with a sinister dialogue about a corpse in the garden—

Has it begun to sprout? Will it bloom this year?
Or has the sudden frost disturbed its bed?

—two Englishmen discussing their tulips, with a note of the terrible intimacy with which murderers imagine themselves being taunted. The traditional British murderer—unlike his American counterpart, who in a vast land instinctively puts distance between himself and the corpse—prefers to keep it near at hand; in the garden, or behind the wainscoting, or

> bones cast in a little low dry garret,
> Rattled by the rat's foot only, year to year.

The *Fire Sermon* opens with despairing fingers clutching and sinking into a wet bank; it closes with Thames-daughters singing from beneath the oily waves. The drowned Phlebas in Section IV varies this theme; and at the close of the poem the response to the last challenge of the thunder alludes to something that happened in a boat:

> your heart would have responded
> Gaily, when invited, beating obedient
> To controlling hands

—but what in fact did happen we are not told; perhaps nothing, or perhaps the hands assumed another sort of control.

In *The Waste Land* as in *The Family Reunion*, the guilt of the protagonist seems coupled with his perhaps imagined responsibility for the fate of a perhaps ideally drowned woman.

> One thinks to escape
> By violence, but one is still alone
> In an over-crowded desert, jostled by ghosts.

(Ghosts that beckon us under the shadow of some red rock)

> It was only reversing the senseless direction
> For a momentary rest on the burning wheel
> That cloudless night in the mid-Atlantic
> When I pushed her over

It must give this man an unusual turn when Madame Sosostris spreads her pack and selects a card as close to his secret as the Tarot symbolism can come:

Here, said she,
Is your card, the drowned Phoenician Sailor,
(Those are pearls that were his eyes. Look!)—

and again:

this card,
Which is blank, is something he carries on his back,
Which I am forbidden to see.

(In what posture did they come back, late, from the Hyacinth Garden, her hair wet, before the planting of the corpse?) It is not clear whether he is comforted to learn that the clairvoyante does not find the Hanged Man.

Hence, then, his inability to speak, his failed eyes, his stunned movement, neither living nor dead and knowing nothing: as Sweeney later puts it,

He didn't know if he was alive
and the girl was dead
He didn't know if the girl was alive
and he was dead
He didn't know if they both were alive
or both were dead....

The heart of light, the silence, seems to be identified with a waste and empty sea, *Oed' und leer das Meer*; so Harry, Lord Monchensey gazed, or thought he remembered gazing, over the rail of the liner:

You would never imagine anyone could sink so quickly....
That night I slept heavily, alone....
I lay two days in contented drowsiness;
Then I recovered.

He recovered into an awareness of the Eumenides.

At the end of *The Burial of the Dead* it is the speaker's acquaintance Stetson who has planted a corpse in his garden and awaits its fantastic blooming "out of the dead land": whether a hyacinth bulb or a dead mistress there is, in this phantasmagoric cosmos, no knowing. Any man, as Sweeney is to put it,

has to, needs to, wants to
Once in a lifetime, do a girl in.

Baudelaire agrees:

> Si le viol, le poison, le poignard, l'incendie,
> N'ont pas encore brodé de leurs plaisants dessins
> Le canevas banal de nos piteux destins,
> C'est que notre âme, hélas! n'est pas assez hardie.

This is from the poem which ends with the line Eliot has appropriated to climax the first section of *The Waste Land*:

> You! hypocrite lecteur!—mon semblable,—mon frère!

Part Two, *A Game of Chess*, revolves around perverted nature, denied or murdered offspring; Part Three, *The Fire Sermon*, the most explicit of the five sections, surveys with grave denunciatory candor a world of automatic lust, in which those barriers between person and person which so troubled Prufrock are dissolved by the suppression of the person and the transposition of all human needs and desires to a plane of genital gratification.

> The river's tent is broken: the last fingers of leaf
> Clutch and sink into the wet bank. The wind
> Crosses the brown land, unheard. The nymphs are departed.
> Sweet Thames, run softly, till I end my song.

The "tent," now broken would have been composed of the overarching trees that transformed a reach of the river into a tunnel of love; the phrase beckons to mind the broken maidenhead; and a line later the gone harmonious order, by a half-realizable metamorphosis, struggles exhausted an instant against drowning. "The nymphs are departed" both because summer is past, and because the world of Spenser's *Prothalamion* (when nymphs scattered flowers on the water) is gone, if it ever existed except as an ideal fancy of Spenser's.

> The river bears no empty boxes, sandwich papers,
> Silk handkerchiefs, cardboard boxes, cigarette ends
> Or other testimony of summer nights. The nymphs are departed.

From the "brown land," amorists have fled indoors, but the river is not restored to a sixteenth-century purity because the debris of which it is now freed was not a sixteenth-century strewing of petals but a discarding of twentieth-century impedimenta. The nymphs who have this year departed are not the same nymphs who departed in autumns known to Spenser; their friends are "the loitering heirs of city directors," who, unwilling to assume responsibility for any untoward pregnancies,

> Departed, have left no addresses.

Spring will return and bring Sweeney to Mrs. Porter; Mrs. Porter, introduced by the sound of horns and caressed by the moonlight while she laves her feet, is a latter-day Diana bathing; her daughter perhaps, or any of the vanished nymphs, a latter-day Philomel

> (So rudely forc'd.
> Tereu.)

Next Mr. Eugenides proposes what appears to be a pederastic assignation; and next the typist expects a visitor to her flat.

The typist passage is the great *tour de force* of the poem; its gentle lyric melancholy, its repeatedly disrupted rhythms, the automatism of its cadences, in alternate lines aspiring and falling nervelessly—

> The time is now propitious, as he guesses,
> The meal is ended, she is bored and tired,
> Endeavours to engage her in caresses
> Which still are unreproved, if undesired.

—constitute Eliot's most perfect liaison between the self-sustaining, gesture of the verse and the presented fact. Some twenty-five lines in flawlessly traditional iambic pentameter, alternately rhymed, sustain with their cadenced gravity a moral context in which the dreary business is played out; the texture is lyric rather than dramatic because there is neither doing nor suffering here but rather the mutual compliance of a ritual scene. The section initiates its flow with a sure and perfect line composed according to the best eighteenth-century models:

> At the violet hour, when the eyes and back

which, if the last word were, for instance, "heart," we might suppose to be by a precursor of Wordsworth's. But the harsh sound and incongruous specification of "back" shift us instead to a plane of prosodic disintegration:

when the eyes and back
Turn upward from the desk, when the human engine waits
Like a taxi throbbing waiting,

The upturned eyes and back—nothing else, no face, no torso—recall a Picasso distortion; the "human engine" throws pathos down into mechanism. In the next line the speaker for the first time in the poem identifies himself as Tiresias:

I Tiresias, though blind, throbbing between two lives,
Old man with wrinkled female breasts, can see ...

There are three principal stories about Tiresias, all of them relevant. In *Oedipus Rex*, sitting "by Thebes below the wall" he knew why, and as a consequence of what violent death and what illicit amour, the pestilence had fallen on the unreal city, but declined to tell. In the *Odyssey* he "walked among the lowest of the dead" and evaded predicting Odysseus' death by water; the encounter was somehow necessary to Odysseus' homecoming, and Odysseus was somehow satisfied with it, and did get home, for a while. In the *Metamorphoses* he underwent a change of sex for watching the coupling of snakes: presumably the occasion on which he "foresuffered" what is tonight "enacted on this same divan or bed." He is often the prophet who knows but withholds his knowledge, just as Hieronymo, who is mentioned at the close of the poem, knew how the tree he had planted in his garden came to bear his dead son, but was compelled to withhold that knowledge until he could write a play which, like *The Waste Land*, employs several languages and a framework of allusions impenetrable to anyone but the "hypocrite lecteur." It is an inescapable shared guilt that makes us so intimate with the contents of this strange deathly poem; it is also, in an age that has eaten of the tree of the knowledge of psychology and anthropology ("After such knowledge, what forgiveness?"), an inescapable morbid sympathy with everyone else, very destructive to the coherent personality, that (like Tiresias' years as a woman) enables us to join with him in "foresuffering all." These sciences afford us an *illusion* of understanding other people, on which we build sympathies that in an ideal era would have gone out with a less pathological generosity, and that are as likely as not projections of our self-pity and self-absorption, vices for which Freud and Frazer afford dangerous nourishment. Tiresias is he who has lost the sense of other people as inviolably other, and who is capable neither of pity nor terror but only of a fascination, spuriously related to compassion, which is merely the twentieth century's special mutation of indifference. Tiresias can see

> At the violet hour, the evening hour that strives
> Homeward, and brings the sailor home from sea,
> The typist home at teatime, clears her breakfast, lights
> Her stove, and lays out food in tins.

Syntax, like his sensibility and her routine, undergoes total collapse. A fine throbbing line intervenes:

> Out of the window perilously spread

and bathos does not wholly overtopple the completing Alexandrine:

> Her drying combinations touched by the sun's last rays.

"Combinations" sounds a little finer than the thing it denotes; so does "divan":

> On the divan are piled (at night her bed)
> Stockings, slippers, camisoles and stays.

Some transfiguring word touches with glory line after line:

> He, the young man carbuncular, arrives,

If he existed, and if he read those words, how must he have marvelled at the alchemical power of language over his inflamed skin! As their weary ritual commences, the diction alters; it moves to a plane of Johnsonian dignity without losing touch with them; they are never "formulated, sprawling on a pin."

"Endeavours to engage her in caresses" is out of touch with the small house-agent's clerk's speech, but it is such a sentence as he might *write*; Eliot has noted elsewhere how "an artisan who can talk the English language beautifully while about his work or in a public bar, may compose a letter painfully written in a dead language bearing some resemblance to a newspaper leader and decorated with words like 'maelstrom' and 'pandemonium.'" So it is with the diction of this passage: it reflects the words with which the participants might clothe, during recollection in tranquillity, their own notion of what they have been about, presuming them capable of such self-analysis; and it maintains simultaneously Tiresias' fastidious impersonality. The rhymes come with a weary inevitability that parodies the formal elegance of Gray; and the episode modulates at its close into a key to which Goldsmith can be transposed:

> When lovely woman stoops to folly and
> Paces about her room again, alone,
> She smoothes her hair with automatic hand,
> And puts a record on the gramophone.

With her music and her lures "perilously spread" she is a London siren; the next line, "This music crept by me upon the waters," if it is lifted from the *Tempest*, might as well be adapted from the twelfth book of the *Odyssey*.

After the Siren, the violated Thames-daughters, borrowed from Wagner, the "universal artist" whom the French Symbolists delighted to honor. The opulent Wagnerian pathos, with its harmonic rather than linear development and its trick of entrancing the attention with *leitmotifs*, is never unrelated to the methods of *The Waste Land*. One of the characters in "A Dialogue on Dramatic Poetry," though he has railed at Wagner as "pernicious," yet would not willingly resign his experience of Wagner; for Wagner had more than a bag of orchestral tricks and a corrupt taste for mythologies, he had also an indispensable sense of his own age, something that partly sustains and justifies his methods. "A sense of his own age"—the ability to "recognize its pattern while the pattern was yet incomplete"—was a quality Eliot in 1930 was to ascribe to Baudelaire.[3] One who has possessed it cannot simply be ignored, though he is exposed to the follies of his age as well as sensitive to its inventions. At the very least he comes to symbolize a phase in "the mind of Europe" otherwise difficult to locate or name; at best, his methods, whether or not they merited his own fanaticism, are of permanent value to later artists for elucidating those phases of human sensibility to the existence of which they originally contributed. This principle is quite different from the academic or counter-academic notion that art must be deliberately adulterated because its preoccupations are.

Wagner, more than Frazer or Miss Weston, presides over the introduction into *The Waste Land* of the Grail motif. In Wagner's opera, the Sangreal quest is embedded in an opulent and depraved religiosity, as in Tennyson's *Holy Grail* the cup, "rose-red, with beatings in it, as if alive, till all the white walls of my cell were dyed with rosy colours leaping on the wall," never succeeds in being more than the reward of a refined and sublimated erotic impulse. Again Eliot notes of Baudelaire that "in much romantic poetry the sadness is due to the exploitation of the fact that no human relations are adequate to human desires, but also to the disbelief in any further object for human desires than that which, being human, fails to satisfy them." The Grail was in mid-nineteenth-century art an attempt to postulate such an object; and the quest for that vision unites the poetry of baffled sadness to "the poetry of flight," a genre which Eliot distinguishes in quoting Baudelaire's "Quand partons-nous vers le bonheur?" and characterizes as "a dim recognition of the direction of beatitude."

So in Part V of *The Waste Land* the journey eastward among the red rocks and heaps of broken images is fused with the journey to Emmaus ("He who was living is now dead. We who were living are now dying") and the approach to the Chapel Perilous.

The quester arrived at the Chapel Perilous had only to ask the meaning of the things that were shown him. Until he has asked their meaning, they have none; after he has asked, the king's wound is healed and the waters commence again to flow. So in a civilization reduced to "a heap of broken images" all that is requisite is sufficient curiosity; the man who asks what one or another of these fragments means—seeking, for instance, "a first-hand opinion about Shakespeare"—may be the agent of regeneration. The past exists in fragments precisely because nobody cares what it meant; it will unite itself and come alive in the mind of anyone who succeeds in caring, who is unwilling that Shakespeare shall remain the name attached only to a few tags everyone half-remembers, in a world where "we know too much, and are convinced of too little."

Eliot develops the nightmare journey with consummate skill, and then maneuvres the reader into the position of the quester, presented with a terminal heap of fragments which it is his business to inquire about. The protagonist in the poem perhaps does not inquire; they are fragments he has shored against his ruins. Or perhaps he does inquire; he has at least begun to put them to use, and the "arid plain" is at length behind him.

The journey is prepared for by two images of asceticism: the brand plucked from the burning, and the annihilation of Phlebas the Phoenician. *The Fire Sermon*, which opens by Thames water, closes with a burning, a burning that images the restless lusts of the nymphs, the heirs of city directors, Mr. Eugenides, the typist and the young man carbuncular, the Thames-daughters. They are unaware that they burn. "I made no comment. What should I resent?" They burn nevertheless, as the protagonist cannot help noticing when he shifts his attention from commercial London to commercial Carthage (which stood on the North African shore, and is now utterly destroyed). There human sacrifices were dropped into the furnaces of Moloch, in a frantic gesture of appeasement. There Augustine burned with sensual fires: "a cauldron of unholy loves sang all about mine ears"; and he cried, "O Lord, Thou pluckest me out." The Buddhist ascetic on the other hand does not ask to be plucked out; he simply turns away from the senses because (as the Buddhist Fire Sermon states) they are each of them on fire. As for Phlebas the Phoenician, a trader sailing perhaps to Britain, his asceticism is enforced: "A current under sea picked his bones in whispers," he forgets the benisons of sense, "the cry of gulls and the deep sea swell" as well as "the profit and loss," and he spirals down, like Dante's Ulysses, through circling memories of his age and youth, "as Another chose." (An account of a shipwreck, imitated from the Ulysses episode in Dante, was one of the long sections deleted from the original *Waste Land*.) Ulysses in hell was encased in a tongue of flame, death by water having in one instance secured not the baptismal renunciation of the Old Adam, but an eternity of fire. Were there some simple negative formula for dealing with the senses, suicide would be the sure way to regeneration.

Part V opens, then, in Gethsemane, carries us rapidly to Golgotha, and then leaves us to pursue a nightmare journey in a world now apparently deprived of meaning.

> Here is no water but only rock
> Rock and no water and the sandy road
> The road winding above among the mountains
>   Which are mountains of rock without water
>   If there were water we should stop and drink....

The whirling, obsessive reduplication of single words carries the travellers through a desert, through the phases of hallucination in which they number phantom companions, and closes with a synoptic vision of the destruction of Jerusalem ("Murmur of maternal lamentation" obviously recalling "daughters of Jerusalem, weep not for me, but for yourselves and your children") which becomes *sub specie aeternitatis* the destruction by fire of civilization after civilization

> Jerusalem Athens Alexandria
> Vienna London
> Unreal

The woman at the dressing-table recurs:

> A woman drew her long black hair out tight
> And fiddled whisper music on those strings;

her "golden Cupidons" are transmogrified:

And bats with baby faces in the violet light
Whistled, and beat their wings
And crawled head downward down a blackened wall

and where towers hang "upside down in air" stability is imaged by a deserted chapel among the mountains, another place from which the life has gone but in which the meaning is latent, awaiting only a pilgrim's advent. The cock crows as it did when Peter wept tears of penitence; as in *Hamlet*, it disperses the night-spirits.

Then a damp gust
Bringing rain.

There the activity of the protagonist ends. Some forty remaining lines in the past tense recapitulate the poem in terms of the oldest wisdom accessible to the West. The thunder's DA is one of those primordial Indo-European roots that recur in the *Oxford Dictionary*, a random leaf of the Sibyl's to which a thousand derivative words, now automatic currency, were in their origins so many explicit glosses. If the race's most permanent wisdom is its oldest, then DA, the voice of the thunder and of the Hindu sages, is the cosmic voice not yet dissociated into echoes. It underlies the Latin infinitive "dare," and all its Romance derivatives; by a sound-change, the Germanic "geben," the English "give." It is the root of "datta," "dayadhvam," "damyata": give, sympathize, control: three sorts of giving. To sympathize is to give oneself; to control is to give governance.

Then spoke the thunder
DA
Datta: what have we given?
My friend, blood shaking my heart
The awful daring of a moment's surrender
Which an age of prudence can never retract
By this, and this only, we have existed.

The first surrender was our parents' sexual consent; and when we are born again it is by a new surrender, inconceivable to the essentially satiric sensibility with which a Gerontion contemplates

... De Bailhache, Fresca, Mrs. Cammel, whirled
Beyond the circuit of the shuddering Bear,

and requiring a radical modification of even a Tiresias' negative compassion.

> The awful daring of a moment's surrender ...
> Which is not to be found in our obituaries
> Or in memories draped by the beneficent spider
> Or under seals broken by the lean solicitor
> In our empty rooms.

The lean solicitor, like the inquiring worm, breaks seals that in lifetime were held prissily inviolate; the will he is about to read registers not things given but things abandoned. The thunder is telling us what Tiresias did not dare tell Oedipus, the reason for the universal curse: "What have we given?" As for "Dayadhvam," "sympathize":

> DA
> *Dayadhvam*: I have heard the key
> Turn in the door once and turn once only
> We think of the key, each in his prison
> Thinking of the key, each confirms a prison

—a prison of inviolate honor, self-sufficiency, like that in which Coriolanus locked himself away. Coriolanus' city was also under a curse, in which he participated. His energies sufficed in wartime (Eliot's poem was written three years after the close of the Great War), but in peacetime it becomes clear that "he did it to please his mother, and to be partly proud." He is advised to go through the forms of giving and sympathy, but

> [Not] by the matter which your heart prompts you,
> But with such words that are but rooted in
> Your tongue ...

After his banishment he goes out "like to a lonely dragon," and plots the destruction of Rome. His final threat is to stand

> As if a man were author of himself
> And knew no other kin.

He is an energetic and purposeful Prufrock, concerned with the figure he cuts and readily humiliated; Prufrock's radical fault is not his lack of energy and purpose. Coriolanus is finally shattered like a statue; and if

Only at nightfall, aethereal rumours
Revive for a moment a broken Coriolanus,

it may be only as the Hollow Men in Death's dream kingdom hear voices "in the wind's singing," and discern sunlight on a broken column. Do the rumors at nightfall restore him to momentary life, or restore his memory to the minds of other self-sufficient unsympathizing men?

DA
Damyata: The boat responded
Gaily, to the hand expert with sail and oar
The sea was calm, your heart would have responded
Gaily, when invited, beating obedient
To controlling hands

Unlike the rider, who may dominate his horse, the sailor survives and moves by cooperation with a nature that cannot be forced; and this directing, sensitive hand, feeling on the sheet the pulsation of the wind and on the rudder the momentary thrust of waves, becomes the imagined instrument of a comparably sensitive human relationship. If dominance compels response, control invites it; and the response comes "gaily." But—"would have": the right relationship was never attempted.

I sat upon the shore
Fishing, with the arid plain behind me

The journey eastward across the desert is finished; though the king's lands are waste, he has arrived at the sea.

Shall I at least set my lands in order?

Isaiah bade King Hezekiah set his lands in order because he was destined not to live; but Candide resolved to cultivate his own garden as a way of living. We cannot set the whole world in order; we can rectify ourselves. And we are destined to die, but such order as lies in our power is nevertheless desirable.

London Bridge is falling down falling down falling down
Poi s'ascose nel foco che gli affina
Quando fiam uti chelidon—O swallow swallow
Le Prince d'Aquitaine à la tour abolie
These fragments I have shored against my ruins

An English nursery rhyme, a line of Dante's, a scrap of the late Latin *Pervigilium Veneris*, a phrase of Tennyson's ("O swallow, swallow, could I but follow") linked to the fate of Philomel, an image from a pioneer nineteenth-century French visionary who hanged himself on a freezing January morning: "a heap of broken images," and a fragmentary conspectus of the mind of Europe. Like the Knight in the Chapel Perilous, we are to ask what these relics mean; and the answers will lead us into far recesses of tradition.

The history of London Bridge (which was disintegrating in the eighteenth century, and which had symbolized, with its impractical houses, a communal life now sacrificed to abstract transportation—

> A crowd flowed over London Bridge, so many,
> I had not thought death had undone so many.)

is linked by the nursery rhyme with feudal rituals ("gold and silver, my fair lady") and festivals older still. Dante's line focuses the tradition of Christian asceticism, in which "burning" is voluntarily undergone. Dante's speaker was a poet:

> Ieu sui Arnaut, que plor e vau cantan;
> Consiros vei la passada folor,
> E vei jausen lo jorn, que'esper, denan....

"Consiros vei la passada folor": compare "With the arid plain behind me." "Vau cantan": he goes singing in the fire, like the children in the Babylonian furnace, not quite like Philomel whose song is pressed out of her by the memory of pain. The *Pervigilium Veneris* is another rite, popular, post-pagan, pre-Christian, welcoming in the spring and inciting to love: "Cras amet qui numquam amavit"; he who has never loved, let him love tomorrow; secular love, but its trajectory leads, via the swallow, aloft. Tennyson's swallow nearly two thousand years later ("Could I but follow") flies away from an earthbound poet, grounded in an iron time, and meditating "la poésie des départs." That poem is a solo, not a folk ritual. As for the Prince of Aquitaine with the ruined tower, he is one of the numerous *personae* Gérard de Nerval assumes in *El Desdichado*: "Suis-je Amour ou Phébus, Lusignan ou Biron?" as the speaker of *The Waste Land* is Tiresias, the Phoenician Sailor, and Ferdinand Prince of Naples. He has lingered in the chambers of the sea

> J'ai rêvé dans la grotte où nage la sirène ...

and like Orpheus he has called up his love from the shades:

Et j'ai deux fois vainqueur traversé l'Achéron
Modulant tour à tour sur la lyre d'Orphée
Les soupirs de la sainte et les cris de la fée.

So *The Waste Land* contains Augustine's cries and the song of the Thames-daughters; but de Nerval, the pioneer Symbolist, is enclosed in a mood, in a poetic state, surrounded by his own symbols ("Je suis le ténébreux,—le veuf,—l'inconsolé"), offering to a remembered order, where the vine and the rose were one, only the supplication of a dead man's hand, "Dans la nuit du tombeau," where "ma seule étoile est morte": under the twinkle of a fading star. It is some such state as his, these images suggest, that is to be explored in *The Hollow Men*; he inhabits death's dream kingdom. The mind of Europe, some time in the nineteenth century, entered an uneasy phase of sheer dream.

These fragments I have shored against my ruins
Why then Ile fit you. Hieronymo's mad againe.

Here Eliot provides us with a final image for all that he has done: his poem is like Hieronymo's revenge-play. Hieronymo's enemies—the public for the poet in our time—commission an entertainment:

It pleased you,
At the entertainment of the ambassador,
To grace the king so much as with a show.
Now, were your study so well furnished,
As for the passing of the first night's sport
To entertain my father with the like
Or any such-like pleasing motion,
Assure yourself, it would content them well.
HIER: Is this all?
BAL.: Ay, this is all.
HIER: Why then, I'll fit you. Say no more.
When I was young, I gave my mind
And plied myself to fruitless poetry;
Which though it profit the professor naught,
Yet is it passing pleasing to the world.

It profits the professor naught, like Philomel's gift of song; and pleases those who have no notion of what it has cost, or what it will ultimately cost them. Hieronymo goes on to specify:

Each one of us
Must act his part in unknown languages,
That it may breed the more variety:
As you, my lord, in Latin, I in Greek,
You in Italian, and for because I know
That Bellimperia hath practised the French,
In courtly French shall all her phrases be.

Each of these languages occurs in *The Waste Land*; all but Greek, in the list of shored fragments. Balthasar responds, like a critic in *The New Statesman*,

But this will be a mere confusion,
And hardly shall we all be understood.

Hieronymo, however, is master of his method:

It must be so: for the conclusion
Shall prove the invention and all was good.

Hieronymo's madness, in the context provided by Eliot, is that of the Platonic bard. If we are to take the last two lines of *The Waste Land* as the substance of what the bard in his sibylline trance has to say, then the old man's macaronic tragedy appears transmuted into the thunder's three injunctions, Give, Sympathize, Control, and a triple "Peace," "repeated as here," says the note, "a formal ending to an Upanishad."

iii

Within a few months Eliot found himself responsible for a somewhat bemusing success. The poem won the 1922 *Dial* award; the first impression of one thousand copies was rapidly succeeded by a second; it was rumored that the author had perpetrated a hoax; the line "Twit twit twit" was not liked; the "parodies" were pronounced "inferior" by Mr. F. L. Lucas; Arnold Bennett inquired of the author whether the notes were "a lark or serious," and was careful to specify that the question was not insulting. The author said that "they were serious, and not more of a skit than some things in the poem itself." Mr. Bennett said that he couldn't see the point of the poem. The *Times Literary Supplement* reviewer felt that Mr. Eliot was sometimes walking very near the limits of coherency, but that when he had recovered control we should expect his poetry to have gained in variety and strength from this ambitious experiment.

He had written a poem which expressed for many readers their sense of not knowing what to do with themselves; as he later put it, with Bradleyan subtlety, "their illusion of being disillusioned." He was credited with having created a new mode of poetic organization, as he had, though specific instances of the cinematic effect were as likely as not attributable to Pound's cutting. Also he was singled out as the man who had written an unintelligible poem, and *with notes*. The author and annotator of this "piece that passeth understanding" was not insensitive to the resulting climate of jest. Six years later he capped a comparison between Crashaw and Shelley by calling for elucidation of the "Keen as are the arrows" stanza of *To a Skylark*: "There may be some clue for persons more learned than I; but Shelley should have provided notes."

Notes

1. Two of them, *The wind sprang up* and *Eyes that last I saw in tears*, are preserved in the collected volume as *Minor Poems*. The third is now part iii of *The Hollow Men*. The poem in *The Tyro* is called *Song to the Opherian* and signed "Gus Krutzsch," a portmanteau-name of which Kurtz seems to be one of the components. There are many small signs that *The Hollow Men* grew from rejected pieces of *The Waste Land*.

2. This incredibly illiterate literary society seems to have been wholly unaware of the methods of Pope, or else to have supposed that a period allegedly devoted to "profuse strains of unpremeditated art" had rendered such methods obsolete.

3. The quoted phrases are from a book by Peter Quennell, which Eliot cites in his essay on Baudelaire.

ELEANOR COOK

T. S. Eliot and the Carthaginian Peace

The Waste Land requires three maps for its place-names. One is a map of Greater London and the lower Thames, for the poem is a London poem even in its final form. One early plan, as Hugh Kenner has argued,[1] conceived of Part III as a vision of London through various Augustan modes, making of the city almost another character, and suggesting a geographical unity as focal point for the poem. At this stage, says Kenner, "the rest of the poem seems to have been planned around it [Part III], guided by the norms and decorums of an Augustan view of history" (p. 35). Then Eliot wrote Part V, the vision of an urban apocalypse became dominant, and Part III was cut accordingly.

The Waste Land is not only a London poem; it is also a European poem, or more precisely a Mediterranean poem. It was always so through the early drafts, and it became noticeably so when, in Part V, London was listed as the last in a series of five great cities, Jerusalem, Athens, Alexandria, Vienna, London. The poem therefore requires a second map for those place-names that are not from the London area, leaving aside the names of Ganga and the Himavant. If those place-names are plotted on a map, they may be seen to ring the Mediterranean in the following sense. The northerly names are not seen as centers, in the way our twentieth-century eyes see them. Rather, they balance Carthage and Mylae to the south, and Jerusalem and Smyrna (now

From *English Literary History* 46 (1979): 341-355.

Izmir) to the east. This map coincides roughly with the Roman Empire at its most expansive, and therefore also coincides roughly with the theater of war during World War I. The center of this second map is Rome.

This leaves us with the names of Ganga and the Himavant. The map that is useful here is a very simple and a very symmetrical one: it is Dante's map of the inhabited world.[2] The exact center of this world is Jerusalem. Ninety degrees to the east is the eastern limit, the mouths of the Ganges, which is also the eastern limit of *The Waste Land*. Ninety degrees to the west is the western limit, Gibraltar or the western end of the Mediterranean, which is also the western limit of *The Waste Land*. Precisely halfway between Gibraltar and Jerusalem is Rome. We have thus three maps, one of a city, one of an empire, one of a world. They are not set side by side; that is, we do not make orderly progression from one map to the next in the poem. Rather, it is as if they were layered, and we read meaning from one map into another. Urban vision, imperial vision, world vision: each illuminates the other.

The English Augustans, Mr. Kenner observes, saw encouraging parallels between their London and Rome at the time of Augustus. Eliot's early plan for *The Waste Land*, mentioned above, was to develop satiric parallels between modern London and Augustan London. Mr. Kenner argues persuasively that Eliot "may well have had in mind at one time a kind of modern *Aeneid*, the hero crossing seas to pursue his destiny, detained by one woman and prophesied to by another, and encountering visions of the past and the future, all culminated in a city both founded and yet to be founded, unreal and oppressively real, the Rome through whose past Dryden saw London's future" (pp. 39–40). London was to be "the original Fisher King as well as the original Waste Land, resembling Augustine's Carthage as Dryden's London had resembled Ovid's Rome" (p. 28). With the final revisions, however, the center of the poem became "the urban apocalypse, the great City dissolved into a desert ..." (p. 46).

But I wonder whether the pre-eminent pattern for London from first to last was not Rome. Of course, in one sense all the cities in the final version of *The Waste Land* are the same: they are Cities of Destruction. But the poem nonetheless focuses on one particular city, London. Similarly, I think that the poem focuses on one prototype for London, and that the prototype is Rome, the center of the second map, and the center of the western half of the third map. Among these three maps, studies of *The Waste Land* have tended to concentrate on the first and the third, Eliot's urban vision and his world vision. But London in 1922 was still the center of an empire. What I want to concentrate on here is Eliot's vision of imperial apocalypse in *The Waste Land*, working from the hypothesis that a vision of Rome and the Roman Empire lies behind Eliot's vision of London and the British Empire.

Rome could provide a pattern for London in *The Waste Land* for good reason. The most obvious is that Rome was once both a great city and the capital of a great empire. In this, she is no different from those other great cities in Part V that were also capitals of great though very different empires: "Jerusalem, Athens, Alexandria, / Vienna, London." This list is worth examining. Eliot preserves the chronological order of the flourishing of each empire. He lists three ancient empires in one line, two modern ones in the following line. The large gap between the three ancient and two modern empires is dominated by Rome, who—and here she differs from the other cities—held sway over all three old empires. The name of Vienna, capital of the Austro-Hungarian Empire, suggests a line of succession, for the Austro-Hungarian Empire saw itself as heir to the Holy Roman Empire, which in turn saw itself as heir to the Roman Empire. Eliot was explicit about part of this line of succession in 1951:

> For Virgil's conscious mind, it [destiny] means the *imperium romanum*.... I think that he had few illusions and that he saw clearly both sides of every question—the case for the loser as well as the case for the winner.... And do you really think that Virgil was mistaken? You must remember that the Roman Empire was transformed into the Holy Roman Empire. What Virgil proposed to his contemporaries was the highest ideal even for an unholy Roman Empire, for any merely temporal empire. We are all, so far as we inherit the civilization of Europe, still citizens of the Roman Empire.... It remains an ideal, but one which Virgil passed on to Christianity to develop and to cherish.[3]

This is the older Eliot speaking. The younger Eliot was quite detached about Christianity, but Eliot always saw himself as heir to the riches of classical civilization, and especially Roman civilization. "Tradition and the Individual Talent" appeared in 1919, and in 1923 Eliot wrote in the *Criterion*: "If everything derived from Rome were withdrawn—everything we have from Norman-French society, from the Church, from Humanism, from every channel direct and indirect, what would be left? A few Teutonic roots and husks. England is a 'Latin' country ..." (*Criterion*, 2 [October 1923], 104).

"For at least seven years, it would seem," writes Kenner, "an urban apocalypse had haunted Eliot's imagination" (p. 42). To an imagination thus haunted, and brooding from 1919 onward[4] over material for what was to be *The Waste Land*, it might very well have appeared that the inheritance of Rome was disintegrating. "I am all for empires," wrote Eliot in January of 1924, "especially the Austro-Hungarian Empire."[5] But the Austro-

Hungarian Empire had just been broken up by the Treaty of Versailles in 1919. And Christianity, considered simply as a force in history in the way Henry Adams saw it, might also be disintegrating. "The struggle of 'liberal' against 'orthodox' faith is out of date," Eliot wrote as early as 1916. "The present conflict is far more momentous than that."[6] The ghost of Rome prevails in *The Waste Land* because Rome evolved from the greatest of Western empires into a Christian one; because the various European empires that followed Rome, all the way down to the British Empire, retained something of this inheritance, including the association of church and state (at least, officially); and because Eliot at the time of *The Waste Land* sees the possibility that this inheritance and this association will come to an end in the disintegration of church and state and civilization as we know them. "Eliot ... once said to me," Spender recalls, "that *The Waste Land* could not have been written at any moment except when it was written—a remark which, while biographically true in regard to his own life, is also true of the poem's time in European history after World War I. The sense that Western civilization was in a state which was the realization of historic doom lasted from 1920 to 1926."[7]

The decline of Western civilization and the parallel between Roman and modern civilization: this suggests Spengler. We tend to associate *The Waste Land* with Spengler, in general because of this sense of the decline of civilization, and in particular because Spengler's seasonal cycle so neatly fits Eliot's allusions to English literature in Parts I to IV of the poem. But Eliot's view of history in *The Waste Land* seems to me less Spengler's than that of Henry Adams, though Stuart Hughes reminds us in his *Oswald Spengler* that the Adams brothers were precursors of Spengler. (Eliot's own dismissal of Spengler is brisk: "These are only a few of the questions suggested by Mr. Perry's work; which compels more attention, I think, than the work of such abstract philosophers of history as Otto [sic] Spengler."[8]) In *The Education of Henry Adams*, Adams argues that Christianity is the last great force that the West has known, but that its strength is coming to an end. The twentieth century will see a major shift in civilization, like the last major shift, which began at about the time of Augustine. For Spengler, the modern cycle begins in 900 AD, Augustine is not a pivotal figure as he is for Adams, and Christianity is not the latest force the West has known. Our age, according to Spengler, parallels that of the shift from Greek to Roman dominance in the Mediterranean, and we are at the beginning of another "Roman" age. "*Rome*, with its rigorous realism—uninspired, barbaric, disciplined, practical, Protestant, *Prussian*—will always give us, working as we must by analogies, the key to understanding our own future" (I.x). Adams makes no such forecasts, being altogether more tentative, at least in *The Education*. But within what Eliot called the "sceptical patrician," there lay a strong sense of apocalypse. Augustine's *Confessions* do not lie behind *The Education of Henry Adams* for nothing. In 1919, Eliot wrote a review of *The Education of Henry Adams* in which he makes no mention of Adams's view of history. But then, he makes no mention of the Maryland spring, which finds a place in *Gerontion*.[9] (Odd that Eliot says "there is nothing to indicate that Adams's senses either flowered or fruited," while his subconscious tucked away that sensual, flowering Maryland spring for poetic use.) Nor does he mention Adams's image of the Hudson and the Susquehanna, perhaps the Potomac, and the Seine rising to drown the gods of Walhalla, nor the argument that the *Götterdämmerung* was understood better in New York or in Paris than in Bayreuth. Yet in *The Waste Land* Wagner's Rhine-daughters from the *Götterdämmerung* are given equivalents in the Thames, and it may be that Adams suggested to Eliot the usefulness of the *Götterdämmerung* in a poem about the end of things and about (in part) the life of a river. For Adams, the beginning of the end of the Roman Empire was the beginning of the age we know, and the coming change will not be the end of things, and thus not a true apocalypse. But his imagery and his sense of cataclysm are such that they would have fed an imagination already haunted by the theme of apocalypse.

So would Conrad, and so possibly would Henry James, two writers whom Eliot read and admired. Conrad, of course, enters into *The Waste Land*. Neither James in *The Golden Bowl* nor Conrad in *Heart of Darkness* looks ahead like Adams to a change in civilization such as the world has not seen in some fifteen centuries. But both books present a dark and troubled vision of empire, and both make use of a parallel between Rome and London. Here are the opening sentences of *The Golden Bowl*:

> The Prince had always liked his London, when it had come to him; he was one of the Modern Romans who find by the Thames a more convincing image of the truth of the ancient state than any they have left by the Tiber. Brought up on the legend of the City to which the world paid tribute, he recognised in the present London much more than in contemporary Rome the real dimensions of such a case. If it was a question of an *Imperium*, he said to himself, and if one wished, as a Roman, to recover a little the sense of that, the place to do so was on London Bridge....

Parallels between Rome and London were common enough at the turn of the century, but only rarely did they serve to set a question-mark against the enterprise of empire itself, its uses as well as its abuses, its civilization as well as its corruption. Both *The Golden Bowl* and *Heart of Darkness* do this, though

Conrad's reaction to the kind of power that underlies the rhetoric of empire is beyond even James's darkness: it is horror. Conrad offers us an ancient Roman view of Londinium at the beginning of *Heart of Darkness*, and a parallel between contemporary London and ancient Rome is implicit. His red-sailed barges in the Thames are also from the beginning of *Heart of Darkness*, and they are already present in the early drafts of Part III of *The Waste Land*.

Something of the force of Conrad's great dark vision of empire on Eliot's imagination in 1919 may be seen in a review of Kipling that Eliot published two weeks before his review of *The Education of Henry Adams*.[10] In 1941, when Eliot wrote an introduction to his selection of Kipling's poems, he outlined sympathetically Kipling's idea of empire. It was for Kipling "not merely an idea ... it was something the reality of which he felt." And Eliot went on to analyze Kipling's sense of the Empire as an awareness of responsibility. But not in 1919. Then, his reaction to Kipling's imperialism was contemptuous, and his sympathies clearly lay with Conrad, who provides the contrast to Kipling in the 1919 review.

> Both of the poets [Kipling and Swinburne] have a few simple ideas. If we deprecate any philosophical complications, we may be allowed to call Swinburne's Liberty and Mr. Kipling's Empire "ideas." They are at least abstract, and not material which emotion can feed long upon. And they are not (in passing) very dissimilar. Swinburne had the Risorgimento, and Garibaldi, and Mazzini, and the model of Shelley, and the recoil from Tennyson, and he produced Liberty. Mr. Kipling, the Anglo-Indian, had frontier welfare, and rebellions, and Khartoum, and he produced the Empire. And we remember Swinburne's sentiments toward the Boers: he wished to intern them all. Swinburne and Mr. Kipling have these and such concepts; some poets, like Shakespeare or Dante or Villon, and some novelists, like Mr. Conrad, have, in contrast to ideas or concepts, points of view, or "worlds"—what are incorrectly called "philosophies." Mr. Conrad is very germane to the question, because he is in many ways the antithesis of Mr. Kipling. He is, for one thing, the antithesis of Empire (as well as of democracy); his characters are the denial of Empire, of Nation, of Race almost, they are fearfully alone with the Wilderness. Mr. Conrad has no ideas, but he has a point of view, a "world"; it can hardly be defined, but it pervades his work and is unmistakable. It could not be otherwise. Swinburne's and Mr. Kipling's ideas could be otherwise. Had Mr.

> Kipling taken Liberty and Swinburne the Empire, the alteration would be unimportant.
>
> And that is why both Swinburne's and Mr. Kipling's verse in spite of the positive manner which each presses to his service, appear to lack cohesion—to be, frankly, immature. There is no point of view to hold them together.

Eliot is here working out the function of ideas as against the function of a point of view. (The distinction had appeared already in 1918 in his analysis of Henry James, the analysis that includes the well-known sentence: "He had a mind so fine that no idea could violate it."[11]) But there is no doubt about Eliot's opinion of Kipling's idea as idea. In the later essay, it is Eliot's reaction to that idea that has changed. This time, he compares Kipling not with Swinburne, but with Dryden, "one other great English writer who put politics into verse."

There is another work that I think entered into the making of *The Waste Land*. It is a book contemporary with the poem; it sheds light on some of the allusions in *The Waste Land*, ties the poem to post-World-War-I history, and incidentally relates Eliot's work at Lloyd's Bank to his poetry. It treats the theme of imperial collapse, and it uses Rome as an implicit example. It is John Maynard Keynes's *The Economic Consequences of the Peace*.

Eliot in 1951 observed that Virgil knew the case for the loser as well as the case for the winner. When he cut and revised the drafts of *The Waste Land*, he deleted several references to Virgil. The one specific reference he chose to retain is an allusion to Dido, a reference that stresses the price rather than the glory of empire. Virgil's Sibyl of Cumae knew the price of empire too. (Mr. Kenner notes that we are meant to recall Virgil's Sibyl, if we have any sibylline knowledge at all, when we see the ruined Sibyl of Cumae in the poem's epigraph.) In Book VI of the *Aeneid*, the Sibyl of Cumae warns Aeneas of the realities on which empires are founded: *bella, horrida bella et Thybrim multo spumentem sanguine cerno* (86–87). And the Tiber, running with blood, takes its place behind the great rivers of the poem, Cleopatra's Nile, the Rhine so recently also running with blood, the Thames. Beyond that, it merges into the larger bodies of water that provided routes for the great maritime empires. All the cities of Part V are associated with famous waters. And the great maritime empire of 1922, on which the sun never set, has behind her the great maritime empire of Rome, and behind that the greatest (we are told) maritime empire of them all, Phoenicia's, whose sailors and ships were a source of power for centuries, and a byword for good seamanship. (One of her sailors appears in Part I and Part IV of *The Waste Land*.) At the naval battle of Mylae in the First Punic War, her erstwhile colony Carthage was defeated by Rome. In the Second and Third Punic Wars, she was again defeated; in the Third War, Carthage was besieged, and, when the city had been taken, her citizens were slaughtered, the city levelled and sown with salt in order to make the soil sterile, and the site dedicated to the infernal gods. The Carthage to which Augustine came was a rebuilt Carthage.

The phrase "a Carthaginian Peace" would therefore mean a peace settlement so punitive as to destroy the enemy entirely and even to make sterile the land on which he lives. What it does to the victor is another question. In December 1919, John Maynard Keynes published his book, *The Economic Consequences of the Peace*, in which he passionately denounced the Treaty of Versailles as a "Carthaginian Peace." (He had resigned as representative of the British Treasury at the Peace Conference.) The book was widely read (according to Etienne Mantoux's *The Carthaginian Peace*, it had been translated into eleven languages and sold some 140,000 copies by 1924), and whether or how far the peace treaties were a Carthaginian Peace was widely disputed. Eliot, as the Lloyd's representative "in charge of settling all the pre-War Debts between the Bank and the Germans, 'an important appointment, full of interesting legal questions', ... was kept busy 'trying to elucidate knotty points in that appalling document the Peace Treaty.'"[12] It is unlikely he would not have read Keynes; he would certainly have known the argument of the book. (In a "London Letter" in the *Dial* for March 1921, Eliot referred to the "respect ... with which Clemenceau and Lloyd George bonified President Wilson" [p. 450]. The view of the respect and bonifying among the three men is Keynes's view, though the remark hardly proves Eliot had read Keynes's book. Nor does Eliot's later remark, cited above, "I am all for empires, especially the Austro-Hungarian Empire," though the view of the Austro-Hungarian Empire is also Keynes's.)

The phrasing in *The Economic Consequences of the Peace* evokes an apocalyptic foreboding and sense of nightmare very like that in *The Waste Land*.[13] Keynes wrote that he himself came to be "haunted by other and more dreadful specters. Paris was a nightmare, and everyone there was morbid. A sense of impending catastrophe overhung the frivolous scene ... the mingled significance and unreality of decisions.... The proceedings of Paris all had this air of extraordinary importance and unimportance at the same time. The decisions seemed charged with consequences to the future of human society; yet the air whispered that the word was not flesh, that it was futile, insignificant, of no effect, dissociated from events." In the "hot, dry room in the President's house ... the Four fulfilled their destinies in empty and arid intrigue." Clemenceau, "dry in soul and empty of hope, very old and tired," schemed on behalf of the "policy of an old man, whose most vivid impressions and most lively imagination are of the past and not of the future." Paris was a "morass," its atmosphere "hot and poisoned," its halls "treacherous." "Then began the weaving of that web of sophistry and Jesuitical exegesis...." "In this autumn of 1919, in which I write, we are at the dead season of our fortunes.... Our power of feeling or caring beyond the immediate questions of our own material well-being is temporarily eclipsed." This is not Pound speaking, or Hesse: it is Keynes, who supports his plea with pages of detailed economic argument that would have interested Eliot professionally. ("I want to find out something about the science of money while I am at it: it is an extraordinarily interesting subject," Eliot wrote to his mother on April 11, 1917, just after joining Lloyd's.[14] And to Lytton Strachey on June 1, 1919: "You are very—ingenuous—if you can conceive me conversing with rural deans in the cathedral close. I do not go to cathedral towns but to centres of industry. My thoughts are absorbed in questions more important than ever enters the heads of deans—as *why* it is cheaper to buy steel bars from America than from Middlesbrough, and the probable effect—the exchange difficulties with Poland—and the appreciation of the rupee."[15])

Ezra Pound saw London as another Carthage: "London has just escaped from the First World War, but it is certain to be destroyed by the next one, because it is in the hands of the international financiers. The very place of it will be sown with salt, as Carthage was, and forgotten by men; or it will be sunk under water."[16] But in 1922, I think Eliot saw London as primarily another Rome, who had brought a famous trading enemy to her knees. Cleanth Brooks, commenting on the use of Mylae in *The Waste Land*, notes that the "Punic War was a trade war—might be considered a rather close parallel to our late war."[17] And Keynes quotes Clemenceau's view that England in the First World War, as in each preceding century, had destroyed a trade rival. The poem's one-eyed merchant and Mr. Eugenides from Smyrna with his shorthand trading terms are figures of importance in an empire.[18] "Money is, after all, life blood," Spender reminds us. The sense of doom in the twenties "emanated from the revolutionary explosions and still more from the monetary collapse of central Europe."[19] Carthage is in *The Waste Land* not only because of its connections with Dido and Aeneas, *The Tempest*, and St. Augustine; not only as a colony of Phoenicia, Phoenicia who had given the Greeks most of their alphabet, which in turn was given to the Romans (by Greeks at Cumae, say Crosby and Schaffer); not only as part of a great maritime empire. It is in the poem also because Carthage is for Rome the great rival, as she is at the beginning of the *Aeneid*, and the relations between the two a pattern for enmity so established that Keynes could use the phrase "a Carthaginian Peace" without further explanation. The argument for declaring the third war against Carthage (repeated again and again by Cato the Censor, with his famous refrain *Carthago delenda est*) was the argument at the center of the controversy over the peace treaties: whether the reviving prosperity of a defeated trade rival could become a danger to the victor. In a poem of 1922, to introduce the battle of Mylae where the reader expects a reference to a World War I battle is to raise chilling questions. The line out of Baudelaire's Paris, which follows the spectral Mylae speech and ends Part I, does not help either, for those who had read Keynes: "You! hypocrite lecteur!—mon semblable,—mon frère!"

For a Carthaginian peace is one that slowly but surely deflects back upon the victor. It is a common argument that Roman life began to decline after the Punic wars. As long as Rome was in a state of war, Augustine writes near the beginning of *The City of God*, she could maintain concord and high standards of civic life. "But after the destruction of Carthage," he continues, quoting Sallust, "there came the highest pitch of discord, greed, ambition, and all the evils which generally spring up in times of prosperity" (II.18).[20] The argument was repeated by Lecky in 1877: "complete dissolution of Roman morals began shortly after the Punic wars" (*OED*, "Punic," A.1). Keynes similarly argues his case as much on behalf of the victors as the vanquished: "they [France and Italy] invite their own destruction also, being so deeply and inextricably intertwined with their victims by hidden psychic and economic bonds." "If we aim deliberately at the impoverishment of Central Europe.... nothing can then delay for very long that final civil war ... which will destroy, whoever is victor, the civilization and progress of our generation." For Rome the victor, and so long the victor that she must have seemed invincible, the eventual turn of time brings Alaric and Attila. Rome itself experiences destruction. St. Augustine, who telescopes history much as Eliot does, argues that the destruction of Rome is only fitting, for the outward devastation only matches the collapse of the inner fabric of society. "For in the ruin of our city it was stone and timber which fell to the ground; but in the lives of those Romans we saw the collapse not of material but of moral defences, not of material but of spiritual grandeur. The lust that burned in their hearts was more deadly than the flame which consumed their dwellings" (II.1). This is true not only of public life, but also of private. "Now a man's house ought to be the beginning, or rather a small component part of the city, and every beginning is directed to some end of its own kind .... domestic peace contributes to the peace of the city" (XIX.16).

No argument that Rome provides the pre-eminent pattern for London in *The Waste Land* can ignore the classic exposition of the *civitas Romae* and the *civitas Dei*, Augustine's *City of God*. Spender speaks of the implicit contrast in *The Waste Land* of the two cities, and he is surely right about this.[21] The original drafts twice included references to an ideal city, though in the end Eliot omitted any explicit reminder of a *civitas Dei*. One reference was in Part III, and read as follows: "Not here, O Glaucon [originally Ademantus], but in another world" (l. 120), which is annotated in Valerie Eliot's edition of the drafts of the poem: "Adeimantus and Glaucon, brothers of Plato, were two of the interlocutors in *The Republic*. Appalled by his vision of the 'Unreal City', Eliot may be alluding to the passage (Book IX, 592 A-B) which inspired the idea of the City of God among Stoics and Christians, and found its finest exponent in St. Augustine" (pp. 127–28). As the poem's shape changed, the ideal city shifted. In a draft of the speech of Madame Sosostris in Part I, the following line is inserted in a bracket after the present line 56: "I John saw these things, and heard them"; the quotation, from near the end of Revelations, refers not only to John's vision of judgment, but more particularly to his vision of the New Jerusalem, which immediately precedes it. Eliot finally cut all references to an ideal city, because, I think, the developing theme of urban and imperial apocalypse refused to accommodate so firm a hope as that in *The Republic* or Revelations. What Eliot kept from the Johannine vision was the dark view of the earthly city or Babylon. The sense of an impending *dies irae* hangs over most of his poem.

Augustine's earthly city is of course Babylon also, together with Babylon's daughter, Rome (*Babylonia, quasi prima Roma ... ipsa Roma quasi secunda Babylonia* [XVIII.2]). And over Augustine's earthly city, the *civitas Romae*, there also hangs a sense of doom in *The City of God*. Rome had been forewarned of her destruction, writes Augustine, by Sibylline prophecy, and the same prophecies warn her of the final apocalypse. Augustine is one of the Church fathers responsible for the conversion of Virgil's Sibyl into Christian prophetess, and, if Virgil's Sibyl of Cumae lives behind the Sibyl of Cumae in *The Waste Land*, so also, I think, may the later Christian Sibyl. "The Sibyl of Erythrae or, as some are inclined to believe, of Cumae ... is evidently to be counted among those who belong to the City of God," writes Augustine (XVIII.24). And he goes on to quote in full the Sibylline oracle which prophesies a day of judgment, using sources from both the Old and New Testaments, the oracle especially famed because its initial letters form an acrostic in Greek that spells "fish," one of the common symbols for Christ in the early Church.[22] There are other fates for the Sibyl than the fate Petronius portrayed and Eliot quoted, though they offer no comfort to the inhabitant or the reader of *The Waste Land*. The Sibyl may find her way into the words of the *dies irae* (*teste David cum Sibylla*), and her verses may be called the fifteen signs of the judgment and sung in some places as late as 1549.[23] Whatever evidence is chosen, this Sibyl is associated with the collapse of Rome and also with the final apocalypse and the day of judgment.

In 1921, Eliot was considering poetic treatments of the day of judgment at least enough to make clear how not to treat it: some poets, he wrote in the Spring issue of *Tyro*, "could imagine the Last Judgment only as a lavish display of Bengal lights, Roman candles, catherine wheels, and inflammable fire-balloons. *Vous, hypocrite lecteur....*"

Eliot's dark vision of the earthly city may be close to Augustine's dark vision of the *civitas Romae*, but it goes without saying that for Augustine the activities associated with any Fisher King, like those in *The Waste Land*, would be evidence only of superstition. *The City of God* includes references to such activities only to attack them. The belief, for example, that the Delphic Apollo might have inflicted sterility upon the land is mere superstition (XVIII.12); so are fears of an evil spell cast upon the land that motivate the fertility rites (VII.24). It is likewise superstition that inspires the familiar proverb, *Pluuia defit, causa Christiani sunt* ("No rain! It's all the fault of the Christians" [II.3]). Welldon's edition of *The City of God* notes that Augustine makes use of this proverb frequently, and it is a proverb that, read with varying degrees of irony, may be applied very handily to *The Waste Land*.

In an apocalyptic mode, the world may seem split into the sweetness of a visionary, ideal and virtually unattainable world, and the sordidness of an actual, present, and virtually inescapable world. There is no middle ground, and practical, temporal concerns and governance are left to others. This kind of painful contrast is what gives *The Waste Land* its poignancy. It is the viewpoint of someone not at home in the world, a peregrine, like Augustine. Augustine was an outsider in more than one sense: not only was his overwhelming allegiance given to another world, but he was a provincial in the Roman Empire, one of the *peregrini* or resident aliens during his stay in Milan.[24] In *The Waste Land*, he takes his place among those other great exiles or provincials who perhaps understood their city and their empire all the better for having been exiles or provincials: Ezekiel, Ovid, Dante. And Eliot? One of Eliot's quotations is from the psalm of exile, with its passionate love of Jerusalem, and its cry, "How shall we sing the Lord's song in a strange land?" The cry echoes behind the homeless voices of *The Waste Land*.

But the Jewish voices were able to utter this psalm or to include an Ezekiel. In the twentieth century, there remain only fragmented voices, a desiccated Sibyl. The apocalyptic mode in *The Waste Land* moves toward its own destruction in the disintegration of the uses of language. Augustine, whose etymology is highly idiosyncratic, thought that the name Babylon was connected with the name Babel. Babylon may thus also be called "confusion," and "punishment in the form of a change of language" is the fate of a Babel or of any Babylon or of any Rome—a punishment which some readers may feel Eliot demonstrates with peculiar force. (Another twentieth-century example of this punishment had been seen at the Peace Conference, where the difficulties of negotiating had been compounded by the fact that only Clemenceau, among the Four, spoke both French and English.)

The dangers of abandoning the middle ground of practical, temporal affairs are all too apparent. At the end of *The Waste Land*, there is a turning, or rather a returning, toward this middle earth and away from exile or private grief. The apocalyptic mode is useful, but not for long. It provides an ideal, but no working pattern for living in this world. A working pattern without an ideal may very well collapse sooner or later, but an ideal with no working pattern can find terrible ways to translate itself into action, or can find itself readily outmanoeuvred and paralysed. Augustine does not ignore the question of how to live in the earthly city. And Keynes, at the end of *The Economic Consequences of the Peace*, tempers his own dark vision with practical suggestions for relieving the nightmare.

The Waste Land, in the end, retains its geographical unity, but the unity becomes far more complex. London as a city forms one focal point. The maps shift, as we muse on the poem, and London becomes a center of empire, another Rome. Do they ever shift again, so that London and Rome become Jerusalem, the center of Dante's world? Never, in the old sense, and not until *Little Gidding* in a mystical sense, and by this time the center may be anywhere, "England and nowhere. Never and always."

Notes

1. "The Urban Apocalypse," in A. Walton Litz, ed., *Eliot in His Time: Essays on the Occasion of the Fiftieth Anniversary* of The Waste Land (Princeton, 1973), pp. 23–49.

2. *The Divine Comedy* (Temple Classics edition), *Paradiso*, canto xxvii, n. 11.

3. "Virgil and the Christian World," broadcast from London, Sept. 9, 1951; reprinted in *T. S. Eliot: Selected Prose*, ed. John Hayward (London, 1953), p. 97.

4. And perhaps earlier. "I hope to get started on a poem I have in mind" (Eliot to John Quinn, Nov. 5, 1919); he hopes "to write a long poem I have had on my mind for a long time" (Eliot to his mother, Dec. 18, 1919); in *The Waste Land: A Facsimile and Transcript of the Original Drafts including the Annotations of Ezra Pound*, ed. Valerie Eliot (London 1971), xviii.

5. *Transatlantic Review*, 1 (January 1924), 95.

6. International Journal of Ethics, 27 (1916), 117.

7. Stephen Spender, *T. S. Eliot* (New York, 1975), pp. 117–18.

8. *Criterion*, 2 (1924), 491.

9. *Athenaeum* (May 23, 1919), 361–62. On the use in *Gerontion* of material from the beginning of chap. XVIII of *The Education of Henry Adams*, see F. O. Matthiessen, *The Achievement of T. S. Eliot* (3rd ed., Oxford, 1958), p. 73.

10. *Athenaeum* (May 9, 1919), 297–98. For the 1941 essay, see *A Choice of Kipling's Verse, made by T. S. Eliot with an essay on Rudyard Kipling* (London, 1941).

11. *Little Review*, 5.4 (1918), 46.

12. *The Waste Land*, ed. Valerie Eliot, p. xviii; the two quotations are from letters of February 1920 to Eliot's mother.

13. And, for that matter, in *Gerontion*, though *Gerontion* was ready for publication on May 25, 1919 (*The Waste Land*, ed. Valerie Eliot, p. xvi) and Keynes wrote his book during August and September 1919 (Roy Harrod, *The Life of John Maynard Keynes* [London, 1951], p. 288).

Quotations from *The Economic Consequences of the Peace* are from the first United States edition (New York, 1920), pp. 5–6, 7, 32, 56, 64, 48, 49, 51, 297. Later references are to pp. 33, 5, and 268.

Keynes was fond of poetry, and was reading *The Waste Land* soon after its first appearance in the October 1922 issue of the *Criterion*. Sir Roy Harrod remembers "coming into his rooms in the autumn of 1922, to find that he was reading aloud *The Waste Land* by T. S. Eliot, a poet of whom I had so far not heard. His reading was intelligent and moving, and served to win one's admiration for this strange new form of expression" (in his *Life of John Maynard Keynes*, p. 29). Early in 1923, Keynes, as the new chairman of the board of the *Nation and Athenaeum*, strongly supported Eliot for the position of literary editor, against much opposition from fellow directors (Michael Holroyd, *Lytton Strachey* [New York, 1967, 1968], II, pp. 368–69). I do not know when Eliot first met Keynes; Clive Bell recalls first meeting Eliot in 1916 when he came for dinner to Gordon Square, where Bell was living with Keynes, but Keynes was out that evening (Clive Bell, *Old Friends* [London, 1956], p. 119).

14. *The Waste Land*, ed. Valerie Eliot, p. xii.

15. Holroyd, *Lytton Strachey*, II, p. 365.

16. Cited by William Empson, *Essays in Criticism*, 22 (1972), 419.

17. From *Modern Poetry and the Tradition*, reprinted in *T. S. Eliot*, The Waste Land: *A Casebook*, ed. C. B. Cox and Arnold P. Hinchcliffe (London, 1968), p. 136.

18. The perennial power of money and craft of bartering are central themes in both *The Golden Bowl* and *Heart of Darkness*.

19. *T. S. Eliot*, p. 118. On Eliot's "present decay of eastern Europe" (head-note to the notes to *The Waste Land*, Part V), see Keynes, for example, p. 4: "But perhaps it is only in England (and America) that it is possible to be so unconscious. In continental Europe the earth heaves and no one but is aware of the rumblings. There it is not just a matter of extravagance or 'labor troubles'; but of life and death, of starvation and existence, and of the fearful convulsions of a dying civilization." Or p. 250n.: "For months past, the reports of the health conditions in the Central Empires have been of such a character that the imagination is dulled, and one almost seems guilty of sentimentality in quoting them. But their general veracity is not disputed...."

20. *The City of God*, tr. Henry Bettenson, ed. David Knowles (London, 1972); all quotations in English are from this edition.

21. *T. S. Eliot*, pp. 121–22.

22. Northrop Frye (who calls Eliot's poem "intensely Latin") mentions the symbolism of fishing in the Gospels in connection with *The Waste Land* (*T. S. Eliot*) [New York, 1963, 1972], pp. 67, 71.

23. Du Bellay, *Defence and Illustration of the French Language*, VIII.

24. On the theme of *peregrinatio*, the status of a *peregrinus*, and his sense of exile, see Peter Brown, *Augustine of Hippo* (Berkeley, 1967), pp. 323–24.

JAMES E. MILLER

Personal Mood Transmuted into Epic: T. S. Eliot's "Waste Land"

1

One of the several handbooks on *The Waste Land* has characterized it as "something like the modern epic," but with a difference: "If an epic is 'that rich vessel which contains the ideals and aspirations of the race,' this poem is a mirror of a certain modern fatigue and dismay."[1] Earlier, I. A. Richards categorized *The Waste Land* as an epic in defending its density of literary allusions: "Allusion in Mr. Eliot's hands is a technical device for compression. *The Waste Land* is the equivalent in content to an epic. Without this device twelve books would have been needed."[2] Whether the reader agrees with the effect claimed for allusion, he is likely to feel *The Waste Land* is in some obscure sense "epic." But in what sense?

In the Whitmanian sense? It is difficult to find two more unlike poets than Eliot and Whitman. But their very unlikeness may be the clue to their community of aim: to express an age through expression of self. Of course, if we take Eliot at his word in "Tradition and the Individual Talent," he would have none of any "expression of the self."[3] But in fact, with what we know now after the publication of the earlier version of *The Waste Land*, and with Eliot's critical comments later in life that seem to refer to *The Waste Land*, we may easily envision Eliot bent on "expression of self" in his most famous poem (as, indeed, we might argue easily that Whitman found his "objective

From *The American Quest for a Supreme Fiction: Whitman's Legacy in the Personal Epic*, pp. 101–125.

correlative" in such "personal" poems as "Song of Myself" or "When Lilacs Last in the Dooryard Bloom'd").

M. L. Rosenthal, in one of the most perceptive analyses of the *Waste Land* manuscripts ("*The Waste Land* as an Open Structure"), intuitively reached back to Whitman via D. H. Lawrence for a major point of comparison:

> ... because of certain different emphases while the poem [*The Waste Land*] was still in the making, the sense of improvisation at the high pitch of genius that struck the first readers of the printed text is reinforced. One almost does well to forget Pound and think of someone as unlikely as Lawrence, with his idea of Whitman as the poet of the "open road," and of a poetry "of the present"; Lawrence wrote in 1918 of "the poetry of that which is at hand: the immediate present. In the immediate present there is no perfection, no consummation, nothing finished. The strands are all flying, quivering, intermingling into the web, the waters are shaking the moon .... This is the unrestful, ungraspable poetry of the sheer present, poetry whose very permanency lies in its wind-like transit. Whitman's is the best poetry of this kind."[4]

In examining the passages Eliot (often on Pound's advice) discarded from the original version of *The Waste Land*, Rosenthal astutely observed:

> And yet Eliot, had he kept these passages, would have committed himself to a much more confessional and vulnerable role in the structure of the poem. He would have had to set his own finicky and precious attitudes, and his abysmal feelings about female physicality, into the scale with other predominant motifs. These were possibilities of commitment toward which he went a fairly long way. In the era of Robert Lowell and Allen Ginsberg, he might well have gone the whole distance. Neither his nor Pound's taste was ready to be confident about doing so in 1922, and doubtless the best available reading public for poetry would not have been ready either.[5]

The implications that flow from the revelation that the deep or original (or originating) structure of *The Waste Land* was "open" and "confessional" in this Whitmanian-Lawrentian sense will be traced out below.[6] It is enough now to suggest that Whitman's so-called optimism and Eliot's pessimism are two sides of the same poetic coin, that both outlooks derived from personal sources and were projected onto worlds that accepted the outlooks as confirming their own.

Eliot's earliest comments on Whitman might well give pause to anyone seeking a link between the two. In fact, Eliot's references to Whitman are such as to raise questions of deeper connections than those admitted. One book has argued the case strongly for a pervasive unconscious influence of Whitman on Eliot.[7] Is it possible that Eliot was so strong in his denunciation because he felt touched, swayed, even influenced? In his Introduction to the 1928 edition of Ezra Pound's *Selected Poems*, Eliot wrote: "I did not read Whitman until much later [than 1908, 1909] in life and had to conquer an aversion to his form, as well as to much of his matter, in order to do so."[8]

One of the strange aspects of Eliot's attitude toward Whitman is his repeated insistence that Whitman could not have influenced Pound—strange, that is, in view of Pound's own admission in his early essay on Whitman (written 1909, published 1955) of just such an influence ("Mentally I am a Walt Whitman who has learned to wear a collar"). In "Ezra Pound: His Metric and Poetry" (1917) Eliot wrote: "Whitman is certainly not an influence; there is not a trace of him anywhere; Whitman and Mr. Pound are antipodean to each other."[9] *Not a trace* is the kind of extreme statement to inspire a contrary critic to find a trace—the kind of statement, in fact, that calls itself by the very nature of its flamboyance into question; and indeed, some critics have found several traces of Whitman in Pound, as for example Donald Davie in his 1964 work, *Ezra Pound: Poet as Sculptor* (referring to the early poetry: "The only poetic voice that [Pound] can command ... is the voice of Whitman.")[10] Eliot would not let the matter lie, and returned to it in his Introduction to *Ezra Pound: Selected Poems* (1928): "I am ... certain—it is indeed obvious—that Pound owes nothing to Whitman"; "Now Pound's originality is genuine in that his versification is a logical development of the verse of his English predecessors. Whitman's originality is both genuine and spurious. It is genuine in so far as it is a logical development of certain English prose; Whitman was a great prose writer. It is spurious in so far as Whitman wrote in a way that asserted that his great prose was a new form of verse. (And I am ignoring in this connection the large part of clap-trap in Whitman's content.)"[11] It is somewhat surprising to find Eliot here resurrecting a disreputable theory that Whitman's poetry was really not poetry, but prose instead. And the parting shot, especially that "clap-trap," betrays an intensity of feeling that the critical point seems hardly to call for. What in Whitman inspired such passionate response?

In a 1926 review of Emory Holloway's biography of Whitman, which had raised a question about Whitman's ambivalent sexuality following Holloway's discovery that a "Children of Adam" poem addressed to a woman had been in manuscript originally addressed to a man, Eliot perhaps touched on the matter that made him so intense in his feeling about Whitman: "Whitman had the ordinary desires of the flesh; for him there was no chasm between the real and the ideal, such as opened before the horrified eyes of Baudelaire. But this, and the 'frankness' about sex for which he is either extolled or mildly reproved, did not spring from any particular honesty or clearness of vision: it sprang from what may be called either 'idealization' or a faculty for make-believe, according as we are disposed. There is, fundamentally, no difference between the Whitman frankness and the Tennyson delicacy, except in its relation to public opinion of the time." This is a strange statement indeed in the context of the revelations of the Holloway book; and the attempt to equate the "Whitman frankness and the Tennyson delicacy" seems far-fetched: clearly Eliot saw himself closer to the Baudelaire "horror." In spite of its general negative thrust, his review of the Whitman biography concluded with a positive assessment, however backhanded: "Beneath all the declamations there is another tone, and behind all the illusions there is another vision. When Whitman speaks of the lilacs or of the mocking-bird, his theories and beliefs drop away like a needless pretext."[12] This last sentence has the passionate ring of one who has been deeply moved by Whitman's major poetry—perhaps even in spite of himself.

In something of a final assessment of Whitman in 1953, in "American Literature and the American Language," Eliot singled him out along with Poe and Twain as "landmarks" of American literature: "To Walt Whitman ... a great influence on modern poetry has been attributed. I wonder if this has not been exaggerated. In this respect he reminds me of Gerard Manley Hopkins—a lesser poet than Whitman, but also a remarkable innovator in style. Whitman and Hopkins, I think, both found an idiom and a metric perfectly suited for what they had to say; and very doubtfully adaptable to what anyone else has to say."[13] In view of Eliot's previous views of Whitman, this statement is nothing short of amazing, and seems to pay homage to both Whitman's form and content. To place Whitman above Hopkins, whose religious poetry would by its very nature have attracted Eliot's deep appreciation, and whose dazzling metrics and sound patterns would have held his deep interest, is astonishing. And to conclude of Whitman that he found "an idiom and a metric perfectly suited" for what he had to say is a long, long way from his early view that both his form and content were suspect. Can we detect here, perhaps, the genuine view of a poet now secure in his own style and reputation, with no longer a need to deny his precursors?

Although it would serve no purpose to go through Eliot's poetry tracking every Whitmanian echo,[14] there are one or two highly relevant to my purposes here. The first, little noticed, appears in "Ode," a poem that Eliot published in *Ara Vos Prec*, 1920 limited edition, never reprinted; thus it does not appear among his collected poems, and has escaped the attention of most of his critics. Space does not permit full analysis of this poem (for my reading of it as a confessional poem see *T. S. Eliot's Personal Waste Land*), but the second stanza appears intelligible only in a Whitmanian context:

Misunderstood
The accents of the now retired
Profession of the calamus.[15]

Eliot's pervasive technique of literary allusion renders it inevitable that, on encountering "calamus," the reader recall the only literary use of the word—in Whitman's *Leaves of Grass*. "Calamus" is a cluster of poems devoted to comradeship, "adhesive" love, and man–man relationships, coming directly after and in contrast to the "Children of Adam" cluster of procreational, sexual, or man–woman poems. (*Calamus* was the title, too, given to a volume of Whitman's passionately intense letters to his "Young Friend," Peter Doyle, published in 1897.) Eliot would surely never have used the word without expecting his readers to make the Whitman connection. We can only assume, then, that the speaker of "Ode" has been a writer whose work has been "misunderstood"—the previous work that was written with the "accents" of the "profession of the calamus." The "accents" of comradeship, man–man love? "Ode" was probably written in 1918, and Eliot had published in 1917 *Prufrock and Other Observations*, a book containing such poems as "The Love Song of J. Alfred Prufrock," and "Portrait of a Lady"—poems portraying (among other things) men who cannot love women.

Another important echo of *Leaves* appears in a passage of *The Waste Land* that Eliot designated as his favorite—what he called the "30 good lines" of the poem, lines of "the water-dripping song in the last part" ("What the Thunder Said"). Among these lines appear the following:

If there were the sound of water only
Not the cicada
And dry grass singing
But sound of water over a rock
Where the hermit-thrush sings in the pine trees
Drip drop drip drop drop drop drop
But there is no water.
(p. 144)[16]

In view of Eliot's own appreciation of "When Lilacs Last in the Dooryard Bloom'd" (as in the comment quoted above concluding his review of the Holloway biography), the Whitman connection here can be missed only at peril of misreading the meaning. The hermit thrush is an American bird, and Whitman made it his own in his Lincoln elegy. We might even take the "dry grass singing" as an oblique allusion to *Leaves of Grass*, where the grass image evoked is usually green, not dry. There is no "sound of water," there is no green grass growing, there is no hermit thrush singing in the pine trees. What is missing, then, is not merely a set of sounds, but what the sounds vitally imply; and what they imply can be fully comprehended only in the context of Whitman's "Lilacs." Whitman's hermit thrush becomes the source of his reconciliation to Lincoln's death, to all death as the "strong deliveress." The poet follows the bird to hear "Death's outlet song of life" as he goes "Down to the shores of the water, the path by the swamp in the dimness, / To the solemn shadowy cedars and ghostly pines so still." Lincoln is never mentioned by name in "Lilacs," but references to him are very much in the "calamus" spirit—the poet mourns for his "comrade lustrous," for the dead he "loved so well."[17] If we follow out all the implications of Eliot's evocation of Whitman's "Lilacs" at this critical moment in *The Waste Land*, we might assume that the modern poem has its origins, too, in a death, in a death deeply felt, the death of a beloved friend. But unlike the Whitman poem, Eliot's *Waste Land* has no retreat on the "shores of the water," no hermit thrush to sing its joyful carol of death; rather, "Only a cock ... on the rooftree" to sound mockingly its ambiguous "Co co rico co co rico" (p. 145).

2

When Valerie Eliot edited and published *The Waste Land: A Facsimile and Transcription of the Original Drafts* in 1971, she prefaced the materials with one of Eliot's few comments about the poem's meaning: "Various critics have done me the honour to interpret the poem in terms of criticism of the contemporary world, have considered it, indeed, as an important bit of social criticism. To me it was only the relief of a personal and wholly insignificant grouse against life; it is just a piece of rhythmical grumbling." Critics have tended to ignore or discount this statement, primarily because they have been unwilling to reconsider the long tradition of interpreting the poem as primarily social criticism. I wish to take Eliot's statement seriously, and, moreover, I would like to link it to the by now familiar description, in "A Backward Glance," of Whitman's aim in *Leaves of Grass*, "to articulate and faithfully express in literary or poetic form, and uncompromisingly, my own physical, emotional, moral, intellectual, and aesthetic Personality, in the midst of, and tallying, the momentous spirit and facts of its immediate days, and of current America."[18]

In making this link with Whitman, I shall not follow the practice of critics of looking back from the 1922 published *Waste Land* to the 1917 essay "Tradition and the Individual Talent," with its ambiguous "Impersonal theory of poetry" (later strongly modified by Eliot); but instead will look forward to the Eliot who would describe his own *Waste Land* as a "personal ... grouse," and who could write of Tennyson's *In Memoriam*: "It is unique: it is a long poem made by putting together lyrics, which have only the unity and continuity of a diary, the concentrated diary of a man confessing himself." In this same 1936 essay on Tennyson, Eliot appeared to have his own *Waste Land* in mind when he wrote: "It happens now and then that a poet by some strange accident expresses the mood of his generation, at the same time that he is expressing a mood of his own which is quite remote from that of his generation."[19] The thrust behind such language as this is very close to that in Whitman's remark quoted above: whether expressing a "Personality" (emotional, moral, intellectual), or expressing his own mood, Whitman, Tennyson—and Eliot himself in *The Waste Land*—seem to be embarked on obscurely related enterprises.

But how is it that critics have for so long missed the personal "mood" in *The Waste Land* that Eliot seems to claim repeatedly as prior and fundamental?[20] The answer, I think, is that there are two *Waste Lands*, the one published in 1922, heavily shaped by Ezra Pound; the other, the original set of manuscripts that Eliot handed over to Pound. It is possible that this "original" poem is the one that Eliot is remembering when he speaks of his relation to the poem. It is, after all, closer to the original sources, feelings, and impulses out of which the poem came. Moreover, there is evidence that Eliot felt the poem slipping out of his grasp as he saw it revised by Pound and as he sometimes reluctantly acquiesced in the revision; as he saw it, in other words, become something other than he had set out to write and had actually written.

Let us take one example, but an important one—the epigraph of the original poem, from Joseph Conrad's *Heart of Darkness*: "Did he live his life again in every detail of desire, temptation, and surrender during that supreme moment of complete knowledge? He cried in a whisper at some image, at some vision—he cried out twice, a cry that was no more than a breath—'The horror! the horror!'" (p. 3). The words are, of course, those of Marlow describing the death of Kurtz, speculating on Kurtz's own awareness of complicity and self-involvement. Pound wrote to Eliot: "I doubt if Conrad is weighty enough to stand the citation." Eliot replied: "Do you mean not use the Conrad quote or simply not put Conrad's name to it? It is much the most appropriate I can find, and somewhat elucidative." At this slight complaint, Pound gave his reluctant permission on the epigraph: "Ditto re Conrad; who am I to grudge him his laurel crown?"[21] But of course, Pound's acquiescence is phrased in such a way as to encourage Eliot to change the quotation—which he did, adopting the now famous passage in Latin and Greek, without indication of its source from Petronius's *Satyricon* (chapter 48): "Yes, and I myself with my own eyes saw the Sibyl of Cumae hanging in the cage; and when the boys cried at her: 'Sibyl, what do you want?', she used to reply, 'I want to die'" (p. 133).

As in instance after instance in the revision, Pound succeeded here in diffusing one dimension of the poem on behalf of another, a "public" or "social" meaning which he perhaps succeeded in making dominant. Indeed, in a letter written in July 1922 Pound defended the social criticism of his own poetry, spoke out for a "profounder didacticism" in art ("It's all rubbish to pretend that art isn't didactic"), and then revealingly referred to *The Waste Land* in a proprietary tone: "Eliot's Waste Land is I think the justification of the 'movement,' of our modern experiment, since 1900. It shd. be published this year."[22] The context makes it clear that Pound saw *The Waste Land* as an example of that "profounder didacticism" which he was defending—the kind of didacticism that would seriously confront the "foeter" of England and the "rotting" of the "British Empire." It takes little imagination, in the light of Eliot's later disclaimers of any major intent of "social criticism," to assume that *The Waste Land*'s author and *The Waste Land*'s reviser were working at odds, consciously or unconsciously, in giving final birth to the poem. The reviser made the poem over into a Poundian poem.

The shift of the epigraph from Conrad to Petronius may be taken as representative. The shift is out and back, to foreign (even "dead") languages and the distant past. And the shift is from the human to the mythic—it is the Sybil who wants to die. The possible personal relevance is highly ambiguous. But the Conrad quotation is another matter. Eliot's remark to Pound—"It is the most appropriate I can find, and somewhat elucidative"—has gone almost unnoticed by *Waste Land* critics. *Appropriate* and *elucidative*: the very fact that Eliot saw the Conrad quotation in this way, and that Pound simply wondered about its "weightiness," suggests a major difference in approach, in comprehension. Moreover, Eliot would seem to be right. There are words and phrases in the Conrad epigraph that are echoed in the poem: "Did he live his life again in every detail of desire, temptation, and surrender during that supreme moment of complete knowledge?" Desire: "memory and desire, stirring / Dull roots with spring rain." Temptation and surrender: "The awful daring of a moment's surrender / Which an age of prudence can never retract." A "supreme moment of complete knowledge": Then spoke the Thunder; "Datta, dayadhvan, damyata": "give, sympathise, control" (pp. 145–46). In *Heart of Darkness*, Kurtz "cried in a whisper at some image, at some vision—he cried out twice, a cry that was no more than a breath—'The horror! the horror!'" The whole of *The Waste Land*, especially as it exists in the manuscripts, appears to be scenes from a life lived over again, scenes flashing by during a "supreme moment of complete knowledge," scenes that make up an interior "image" or "vision," evoking "The horror! the horror!"

In short, the Petronius quotation points outside while the Conrad points inside the consciousness of the poem: indeed, the state of consciousness and self-awareness of Kurtz in *The Heart of Darkness* may be taken as a paradigm for a similar state of consciousness lying behind and unifying *The Waste Land*. It announces (or suggests) that *The Waste Land* is focused not on the world but on an individual's consciousness as he is perceiving himself and the world—in a state of emotional-spiritual crisis. Marlow's statement about Kurtz, then, offers a kind of outline of the "action" of *The Waste Land*, and is indeed, as Eliot told Pound, "appropriate" and "elucidative." This "action" is not an objective statement of social criticism about the world become waste land. Rather, it is a dramatization of an individual consciousness in a precarious state of balance living "his life again in every detail of desire, temptation, and surrender" as he works his way to that "supreme moment of complete knowledge" out of the Thunder's voice (at the end of "What the Thunder Said"). The knowledge is self-knowledge. The final vision is a vision of the self broken and shattered, shoring some literary-intellectual fragments against his "ruins." *The Waste Land* lies within. It may he within us all.

We may, then, read the original *Waste Land* as a dreamlike recapitulation of a life, all the scenes connected with that one life, the characters melding into each other as in a dream, but resolving into figures connected with the life represented by that central consciousness. All of the original poem fits easily into this frame, and the parts form a sequence that moves with a kind of directness and inevitability to the vision brought by the Thunder's voice at the end. With this frame in mind, we may more easily understand those sections of the manuscripts, excised by Pound and Eliot, that had direct connection with Eliot's life—the opening scene of debauchery, for example, which came out of Eliot's Harvard days, or the long sea scene of Part IV, that related to Eliot's youth and his summer vacations in Massachusetts near the Dry Salvages. In presenting a consciousness reliving his moments of "desire, temptation, and surrender," Eliot felt free to draw (or perhaps unconsciously drew) on moments and details of his own life, some of the most clear-cut of which did not survive revision. With the publication of *The Waste Land* facsimile, Valerie Eliot revealed more and more of the poem's "characters" as originating in Eliot's own life (as, for example, the Marie of the opening section, and Stetson at its close).[23]

3

In contrast with most analyses of *The Waste Land*, we might heed Eliot's observations that in his end is his beginning: we shall begin with the "moment" which the original epigraph indicated was in the poem, and to which all the rest of the poem is directed: a life relived up to a moment of "complete knowledge." Since the epigraph indicated that the "details" of the life relived were details of "desire, temptation, and surrender," we might expect the knowledge achieved to have something to do with these matters. And, indeed, this proves to be the case.

Eliot directs our attention in his footnotes to the *Brihadaranyaka Upanishad*, 5, 1, for the source of his "Datta, dayadhvam, damyata," and for the "fable of the meaning of the Thunder." In the *Upanishad*, the god Prajâpati is asked by his sons—gods, men, and Asuras—to instruct them, and he does so through the voice of the Thunder, always in a single syllable. First he says "Da," and the gods understand him to advise self-control; his next "Da" to the men they take to mean "give"; and his third "Da" to the Asuras (Hindu evil deities) they understand to mean "have compassion." As the commentator on this *Upanishad* points out, the uttering of the one syllable forced each group in turn to discover his own weakness within. In other words, the god's advice turns out to be self-advice that is elicited through self-awareness.[24]

Eliot departs from the *Upanishad*, as he inverts the order from *control yourselves*, *give*, and *have compassion* to *give*, *sympathize*, *control*, and as he subtly modulates the meaning to suit his own purposes. The first "Da" the poet hears he takes to be "Datta": give. Whereas the men in the *Upanishad* take this advice to mean "distribute your wealth to the best of your might, for you are naturally avaricious," Eliot applies it in an entirely different context. This should be sufficient signal to the reader that the poet is not simply reproducing the incident from the *Upanishad* but is adapting it to his situation in *The Waste Land*. When the Thunder says "Da," the poet-protagonist responds with a genuine confrontation with the interior self—and the intrusive memory that has haunted him throughout the poem.

The manuscript is helpful in clarifying the nature of that memory. At one time (in probably the earliest version), Eliot had written (italicized words later revised):

Datta. *we brother*, what have we given!
My friend, *my friend, beating in* my heart,

The awful daring of a moment's surrender
Which an age of prudence *cannot* retract—
By this, and this only, we have existed,
Which is not to be found in our obituaries,
Nor in memories *which will busy* beneficent spiders
Nor *in documents eaten* by the lean solicitor
In our empty rooms.

(p. 77)

The partner is unmistakably masculine, the moment is a "moment of surrender," a giving of the self to a friend—a surrender and a giving that "an age of prudence cannot retract." In revising the passage, the meaning was not changed, but slightly dispersed or diffused. The first line dropped the direct address, "we brother." The second line became "My friend, blood shaking my heart"; in the original, it is clearly the friend "beating in" the poet's heart that has been the origin of his passionate intensity.

The meaning of this passage appears to me lucid, and the tone not ironic but deeply moved, deeply moving. It is a confrontation that is also self-confession. The poet and his friend have experienced the "awful daring of a moment's surrender." An age, or lifetime, of "prudence" cannot "retract" that moment, cannot replace it; it exists in time, it endures in the memory. Moreover, this moment has been the essence of their existence, this memory shaping their very selves, giving them their essential, their emotional identity. When they die, this shaping event will not even be listed in their obituaries, nor will it be found in "memories" (mementoes, "treasures") that the spiders will take over, nor in the documents, "under seal," opened after their death by their lawyers (solicitors) going through their "empty rooms." Clearly this passage is clarification for the self, and an affirmation, a confrontation with the truth that the poet-protagonist must learn to live with, not evade, not suppress, not deny, not duplicate or attempt to duplicate.

The second "Da" of the Thunder becomes in the poet's understanding "Dayadhvam," "sympathize." The manuscript version is again helpful (italicized words later revised):

Dayadhvam. *friend, my friend* I have heard the key
Turn in the door, once and once only.
We think of the key, each in his prison,
Thinking of the key, each *has built* a prison.
Only at nightfall, aetherial murmurs
Repair for a moment a broken Coriolanus.

(p. 79)

Once again, Eliot's revisions have slightly diffused the meaning. And his quotations in the footnotes from Dante and F. H. Bradley have deflected the critics from the continuity of meaning in the Thunder passage. It is significant, as revealed in the manuscript, that the passage begins in direct address to the friend. The key that has turned in the door "once and once only" is surely related to the previous "awful daring of a moment's surrender." The self has been genuinely penetrated only once—during that surrender with the friend. The rest of existence has been a memory of that moment, and a contemplation of the key that was once turned. But each is in his prison, a prison (as in the manuscript) "each has built." Though we long for that human or spiritual intermingling, for the soul-sharing that might come with the turn of the key, it does not turn, and we remain alone. *Sympathize. Have compassion*. In a world in which we all exist behind barriers, in fearful isolation, that we ourselves have created, where the very nature of existence itself helps create the prisons we built for ourselves, there is abundant need of sympathy and compassion. The proud Coriolanus may be a supreme example of a man isolated in his own prison. Eliot changed the *repair* to *restore*, and then to *revive the spirits of*. Finally the line read: "Revive for a moment a broken Coriolanus." The precise meaning of these references to Coriolanus may remain obscure,[25] but the general meaning is clear: only occasionally and perhaps transcendentally (or imaginatively) is his (or the poet's, or our) isolation dispelled—and then only momentarily, "aetherially."

The third "Da" spoken by the Thunder evokes from the poet "Damyata," control. In the *Upanishad*, the control is clearly self-control. In Eliot, the control is expanded in meaning. Again, the original manuscript gives us more details with which to construct the meaning (italicized words later revised):

> Damyata: *the wind was fair, and* the boat responded
> Gaily, to the hand expert with sail and *wheel.*
> The sea was calm, *and* your *heart responded*
> Gaily, when invited, beating *responsive*
> To controlling hands. *I left without you*
> *Clasping empty hand: I sit upon the shore*
> *Fishing, with the desolate sunset behind me*
> *Which now at last ....*
>
> (p. 79)

These lines went through several changes, and were finally published:

> Damyata: The boat responded
> Gaily, to the hand expert with sail and oar

The sea was calm, your heart would have responded
Gaily, when invited, beating obedient
To controlling hands.
(p. 146)

In the published *Waste Land*, there is a distinct break at this point, as the image of the poet become fisher king begins the concluding section of the poem.

Given the sequence we have been following in the "Thunder" passages of the manuscripts, there is every reason to believe that the poet is addressing his friend in this sea scene, and it may, in the original version, have been a reconstruction of that moment of daring surrender. In the original manuscript, the moment is consummated: "your heart responded / Gaily, when invited, beating responsive / To controlling hands." By the time the passage is published, the moment is an opportunity passed by: "your heart *would have* responded"; and the beating of the heart would not have been *responsive* but *obedient*. The "controlling hands" are curiously retained. Moreover, the original manuscript describes a separation: "I left without you / Clasping empty hands I sit upon the shore." That "desolate sunset" is clearly the poet's own desolation in the separation from his friend, symbolized by the "clasping empty hands" that once were "controlling."

The third "Da" completes the Thunder's message, and completes, too, the poet's vivid confrontation with the realities of his life that have heretofore evaded him. Though he has not resolved the causes of his agony, he has come to a full recognition of its sources, and he can now set about shaping his life to live as he can with this "complete knowledge." We might summarize the section devoted to the "fable of the meaning of the Thunder"—give, sympathize, control—thus: the poet-protagonist confesses that he has given himself in surrender in a moment whose meaning is beyond calculation; he asks for understanding and sympathy in his impenetrable isolation, an imprisonment that is part of the common human predicament; and he pledges an exchange of one kind of control (of another individual) into self-control, changing controlling hands into clasped hands.

In arriving at this "supreme moment of complete knowledge," the poet presumably relived his life in every detail of "desire, temptation, and surrender." The scenes of *The Waste Land* leading up to this climactic moment should, if we are right, reveal something of these details.

4

We may assume that we are closer not only to the poem's sources but also to its profoundest meanings in reading it through the manuscripts, in the structure it had before the Pound revisions. The various scenes, episodes, or images we may take as flashing fleetingly through the mind of the poet-protagonist on his way to the vision evoked by the Thunder's voice. The original title of the work, "He Do the Police in Different Voices," suggests such a continuity: that is, that all the voices of the poem are those of the poet himself, that the entire drama is interior, that the self of the poet comes forth in the many roles in which he had previously lived his life. In editing the manuscripts, and subsequently, Valerie Eliot has emphasized the biographical sources of the poem. Her persuasive revelations, often coming originally from the poet himself, show the poem as much less independent of its author than once assumed. Indeed, the "I" of the poem appears now to have the kind of connection with the author that Whitman's "I" has in his *Leaves*, or Pound's in *The Cantos*, or (in a complicated way) John Berryman's various "I's" in *The Dream Songs*. Thus in quickly reading through the poem, we shall repeatedly note a biographical dimension.

Perhaps the most biographical of all the lines are those Eliot placed first, a scene of one night's debauchery (or hell-raising) by college youth in a night out on the town in the Boston of Eliot's own college days. Drinking and sex are the aim, but there seems to be more of the first than the latter. By the end of the passage, an "I" has separated out from the various characters, an "I" whom we might identify with the "I" of *The Waste Land*. As his companions race off in a meaningless romp, this individual gets out of the cab and goes off alone: "So I got out to see the sunrise, and walked home." There is an essential innocence to this episode that is part of its tone, a merry boys-will-be-boys fun. Clearly this scene comes from the life of the poet before the events that are the focus of the episode of the Thunder's voice, the subject of his "complete knowledge." His instantaneous review of his life begins with a period of innocence when so much of what he will later view with a kind of horror or revulsion, especially sex, is evoked in a comic context (drunken college boys refused admission to Myrtle's brothel). Moreover, the image of the sunrise at the end of this opening episode, viewed clearly with anticipation and pleasure, provides a strong contrast with the "desolate sunset" to which the "fisher king" turns his back at the very end of the manuscript version of the poem. But by the time Eliot and Pound had finished their revision, both sunrise and sunset had disappeared from *The Waste Land*.

The next passage after this opening college scene is the now famous one that opens the published *Waste Land*: "April is the cruellest month, breeding / Lilacs out of the dead land, mixing / Memory and desire, stirring / Dull roots with spring rain." We may assume that with these lines we are much closer in time to the poet on his way to complete knowledge, the poet who has clearly been severely wounded in the time between those innocent college days and the "now" of the poem. April and lilacs stir "memory and desire," carrying the poet back to the period abroad—a time that we might identify as 1910–11, when Eliot left Harvard for a year to study at the Sorbonne, followed by a summer of travel through Europe, including northern Italy and Munich. All the details fit (Königssee, Hofgarten), including the conversation of Marie—who is, according to Valerie Eliot, Countess Marie Larisch, whom Eliot actually met and whose "description of the sledding, for example, was taken verbatim" from the conversation (pp. 125–26). Although we are not told when this encounter took place, we might assume it to be during that summer trip in Germany. But the important detail of these lines comes in "Winter kept us warm"; "Summer surprised us"; "we stopped in the colonnade." The plural pronoun reveals that the poet is remembering the time with his friend—the friend revealed by the Thunder's voice—but here in the midst of their fulfilled friendship; a friend perhaps met at the Sorbonne who may have accompanied Eliot on his summer travels, the two together encountering the "niece and confidante of the Austrian Empress Elizabeth" and hearing her idle conversation of an idle life.

After the break of the asterisks (in the manuscript only), the poet has slipped from memory back into the agonizing present "What are the roots that clutch, what branches grow / Out of this stony rubbish?" The lifeless scene ("dead tree," "dry stone," "red rock") is highly evocative of death, and the concluding line of the cluster—"I will show you fear in a handful of dust"—suggests (in line with the title of this section, "The Burial of the Dead") that death is the root cause of the present agony. Another set of asterisks indicates the taking over of "memory and desire" once again, confirmed by the Wagnerian love lyric, followed by recollections of a moment in the past, associated with hyacinths, of transcendent love—"I was neither / Living nor dead, and I knew nothing, / Looking into the heart of light, the silence." The closing Wagnerian fragment for this cluster ("Desolate and empty the sea") again shifts the poem from memory to the present.

Are we to assume that the accompanying friend remembered in the present opening of *The Waste Land* is the "hyacinth girl" of these lines? There are many reasons not to so assume. Perhaps the strongest is that the Thunder fable refers clearly to a masculine friend. Moreover, the only reference to the "hyacinth girl" in these lines is placed in a quotation: "You give me hyacinths first a year ago; / They called me the hyacinth girl." With emphasis on *girl*, we might see that the speaker need not be feminine (it was the poet who had presented the hyacinths to the speaker). In addition, there is the classical association of the hyacinth with the calamus-like relationship between Apollo and Hyacinthus, a handsome boy accidentally killed when the two were throwing the disk: in his memory, Apollo created the flower bearing his name as an eternal reminder of his love. Further, the "hyacinth girl" recurs no place else in *The Waste Land* or in the memory of the poet-protagonist, nor does "she" turn up in the hand dealt by Madame Sosostris in the lines next following in "Burial of the Dead." And finally (and perhaps conclusively), the manuscripts of "A Game of Chess" provide a masculine association with the hyacinth image: "I remember / The hyacinth garden. Those are pearls that were his eyes, yes!" (p. 13). Though the "hyacinth garden" reference disappeared in revision, Eliot put in a footnote to the remainder of the line: "Cf. Part I, 1. 37, 48" (p. 147). The first of these contains the "hyacinth garden" image, the second contains the first appearance of the line, "Those are pearls that were his eyes" (parenthetically inserted in Madame Sosostris's speech). Thus Eliot seemed determined that the reader would associate memory of the hyacinth garden with a haunting memory of the drowned sailor.

With Madame Sosostris the poet-protagonist returns from memory to the present, and an ironic assessment of his present condition. The cards dealt by this "famous clairvoyant" are the cards fate has dealt the poet. It is significant that the first is that of the "drowned Phoenician Sailor," causing a momentary catch in the memory of the poet, who meditates to himself as he listens to the Madame: "(Those are pearls that were his eyes. Look!)." Although Pound marked this line for excision, it remained; and it surfaces repeatedly elsewhere in the published *Waste Land* and appears to be a line evoking the friend who is now lost, incarnated in the poem as Phlebas the Phoenician. This first card of fate, then, reveals the basic cause of the poet's present agony: the loss of his companion and friend through drowning, subject of Part IV of the poem. The next card dealt is that of "Belladonna, the Lady of the Rocks, / The lady of situations." This card appears to refer to the woman in the poet's life, and the epithets applied to her suggest her hardness, her craft; we may assume that the poet has become linked to her, probably through marriage, and the relationship has developed into a major source of grief for him. "Belladonna," then, is the second basic fact to account for the poet-protagonist's present critical state, and is a primary subject in Part II of the poem. Grieving for the death of an intimate and beloved friend, trapped in a loveless marriage with a scheming woman, the poet may well view his situation with despair. The next card dealt him is himself and the life he may look forward to: "Here is the man with three staves, and here the Wheel." In the manuscript Eliot had tried "King fishing" and "fisher king" for the "man with three staves" (p. 9), finally settling on the latter. It is the impotent "fisher king" role that the poet-protagonist will later assume, especially in Part III and in the final Part V of the poem. And the "Wheel" symbolizes the tortured, meaningless suburban life that his present plight had bound him to; the figure of the wheel appears in "The Death of the Duchess," a manuscript poem that yielded many of its lines for Part II of *The Waste Land*—"The inhabitants of Hampstead are bound forever on the wheel" (p. 105).

We may take the first three cards of Madame Sosostris as the cards delineating the poet's present fate. But what of his future? The next cards are not reassuring. "And here is the one-eyed merchant, and this card, / Which is blank, is something he carries on his back, / Which I am forbidden to see." In his footnote to the Sosostris section, Eliot points, out that this merchant (like the Phoenician sailor) appears later in the poem—as in fact he does, in Part III, making what appears to be a homosexual proposition ("a weekend at the Metropole") in his "demotic French" (p. 140). But what is suggested by the blank card signifying something he carries on his back—something that even Madame Sosostris is forbidden to see? Could it be the burden that the proposition carries with it, if accepted? And its sordidness as well as its indeterminateness or vagueness keeps it out of Madame Sosostris's vision? This, then, could be a possible future? Madame Sosostris says (in the manuscript): "I look in vain / For the Hanged Man" (p. 9). Eliot's note tells us: "The Hanged man ... fits my purpose in two ways: because he is associated in my mind with the Hanged God of Frazer, and because I associate him with the hooded figure in the passage of the disciples to Emmaus in Part V" (p. 147). Had Madame Sosostris found the Hanged Man, the poet-protagonist might have had the kind of hope found in the traditional elegy—the hope of resurrection and renewal, the trust in spiritual reuniting with the beloved lost friend. But since this card is not found, the poet can look forward to no surcease of his sorrow and despair. Madame Sosostris advises, "Fear death by water": death will bring no release from the pain the poet feels.

In the closing lines of Part I of *The Waste Land*, we see the poet in his present state greeting a friend in the street, one Stetson (who, according to Valerie Eliot, is based on a real bank-clerk acquaintance),[26] with the kind of badinage friends share, but with a serious undercurrent—"That corpse you planted last year in your garden, / Has it begun to sprout? Will it bloom this year?" Corpses buried in the garden, like memories hidden in the psyche, will out no matter what. In the Madame Sosostris section of the poem, the poet has just reviewed in the cards of his fate all those buried corpses of his past that will not lie quietly buried: but principal among them is the real corpse buried, the lost sailor and friend who haunts the poet and appears to be the moving spirit haunting *The Waste Land*.

In Part II of *The Waste Land*, "A Game of Chess," the poet relives the essence of his relation with his wife. The original title of the section, "In the Cage," after the Henry James story of a telegraphist, offered a kind of specific preparation for the second command of the Thunder—sympathize—with the poet's meditation on each creating his own prison: all the characters who appear in "A Game of Chess" are imprisoned within selves that no turning key can reach. In the first half of the section, the poet and his wife have a talk, but without communication: the wife's voice dominates throughout with a kind of nervous staccato; the only answers she receives are the silent meditations of her husband. She demands: "Do you know nothing? Do you see nothing? Do you remember / Nothing?" He replies (but to himself only): "I remember / The hyacinth garden. Those are pearls that were his eyes, yes!" (p. 13). He is on that Wheel of Madame Sosostris's card. The second half of Part II, the scene in the pub, shifts to a level lower in the social order, but the emptiness of relations between the sexes does not markedly differ: everywhere the poet turns, he sees a reflection of his own agonized state, his own imprisonment. We may take the final voice of the section—"Good night, ladies, good night, sweet ladies, good night, good night"—as the poet's own, the poet in delicate psychic balance, making an ironic comment on a scene overheard, a scene that he has translated into the language of his own personal anguish.

Part III of *The Waste Land*, "The Fire Sermon," consists of a medley of scenes, each of which works some variation of "desire, temptation, and surrender," and each of which connects directly or subterraneously with the poet's own particular spiritual malaise. The opening lines on Fresca, marked for deletion by Pound, may be read as some of the most flagrantly misogynistic of the entire poem, dramatically justified by the total vacuity of the poet's marriage as presented in the preceding section. Fresca may represent a composite portrait of all women for the poet—with her "hearty female stench," her "wit of natural trull" (prostitute), she is reduced by the "same eternal and consuming itch" to the role of "plain simple bitch" (pp. 23, 27). It is no accident that immediately after this devastating portrait, the poet appears as the impotent fisher king fishing "in the dull canal," and soon afterwards he receives his invitation from the Smyrna merchant for a "weekend at the Metropole." And shortly thereafter, he becomes the slightly voyeuristic Tiresias, witnessing at the "violet hour" seduction of the bored typist by the "young man carbuncular." Elizabeth and Leicester float into view next, and their gilt trappings are placed in contrast with the sordid scenes of seduction of three modern maidens, all variations in some sense of the bored typist. The section ends with what seems to be both a confession and a prayer: a confession by the poet that he remains caught up in his desires, temptations, surrenders—he is "burning burning burning burning"—and a prayer to be released: "O Lord thou pluckest me out."

In Part IV of *The Waste Land*, "Death by Water," the poet is carried back further into his past than even his college days at Harvard. The sea narrative that once opened this section begins with a journey starting from the Dry Salvages—a cluster of dangerous rocks off Gloucester, Massachusetts, the vacation home of the Eliots during T. S. Eliot's boyhood (and, of course, the title of the third of "Four Quartets"). There are several indications ("A porpoise snored upon the phosphorescent swell," "the sea rolled asleep" [p. 55]) that this narrative is some kind of dream sequence in which the poet is reliving his life symbolically up to the death of his beloved friend. The ship started out with "kingfisher weather," and nearly "everything went wrong," with the food spoiled and the crew becoming quarrelsome. But then the fish came, and the voyage suddenly turned into a happy one, as the men began to count their earnings. Just as suddenly the voyage again turned threatening—this time into a nightmare, the ship sailing beyond the "farthest northern islands," and ultimately into an iceberg—and total destruction. At a critical point the poet confessed, "I thought, now, when / I like, I can wake up and end the dream." But the dream continued to its nightmare conclusion—and death. It is at this point that the lines (on Phlebas the Phoenician), that survived revision, appear; the drowned sailor is described in his death as in some ways reenacting the experience of the poet in the structure of the poem: "He passed the stages of his age and youth / Entering the whirlpool." Memory of Phlebas lies at the heart of the "memory and desire" of the poem: "Consider Phlebas, who was once handsome and tall as you" (pp. 55–61).

If Part IV of *The Waste Land* presents a sea journey to a confrontation with death, ending with the vivid scene of the drowned sailor disintegrating beneath the waves, Part V ("What the Thunder Said") presents a land journey to a similar confrontation—at the Chapel Perilous in the mountains, amidst the "tumbled graves": "There is the empty chapel, only the wind's house, / It has no windows, and the door swings, / Dry bones can harm no one." The journey has been long and arduous for such an empty discovery; but of course this is not *the* discovery of the section, but a requisite preliminary to it. The realization that "dry bones can harm no one" brings a "damp gust," and then the speech of the Thunder. The discovery brought by the Thunder is a discovery about life that could come only after the confrontation with death, the discovery that we have already examined above, embodied in the Thunder's speech: give, sympathize, control. In confronting the sailor's death, the poet can finally confront the meaning of his relationship with him in life, that "awful daring of a moment's surrender."

Our final view of the poet is in his role as impotent fisher king, picking through the pieces that constituted his life ("These fragments I have shored against my ruins"), yearning for "Shantih, shantih, shantih"—"The Peace which passeth understanding." But he has made his journey to confrontation, and has probed the obscure and elusive meaning of his existence. He does have fragments to work with to shore against his "ruins."

5

Validity of the above reading does not hang on identification of Phlebas the Phoenician in Eliot's life. But as a matter of fact, there is some reason to believe that he was one Jean Verdenal, a French medical student who wrote poetry and lived in Eliot's *pension* in Paris during Eliot's year (1910–11) of study at the Sorbonne. (It should be noted parenthetically that the first critic to make this suggestion, John Peter, was earlier the author of an essay reading *The Waste Land* [without benefit of the manuscripts] along the lines outlined above; and he was threatened by Eliot with a lawsuit and as a result withdrew the article until after Eliot's death, at which time he resurrected it and presented his theory about Jean Verdenal; this fascinating chapter in *Waste Land* criticism requires its own separate treatment.)[27] Eliot's dedication of his first volume of poems, *Prufrock and Other Observations* (1917), to him tells us most of what we know about him: "For Jean Verdenal, 1889–1915 / mort aux Dardanelles." The Dante quotation which came to be included in the dedication is from Canto XXI of the *Purgatorio*, and may be translated—"Now you are able to comprehend the quantity of love that warms me toward you, / When I forget our emptiness / treating shades as if they were solid."[28] Eliot's only other reference to Verdenal is to be found in the editor's column of *Criterion* for April 1934 in a passage in which Eliot was reminiscing about the Paris of his youth: "I am willing to admit that my own retrospect is touched by a sentimental sunset, the memory of a friend coming across the Luxembourg Gardens in the late afternoon, waving a branch of lilac, a friend who was later (so far as I could find out) to be mixed with the mud of Gallipoli."[29]

With the sparse facts that are known, we might construct the following plausible account of the Eliot–Verdenal relationship: At the age of twenty-two, Eliot went to Paris and found living in his same *pension* a charming young Frenchman his own age who was studying medicine and who wrote poetry. Loneliness impelled Eliot into friendship, and proximity made close attachment possible and even probable. It would have been natural for the two to travel in Italy and Germany during the summer (especially Munich, where Eliot completed "Prufrock"), and it is possible that their relationship was renewed in 1914 on Eliot's return to Paris. World War I forced Eliot's departure from Germany to England in 1914 and led to Verdenal's enlisting or being drafted in the French forces. Caught in the campaign to take the Dardanelles in 1915, he was one of the countless young Frenchmen, Englishmen, and Australians who were lost in "the mud of Gallipoli."

According to his military records, he was cited for bravery in evacuating the wounded by sea on 30 April 1915, and he was "killed by the enemy on the 2nd May 1915 in the Dardanelles." A notation on the record indicates he was killed "while dressing a wounded man on the field of battle." There appears to be no record of disposition of the body by land or by sea.[30] Eliot would have heard of his death in May, or at the latest in early June, and his dismay and anguish may well have impelled him into a hasty marriage that was largely meaningless except as an irrational response to his bitter loss. The marriage turned out to be catastrophic; the deeply wounded Eliot seems to have felt revulsion at the thought of intimacy with a woman—a woman that all his friends (and apparently he) found "vulgar";[31] finding himself unstimulated sexually, he seems to have attempted to fill Vivienne's physical needs only some six months after the marriage by sending her off alone on a beach holiday with Bertrand Russell, something of a satyr. But as Vivienne's mental health deteriorated, caused in part at least by the frustrations of an unsatisfying, perhaps unconsummated, marriage, Eliot's health also began to deteriorate, and his ability to write poetry to decline. The critical point was reached in 1921, when he found his only refuge from a breakdown was to take leave from his job (and Vivienne), consult a nerve specialist, or psychologist, in Lausanne, Switzerland, and write a long poem which had been under contemplation for some time—*The Waste Land*.[32]

If this version of Eliot's early years is approximately right, there can be no doubt that the voice of *The Waste Land* is *his* voice, the spiritual crisis of the poem's protagonist *his* crisis. What we have in *The Waste Land*, then, is not an "impersonal" poem, nor yet an autobiographical poem, but a poem much closer in form to such poems of Whitman's *Leaves of Grass* as "Out of the Cradle Endlessly Rocking" or "When Lilacs Last in the Dooryard Bloom'd," poems in which biography has been transfigured into poetic drama. Or, indeed, much closer than formerly thought to Eliot's own later *Four Quartets*, where the spiritual quest has always been assumed to be Eliot's own. We might say of *The Waste Land* what Eliot wrote of Whitman's two poems: "Beneath all the declamations there is another tone, and behind all the illusions there is another vision. When Whitman speaks of the lilacs or of the mocking-bird, his theories and beliefs drop away like a needless pretext."[33]

The reality of Jean Verdenal, or the actual biographical nature of his relationship with Eliot, does not determine the meaning we have been exploring in *The Waste Land*. What Eliot made imaginatively of the reality of some such relationship has determined the meaning deposited in the poem itself. It is along this line of thought that we might be led to say that if Jean Verdenal did not exist, we would have to invent him: *The Waste Land* insists on it and demands of us the invention.[34] In a similar vein, we could say of Milton's "Lycidas" that it demands we invent Edward King, or of Tennyson's *In Memoriam* that we invent Arthur Hallam, or of Whitman's "When Lilacs Last in the Dooryard Bloom'd" that we invent Abraham Lincoln. The parallels are not exact, but they are close enough to render comparison meaningful: each of these poems begins with a private grief and moves out through an ever widening view to a public perspective. The first has shaped the latter, but the latter is shared by the poem's readers in ways that the first could never be. Thus a private and personal anguish becomes the means through poetic experience to a general or universal insight. The poet begins with himself, but ends with the world. *The Waste Land* lies within, but it leads to the world in waste.

6

In 1933 Eliot asserted: "But what a poem means is as much what it means to others as what it means to the author: and indeed, in the course of time a poet may become merely a reader in respect to his own works, forgetting his original meaning—or without forgetting, merely changing."[35] Here Eliot seems to be acknowledging that in spite of his protests, *The Waste Land* has continued to be and will continue to be read as social criticism—and the readers who thus interpret the poem have their right to do so.

We have already noted how the American personal epic, though it begins with individual experience, reaches out to a public or political dimension. Even in his "Calamus" or most "confessional" poems, Whitman projected a political ideal, a state of democratic brotherhood. The pattern of movement from personal to public, from private to political, is repeated in all the American long poems ambitious to be epic. As Eliot implies, it would be foolish to deny that this "meaning" exists in the poem. Any "personal grouse" against life is, to be persuasive, necessarily involved with some of the probably unpleasant realities of life as it objectively "is." There *is* sterility in modern urban life, there *is* spiritual desiccation in modern religious belief, there *is* a deep sense of futility in contemporary experience, meaninglessness in much of modern activity, emptiness in many human relationships and institutions, including marriage.

The Waste Land, then, like Whitman's *Leaves* before it or John Berryman's *Dream Songs* after, does have a dimension of "social criticism" that is important to its totality of meaning. But as in the other poems, it is not independent but dependent—and dependent on that "personal" dimension that is central to the poem's meaning and structure. Of all the American long poems with which we are dealing here, it is in some ways most like Berryman's *Dream Songs*. The secret of Berryman's sequence is the recurring nightmarish memory of the father's suicide—a suicide committed in the young son's presence. This very private, very personal experience is the unspoken event around which the *Dream Songs* revolve; they often take their meaning from this private anguish even when they contain no reference to it. The father's suicide may be said to haunt *The Dream Songs* just as Jean Verdenal's death haunts *The Waste Land*. But both long poems radiate out from this private source, and take a jaundiced view of the world and human experience that exerts its universal appeal.

But *The Waste Land*'s early readers, without benefit of the manuscripts published in 1971, tended to read the poem as social criticism without awareness of the personal dimension. They saw the poem's unrelieved anguish as a supposedly objective view of the world as it "really is," and they struggled to interpret the poem's odd attitude toward sex and women as compatible with the poem's social and religious themes. Ezra Pound helped in his revisions to give the poem this unrelieved look, closer in spirit to those Cantos that often are unrelieved invective or diatribe against some social ill or wrong.

Both Hart Crane and William Carlos Williams took dark views of this dark poem, and their reactions were important in shaping *The Bridge* and *Paterson*—poems that were in some ways "answers" or "replies" to *The Waste Land*. But one of the elements of these "answers" is the personal dimension they include, as much as to say: if Eliot would take poetry down an "impersonal" path, they would remain relentlessly "personal"—but still dedicated to austere art. They did not live to know the manuscripts of Eliot's poem—and just how intimately "personal" Eliot's poem was. Crane saw it as a poem of "complete renunciation" that was "so damned dead," and he saw his "vision" in *The Bridge* as in some way countering Eliot's.[36] Williams believed that *The Waste Land* "gave the poem back to the academics," and returned poetry "to the classroom.[37] Both poets reflected Eliot's influence in their poems, including his dark "vision": but both poets labored to write their poems as in some sense a corrective to the unrelieved darkness of Eliot's vision.

Very often in the history of American poetry, Walt Whitman and T. S. Eliot have been presented as two possible polarities, the two extremes: of the personal and the impersonal; of the optimistic and the pessimistic. They have been painted in unrelieved colors, and poets have taken one or the other as model, or have attempted to thread their way through the straits between. In reality, neither poet is so unrelieved. And they have more in common than has often been thought—in the way they exploit poetically their emotional experience, and in the way they use themselves and their feelings as representative of their time and place. It seems unlikely that Eliot's long poem, in the form in which it was first conceived and written, would have been possible without the precedence of Whitman's own experiments in similar forms. In what he derived from Whitman consciously or unconsciously, and in the way he shaped the poems that came after him, T.S. Eliot must assume a prominent place in the succession of America's poets of the personal epic. And *The Waste Land* must be viewed with double vision: the poem as it exists in history (the 1922 published version) and the poem as it escapes history (as it is glimpsed in manuscript), as it is in and of itself.

A final word:
from
"Fifty Years of American Poetry"

Randall Jarrell

> Won't the future say to us in helpless astonishment: "But did you actually believe that all those things about objective correlatives, classicism, the tradition, applied to his poetry? Surely you must have seen that he was one of the most subjective and daemonic poets who ever lived, the victim and helpless beneficiary of his own inexorable compulsions, obsessions? From a psychoanalytical point of view he was far and away the most interesting poet of your century. But for you, of course, after the first few years, his poetry existed undersea, thousands of feet below that deluge of exegesis, explication, source listing, scholarship, and criticism that overwhelmed it. And yet how bravely, and personally it survived, its eyes neither coral nor mother-of-pearl but plainly human, full of anguish.[38]

Notes

1. Robert E. Knoll, Introduction to *Storm over "The Waste Land"* (Chicago: Scott, Foresman & Co., 1964), p. i.
2. I. A. Richards, *Principles of Literary Criticism* (New York: Harcourt, Brace & Co., 1948), pp. 290–91.

3. T. S. Eliot, "Tradition and the Individual Talent," *Selected Essays* (New York: Harcourt, Brace & Co., 1950), p. 7.

4. M. L. Rosenthal, "*The Waste Land* as an Open Structure," *Mosaic*, Fall 1972, pp. 181–82. This essay was incorporated in Rosenthal's *Sailing into the Unknown: Yeats, Pound, and Eliot* (New York: Oxford University Press, 1978); in this work Rosenthal maintains that the "main artistic contribution" of Yeats, Pound, and Eliot is "the modulation toward a poetry of open process, largely presentative, which tends toward a balancing of volatile emotional states.... We are talking about a significant evolutionary change of which the practitioners are only incompletely conscious (and the theorists almost completely unconscious, so that the main developments occur by a sort of instinctive collusion among the most highly sensitized poets at any given moment)" (p. 205).

5. Rosenthal, "*The Waste Land* as an Open Structure," pp. 188–89.

6. See this position sustained at length in James E. Miller, Jr., *T. S. Eliot's Personal Waste Land: Exorcism of the Demons* (College Park: Pennsylvania State University Press, 1977).

7. Sydney Musgrove, *T. S. Eliot and Walt Whitman* (Wellington: New Zealand University Press, 1952).

8. T. S. Eliot, Introduction to Ezra Pound's *Selected Poems* (London: Faber & Gwyer, 1928), pp. viii–ix.

9. T. S. Eliot, "Ezra Pound: His Metric and Poetry," To *Criticize the Critic* (New York: Farrar, Straus & Giroux, 1965), p. 177.

10. Donald Davie, *Ezra Pound: Poet as Sculptor* (New York: Oxford University Press, 1964), p. 82.

11. T. S. Eliot, Introduction to *Ezra Pound: Selected Poems*, pp. ix, xi.

12. T. S. Eliot, "Whitman and Tennyson," *Walt Whitman: A Critical Anthology*, ed. Francis Murphy (Baltimore: Penguin Books, 1969), p. 207.

13. T. S. Eliot, "American Literature and the American Language," *To Criticize the Critic*, p. 53.

14. But see Sydney Musgrove's *T. S. Eliot and Walt Whitman* (n. 7 above), and James E. Miller, Jr., "Whitman and Eliot: The Poetry of Mysticism," *Quests Surd and Absurd* (Chicago: University of Chicago Press, 1967), p. 112–36.

15. T. S. Eliot, "Ode," *Ara Vos Prec* (London: Ovid Press, 1920), p. 30.

16. Page numbers after quotations from T. S. Eliot's *The Waste Land* or its manuscript version refer to pages in *The Waste Land: A Facsimile and Transcription of the Original Drafts*, ed. Valerie Eliot (New York: Harcourt Brace Jovanovich, 1971). This volume contains, in addition to the manuscripts, important informative footnotes and a reprint of *The Waste Land* as published in 1922 (and its footnotes).

17. Walt Whitman, *Complete Poetry and Selected Prose*, ed. James E. Miller, Jr. (Boston: Houghton Mifflin Co., 1959), pp. 237, 239.

18. Ibid., p. 444.

19. T. S. Eliot, "In Memoriam," *Selected Essays* (New York: Harcourt, Brace & Co., 1950), p. 291.

20. For examination of Eliot's various statements claiming *The Waste Land* as in some sense personal, see Miller, *T. S. Eliot's Personal Waste Land*, pp. 8–11.

21. Ezra Pound, *The Letters* (New York: Harcourt, Brace & World, 1950), pp. 169, 171.

22. Ibid., p. 180.

23. See Miller, *T. S. Eliot's Personal Waste Land*, pp. 66–67, 77.

24. *The Bribadaranyaka Upanishad*, tr. Swami Madhavananda (Calcutta: Advaita Ashrama, 1965), pp. 813, 17.

25. See Miller, *T. S. Eliot's Personal Waste Land*, p. 129.

26. Ibid., p. 77.

27. Ibid., pp. 7–16. See also John Peter, "A New Interpretation of *The Waste Land*," *Essays in Criticism* 2 (July 1952): 245; and "Postscript," *Essays in Criticism* 19 (April 1969): 165–75.

28. See Miller, *T. S. Eliot's Personal Waste Land*, pp. 17–18.

29. T. S. Eliot, "A Commentary," *Criterion* 13 (April 1934): 452.

30. See George Watson, "Quest for a Frenchman," *Sewanee Review* 84 (Summer 1976): 466–75; Miller, *T. S. Eliot's Personal Waste Land*, pp. 20–21.

31. See Miller, *T. S. Eliot's Personal Waste Land*, pp. 25–26.

32. Ibid., pp. 24–27.

33. Eliot, "Whitman and Tennyson," *Walt Whitman*.

34. For a fascinating experiment in the reading of Eliot's *Waste Land* and other poems for what they reveal in and of themselves (without benefit of any biographical data) of Eliot's psychic states, see Leon Edel, *Literary Biography* (Bloomington: Indiana University Press, 1973), pp. 70–88. Edel re-creates an Eliot purely out of the literary data who is quite similar emotionally and psychically to the Eliot we have attempted to delineate through speculation about the biographical data.

35. T. S. Eliot, *The Use of Poetry and the Use of Criticism* (New York: Barnes & Noble, 1933), p. 130.

36. Hart Crane, *The Letters*, ed. Brom Weber (Berkeley: University of California Press, 1965), pp. 127, 105.

37. William Carlos Williams, *The Autobiography* (New York: New Directions, 1951), pp. 146, 174.

38. Randall Jarrell, "Fifty Years of American Poetry," *The Third Book of Criticism* (New York: Farrar, Straus & Giroux, 1969), pp. 314–15.

GREGORY S. JAY

Discovering the Corpus

> Then I—I shall begin again. I shall not cease until I bring the truth to light. Apollo has shown, and you have shown, the duty which we owe the dead. You have my gratitude. You will find me a firm ally, and together we shall exact vengeance for our land and for the god. I shall not rest till I dispel this defilement—not just for another man's sake, but for my own as well. For whoever the assassin—he might turn his hand against me too. Yes, I shall be serving Laius and myself.
>
> Oedipus Tyrannus

The detective and the literary critic are often compared. Each undertakes to solve a mystery, working from scattered clues to piece together the meaning of disparate events. This is a hermeneutic quest, as the detective-critic discloses at last the surprising truths behind apparently random appearances. Ideally, a "totalization" or systematic comprehension of fragments is the result. The figure of the sleuth appeals to every reader's desire to detect a pattern in life's haphazard flow of things; our interest is more intensely fixed when there has been a crime, since the violation of the law stands metaphorically for the negation of meaning in general, for an outbreak of transgression that threatens to bring down the orders of significance established by the law's logos. So it is that many critics take special interest (at least of late) in texts that disobey laws, genres, or

---

From *T. S. Eliot and the Poetics of Literary History*, pp. 137–155.

conventions. Theoretical critics tend to pursue these literary felonies after the formal or aesthetic case is closed, inquiring at the doors of philosophy, linguistics, psychoanalysis, and history, and throughout the neighborhood of the human sciences for the agents of disharmony.

But who has been slain in *The Waste Land*? The intrigue deepens when we realize that the victim, the assailant, and the detective are interchangeable metaphors. The predicament of Oedipus dramatizes this tragic condensation of roles, the entanglements of which will preoccupy much of Eliot's poem. We have seen in an earlier chapter the similar case of the Quester and the Fisher King. The disturbing indistinction between, or identification of, Oedipus and Laius or Quester and King repeats the "peculiar personal intimacy" of poetic sons and fathers. The addition of the detective (a vocation thrust upon both Oedipus and the Quester) to this relation figures the desire to resolve its paradoxes and to reinstitute the power of the law. The poem enacts this effort to unravel the mystery and restore order. Yet simultaneously, in form and conception, it compulsively repeats the crime, transgresses the inherited rules of writing, and dismembers the unity of the fathers' words. Adding another turn of the screw, the poem presents this fragmentation of truth as the death of the speaker or author himself. We are asked to mourn his life as well, though self-murder is the planned escape from "personality" back to the soul's eternal life. The stylistic subordination of personal voice to borrowings, echoes, and allusions performs an askesis that violates the unity of self and tradition. "What happens" to the poet, wrote Eliot in 1919, "is a continual surrender of himself as he is at the moment to something which is more valuable. The progress of an artist is a continual self-sacrifice, a continual extinction of personality" (SE, 7). The body of tradition and the poet himself suffer willingly, or by the will of the poet, the ritual of the *sparagmos*. This is part of the relevance of the vegetation god ceremonies, as they too dramatize an identification of the god with the life of the people who recurrently slay him in the name of fertility. The god's resurrection and the nation's rejuvenation culminate another restricted economy of the *Aufhebung*, in which castration and death are the *via negativa* of potency and life. As I will argue later, this pattern informs *The Waste Land*'s modernist revision of the pastoral elegy, the genre whose laws the poem subjects to uncanny interpretations.

It would be nothing new simply to observe that *The Waste Land* violates literary (and other) laws or that like many such texts it places the reader quite self-consciously in the occupation of the hermeneutic detective. The criminal themes of murder and adultery serve this function and provide self-consuming models for the resolution of the poem as a whole. An avid fan of Conan Doyle and founding member of a Sherlock Holmes fan club, Eliot presents us with a puzzling array of remains that increase our suspicion that a coherent, though horror-filled, story lies behind the "heap of broken images." Dead men turn up everywhere in this unreal city, or their words float to its allusive surface. The story begins like a good melodrama at the victim's burial service and proceeds in disjointed flashbacks to piece together the tale of his loves and losses. But the victim is protean, as are his assailants, and hermaphrodite and polysemous. The corpse's casket is a library, his obituary everyman's. The poem's criminal atmosphere filches much of its scenery from Eliot's reading of Shakespearean and Jacobean tragedy, through numerous allusions to adultery and murder in Webster, Middleton, and others. Eliot's voyeuristic involvement with the sordid had also prompted his earlier verse on urban horrors, his taste for Baudelaire and for *Bubu of Montparnasse*, the story of a Parisian whore for which he wrote a preface. He was fascinated by that English tradition of popular tabloid gossip about the criminal, which seemed to be a modern Jacobeanism. With similar motives Eliot consistently ranks Poe, elegist of dead beauties and inventor of detective fictions, among the three or four American writers worthy of his attention.

The poem's origin in this tradition of low crime, sordid mystery, and dark artistry is evidenced in the manuscripts, where the original title, "He Do the Police in Different Voices," is taken from Dickens' *Our Mutual Friend*. In the passage Eliot has in mind, Sloppy performs a kind of ventriloquism as he reads the newspaper text that tells of ghastly doings, providing an obvious source for *The Waste Land*'s polyvocal method (WLFS, 125). *Our Mutual Friend* contains not only a model for Eliot's revoicings, but a protagonist come back from the dead. John Harmon rises from the waters of the Thames to inhabit London in the disguise of John Rokesmith, covertly observing the fate of his own entailed inheritance, concretely symbolized by the mounds of waste that are the novel's thematic and ironic narrative centers. In erasing his own identity, Harmon, like the Duke in Shakespeare's *Measure for Measure*, compounds and perpetuates the disharmony of his realm. Eliot may also have been thinking of Dickens' *Bleak House*, whose Detective Bucket is one of the first great English comic sleuths. That novel, as J. Hillis Miller has written, brilliantly examines the problems of wills, testaments, and legacies lost in a hopeless mire of documents and interpretations disputed interminably.[1] The novel's characters find themselves bewildered by a mountain of wastepaper. Esther Hawdon, one of the novel's two narrators, tells her tale in an effort to uncover, detective fashion, the truth of her own parentage. Her mother, Lady Dedlock, is an "exhausted deity," an artist of deceptive self-representation. Her dead father, the shadowy Captain Hawdon, was, we are not surprised to learn, a legal copyist—a textual nobody like Melville's Bartleby. His death parallels in implication the farcical court case of Jarndyce and Jarndyce: both represent the breakdown of lawful, authoritative, ordered scripts. The revelations of the novel lead in the end to Esther's marriage and the construction of another Bleak House, an edifice not unlike Dickens' book, which problematically hopes to restore what has been wasted. Eliot agreed that it was Dickens' "best novel" and "finest piece of construction" (SE, 410–11).

The motifs of detection, scattered writings, adulteries, and sacred mysteries may be traced in a second deleted title. Part 2, "A Game of Chess," first bore the designation "In the Cage," the title of Henry James's tale of a young woman whose job in a telegraph-office cage makes her privy to the cryptic secrets of high-society lovers. Valerie Eliot ascribes this title instead tc the passage from Petronius that provided Eliot with his epigraph of the Cumaen sibyl (WLFS, 126). Grover Smith concludes that this explanation "does not hold up," though he declares that James's story "has no particular relevance to Part II of the poem." On the contrary, it strikingly prefigures Eliot's formal and thematic concerns. James uses the figure of the sibyl ironically in his portrait of the girl whose function is "to dole out stamps and postal orders, weigh letters, answer stupid questions, give difficult change and, more than anything else, count words as numberless as the sands of time."[2] She occupies a vortex of writings, exercising her "instinct of observation and detection" in guessing "the high reality, the bristling truth" of the fragmentary messages that pass before her. Although she "was perfectly aware that her imaginative life was the life in which she spent most of her time," supplemented by "greasy" novels "all about fine folks," the girl scarcely perceives the disparity between her projections of sublime Romantic love and the seedier reality of her clients' adulterous liaisons. She finds her ladies and gentlemen "always in communication," and "she read into the immensity of their intercourse stories and meanings without end." Her folly in so mistaking her own wish fulfillment—that Romantic love might sweep her transcendentally out of the plebeian world of her intended Mr. Mudge and into the aristocratic sublime—informs Eliot's placement before his readers of the cryptic evidence of so many sordid or tragic liaisons contemporary and antique. James's tale illustrates a point Eliot would insist upon, that Romanticism looks to relations in this world for a Truth that lies beyond it. James's social point—that her sublime is a trick that cheap romantic novels play on the hearts of the lower class—becomes in Eliot the conviction that he has been seduced by his precursors' imaginative achievement of an erotic union of the mind with the world it reads.

The girl in the cage concentrates her powers upon a single case, that of the adulterous communication between Lady Bradeen and Captain Everard.

(James was shameless in his names!) Like the chess game's king, Everard is the weakest player in James's complicated love game: "he only fidgeted and floundered in his want of power." In this society, like that of *The Waste Land*, "it was much more the women, on the whole, who were after the men than the men who were after the women." Perhaps it was this underscoring of the castration thematic so recurrent in James that led Eliot to decoy his readers with a change of title. Moreover, the figure of the girl as sibyl and decoder would have been assimilated to that of Eliot himself, identifying her Romanticism as the cause of interpretative impotence, since in the end she gets it all quite muddled: "what our heroine saw and felt for in the whole business was the vivid reflexion of her own dreams and delusions and her own return to reality." This acceptance of the reality principle represents the girl's askesis. Her biological femininity does not preclude, but underlies, her participation in a castration psychology that has shaped her search for the missing truth from the start.

James's tale links Eros, truth, writing, and the phallus in the girl's pursuit of Everard's mystery. "It came to her there, with her eyes on his face, that she held the whole thing in her hand, held it as she held her pencil, which might have broken at that instant in her tightened grip. This made her feel like the fountain of fate."[3] Poor Everard! When she grasps the "truth" of his letters and affairs, she purloins the phallus and restores it to her own incomplete self. In this she, as much as any of James's bachelor epistemologists, figures the Romantic author as castrated/castrating in the quest for a condensed logos of sex, writing, and knowledge. At the end, however, she learns that her salvation of Everard through recollection of the lovers' letters only dooms him to Lady Bradeen's clutches. In the economy of phallogocentrism, the truth of the letter always requires the dispossession of its former owner: the girl has unwittingly emasculated Everard in knowing him. The truth she is left with is the "truth" of his castration, as we are left with the uncanny notion that "truth" in writing "castrates" life. Renouncing her sibyl's job and marrying Mr. Mudge, the girl gives up the Romantic and phallogocentric vocations for a less metaphysical career. Eliot's poem takes up her career once more in deciphering the logos of scattered parts. It restages the drama of James's tale, expressing once more the Romantic longing to find Truth through the incarnations of Eros, discovering once more that the truth of sexuality is loss, difference, and the adulteration of identity. In its negative theology, *The Waste Land* repeatedly returns to castration as truth, sublimating the deconstruction of Romantic Eros into another quest for the divine love that can fulfill the desires human life seems to imitate with its carnal appetites. The fragmentation of truth in the poem operates, according to such logic, to spur our critical desire to locate and regenerate what has been lost, and it represses, by its very hyperbole and lamentation, the prerequisite of castration as the "original" scene of the crime. Only in aspects of its conclusion does the poem come round to a reconciliation with the dissemination of the father's word.

Correspondences with James's tale shed light on at least the first two parts of "A Game of Chess," with its evocations of insufferable women, male fear, and marital discord. At the heart of these mournful mysteries lies the retelling of paradise lost. As his footnote tells us, Eliot borrows his "sylvan scene" from Milton (and, quite tellingly behind that, from Spenser's accounts of Venus and Adonis and of the Bower of Bliss) for his own revisionary display of "The change of Philomel, by the barbarous king / So rudely forced." She becomes the genius loci of a "romantic" transmutation of loss into a redemptive, artful song. What Eliot adds to our hearing, literally so in the manuscript, is "lust," the unsublimated drive that violates the virgin garden of woman and man's identity. The element of incest in the rape of Philomel by Tereus may appear irrelevant here unless we understand desire's threat to kinship systems and thus by extension to the structuring of a stable and meaningful economy of differences. Philomel represents woman as an object of prohibited desire, and we are left wondering whether that prohibition originates in genealogy (in which case she would be a metaphor of the mother) or in a "classical" deconstruction of a "romantic" metaphysics of art and Eros.

These complex associations may be further detected, if not resolved, by reference to a clue overheard by that exceptional aural sleuth, John Hollander. He notices that the second reference to Philomel's song, in "The Fire Sermon," reads "So rudely forc'd," and he argues that "there is nothing to explain the peculiar spelling 'forc'd' at this point, except a Miltonic echo," from "Lycidas": "And with forc'd fingers, rude." What correlation can there be, beyond the general "milieu of the drowned poet," between the king's rape of Philomel and Milton's untimely plucking of the berries? The answer, I think, lies in the elegiac strategy of poetic resurrection intrinsic to Milton's transumption of the genre in "Lycidas," that is, in his rebirth as a poet after this "violation" of Mother Nature and the Muse. Milton's "inviolable voice" haunts new poets with its power to create a highly individual beauty out of its "Babylonish" troping of the language and inheritance. Eliot's king is called "barbarous," meaning he literally speaks an unacceptable language, an eccentric tongue. The speaker of "Lycidas" presumes to grasp the laurel crown before his time, pressured into it, he says, by the death of Edward King. To tradition he says he must "Shatter your leaves before the mellowing year," where "Shatter" connotes not only the traditional ritual scattering of leaves but a destructive shattering as well.[4] The song of Philomel, then, once more inscribes the poet's ambivalence toward beginning again his attempt upon the sublime and condenses the problems involved with those of sexuality. Thus, the passage expresses 1) a fear of the father-precursor's prohibition, 2) a desire to scatter the words of the father by violating his Muse, 3) a dread that he may not have the power to regather the leaves in a new volume of love, and 4) a transfiguring urge to reject the whole "romantic" problematic as delusory compared to a complete askesis and retheologization of desires poetic and sexual.

The section had opened, in fact, with a revision of a precursor. Eliot twists Shakespeare's lines on Cleopatra into an elegantly suffocating portrait of the lady, thus contradicting all his warnings about Shakespeare's bad influence in the sense that his defensive parody both confirms Shakespeare's stylistic preeminence in its absence and improves upon it with additions from other dead masters. Frequently cited in Eliot's criticism, *Antony and Cleopatra* holds a high station in his canon. The play's theme of a hero led astray by his infatuation with a beautiful woman illustrates one of Eliot's key obsessions, vacillating as it does between adoration and condemnation. He had given the lines "she looks like sleep, / As she would catch another Antony / In her strong toil of grace" as an example of Shakespeare's "complicated" metaphors, remarking that the trope's additive quality was "a reminder of that fascination of Cleopatra which shaped her history and that of the world, and of that fascination being so strong that it prevails even in death" (SE, 205). The fascination of Cleopatra stands for the fascination of Shakespearean metaphor: both exceed, add, tempt one beyond confirmed identity, whereas Dante's "visual" metaphors reveal truth. Cleopatra seduces as Shakespeare's poetic style can seduce, turning her victims into predecessors of James's deluded romantic girl. Antony's fate echoes Captain Everard's, while Enobarbus is made into yet another blinded prophet. Sifting through Shakespeare's leaves, Eliot is lured but suspicious, and he mocks the folly of Enobarbus and of misreaders who have failed to hear Shakespeare's irony as he dramatically presents yet another victim of Cleopatra's self-representations. Revising Shakespeare's style, Eliot overloads the imagery of his lines to create a dissociation of sensibility. He compounds the Jacobeans, the eighteenth-century baroque, and *fin de siècle* aestheticism in a hyperbolic illustration of the snares of sensual imaginings. He brings to the surface the purport of Shakespeare's speech with the aid of its setting in his own poem, among the fearful females, deluded men, and parodied styles.

The failure of romanticism to find in human experiences the sublime it projects as lost also pervades the disharmony of the nervous couple in the subsequent lines of "A Game of Chess." As the opening section dwelled upon the femme fatale, this conversation, or lack of one, indicates the concurrent absence of the saving woman who provides access to life, creation, presence, and the Absolute. While "nothing" occurs between these two, all the action takes place offstage. The section's title and Eliot's note refer us to Middleton's *Women Beware Women* and Bianca's forced seduction, which occurs while her mother-in-law is distracted by a chess game with the procuress. "The wind under the door" sends us to Webster's *The Devil's Law Case*, in which it brings news of a man's wounding.[5] Another primal scene, then, of woman's violation and man's vital loss takes place within earshot of this couple and within an imagistic and allusive context of reiterated blindness. It was also, Grover Smith notes, "with a noise and shaking, and with a blast of wind, that the dead in Ezekiel's valley of dry bones received the breath of life and stood upon their feet."[6] In the manuscript, what the wind was doing was "Carrying / Away the little light dead people" (WLFS, 13), a theft from the Paolo and Francesca episode in *Inferno*, canto 5. Of them Eliot wrote: "To have lost all recollected delight would have been, for Francesca, either loss of humanity or relief from damnation. The ecstasy, with the present thrill at the remembrance of it, is a part of the torture. Francesca is neither stupefied nor reformed; she is merely damned; and it is part of damnation to experience desires that we can no longer gratify" (SW, 165–66). The speaker in Eliot's poem either cannot gratify his desires or gratifies them at the cost of a greater damnation. Eliot's couple, in Dantean fashion, seem eternally damned to the condition of unsatisfied longing. Intercourse of any kind appears impossible in this "rat's alley / Where the dead men lost their bones."

What obstacle prevents speech, thought, or action here? The "loss" of "bones" imaged in the man's words voices a connection between present impotence and past losses or glories. He is hardly present at all, in fact, as his mind is usurped by repetitive memories that possess him. The significance of this haunting may be seen in a look at Eliot's revisions. The printed draft reads, "I remember / Those are pearls that were his eyes." The manuscript reads: "I remember / The hyacinth garden. Those are pearls that were his eyes, yes!" (WLFS, 13). Pound left these lines unaltered, except to suggest cutting the allusion to Molly's soliloquy in *Ulysses* (a relevant tale of adulteries and wandering paternities). Vivienne Eliot inexplicably penned "Yes & wonderful wonderful" in the margin. The decision to drop this reference to the hyacinth garden was evidently Eliot's own. Perhaps he felt that having his speaker recall that former ecstasy here would be too obvious an irony. He may also have been uncomfortable with the conjunction of a lover's tryst with a father's death or of the loss of love and the loss of eyes. Some have even argued that the excision covers up a reference to Jean Verdenal and Eliot's attraction to him, a sensational and untenable speculation.[7] A more viable biographical reading would be that the passage implies that the man's memory of a former love makes his disillusionment with a present wife crippling and that Eliot, would not have thrown such a message at Vivienne in public, whatever her perception of the lines' import. He was too caring and solicitous toward her feelings for that, even if the lines were simply intended to express impersonally the difference between an ideal regenerative love and a spiritless communication. The juxtaposition of hyacinth garden and Ariel's song would have been helpful, however, in pointing out the links between these two scenes of love, loss, and metamorphosis. They emerge from a "romantic" desire for translation into a beatified state, transfiguring loss into pearls as precious as Molly's final, loving *affirmation* of her moment as Bloom's flower of the mountain. Incoherence plagues the speaker of the scene because, by measure of past or figurally constructed images, his emotions cannot find any available or adequate object. A poetic coherence, however, holds these lines and themes and allusions in a paratactic assemblage that puts the techniques of imagism and symbolism to their best use: a vital tension stays suspended between the incoherence of the represented and the skill with which Eliot draws us on to read his articulations of its origins and ends as we play sibyl to the poem's leaves.

The foregoing investigations of a few intertextual case histories in *The Waste Land* demonstrate how quickly the poem eludes interpretative or aesthetic closure. At the risk of scattering an already shattering poem, these forays seemed strategically prerequisite to theoretical questions about how to read or name this text, since criticism and canon formation have already so tamed its uncanniness for us. It might be healthy to restore our sense of how aberrant the poem is, as any undergraduate would gladly tell us.

Reviewing Eliot's experiment after its initial publication, Louis Untermeyer wrote, "It is doubtful whether 'The Waste Land' is anything but a set of separate poems, a piece of literary carpentry, a scholarly joiner's work, the flotsam and jetsam of desiccated culture," or simply a "pompous parade of erudition."[8] These are pertinent insights, though not in the derogatory sense that Untermeyer intends. Inspection of the published manuscripts now confirms that Eliot did indeed assemble his poem from myriad jottings, some nearly ten years in the keeping. Most of the poem as we have it was set down in 1921 and 1922, undergoing a famous series of revisions at the hands of Eliot, his wife, and Ezra Pound. At the literal level this history exhibits processes ordinarily disguised in the presentation of supposedly unitary, orderly texts ascribable to a single authorial consciousness. Untermeyer's critical a priori posits the existence and privilege of a metaphysically conceived writing, set down instantaneously and forever by a voice speaking an isolable truth. This formalist object would above all things be "separate," individually differentiated, whole, and free of the past. Eliot's "poem," however, is an intertextual phenomenon, conspicuously a process of allusive appropriation. *The Waste Land* demonstrates Eliot's theory of tradition and Harold Bloom's insistence on intertextuality. There are no individual, self-contained poems. The "poem" lies in the relations between poems, in the troping of an ancestor. Has Eliot allowed us to say who "wrote" *The Waste Land*? What do we think we mean if we say that Eliot wrote:

> Frisch weht der Wind
> Der Heimat zu.
> Mein Irisch Kind,
> Wo weilest du?

These lines from Wagner were the German's property, but their properties are in Eliot's hands now.

Untermeyer's metaphors for the poem ("literary carpentry, a scholarly joiner's work") point again to Lévi-Strauss's notion of *bricolage* and to an idea of poetry as the opportune arrangement of whatever happens to be at hand rather than as the mimesis of an organic or transcendent architecture. Yet, before endorsing *bricolage* as a master metaphor of the text, we should recall Derrida's argument that "if the difference between *bricoleur* and engineer is basically theological, the very concept of *bricolage* implies a fall and an accidental finitude."[9] *Bricolage*, like belatedness and other mythologies of lost Golden Ages, retrospectively invests an absent figure with the status of an Origin. Ironically, the bricoleur's technique in *The Waste Land* rebuilds, albeit through lament and eulogy, the value of metaliterary and metaphysical constructs that writing might mirror rather than piece together: "What are the roots that clutch, what branches grow / Out of this stony rubbish?" The possibility of an organic logos springing up out of all this textual rubbish is suggested by the figural language here, but in its contextual allusion to the resurrection of the bones in Ezekiel the passage looks instead to a transcendent power for salvation. The use of *bricolage*, or the allusive method, in *The Waste Land* does transgress the conventions of poetry, but like any transgression it simultaneously re-marks the place of the law.

Bricolage and engineering, like the artificial and the organic or the chaotic and the orderly, fall into a binary opposition of the kind that Hegel puts to work in the following relevant passage.

> The encyclopaedia of philosophy must not be confounded with ordinary encyclopaedias. An ordinary encyclopaedia does not

> pretend to be more than an aggregation of sciences, regulated by no principle, and merely as experience offers them. Sometimes it even includes what merely bear the name of sciences, while they are nothing more than a collection of bits of information. In an aggregate like this, the several branches of knowledge owe their place in the encyclopaedia to extrinsic reasons, and their unity is therefore artificial: they are *arranged*, but we cannot say that they form a *system*. For the same reason, especially as the materials to be combined also depend upon no one rule or principle, the arrangement is at best an experiment, and will always exhibit inequalities.[10]

The distinction between the "ordinary encyclopaedia" and the "encyclopaedia of philosophy" seems to parallel the one between the nineteenth-century poem of organic unity and the twentieth-century poem of fragments. "On Margate Sands / I can connect / Nothing with nothing." How many readers of *The Waste Land* or Pound's *Cantos* have come away thinking that "they are *arranged*, but we cannot say that they form a *system*"? This is not quite the case, however, as with Eliot we have any number of systems alluded to as possible keys—myth, anthropology, mysticism, religion, the tarot, and even literary criticism. The poem experiments with these systems of interpretation by inviting the detective-critic to try them out on the aggregation of entries stolen from other encyclopedias. Eliot's famous dictum bears repeating: "The good poet welds his theft into a whole of feeling which is unique, utterly different from that from which it was torn; the bad throws it into something which has no cohesion" (SE, 182). "Torn" implicitly plays upon the metaphor of the dismembered body, utilizing the traditional aesthetic description of a work as "shapely" or "monstrous," as in the opening of Horace's *Arc Poetica*. Only if the purloined goods are re-membered in a coherent new body, "whole" and "unique," is theft pardonable.

What is this "cohesion"? In contrast to Hegel's "system," Eliot gives us an emotion rather than an epistemology. "I cannot make it cohere," wrote Pound in Canto 116, after a lifetime's work at a poem that, one could argue, never strayed from the method Eliot advanced and then abandoned in *The Waste Land*. Cohesion stems from the Latin *haerere*, to stick together. Its cognates include adherence, adhesion, and hesitation. The principle of connection in each is paratactic: discontinuous elements are held together but not integrally so, their relations being not so much of interiors coordinated as of exteriors juxtaposed in tension or suspension. This sticking may also lead to hesitation, an occupation of the adherent ground between oppositions. In fact, in "Prufrock" and *The Waste Land*, it is this condition of hesitation that is the "whole of feeling." In a letter to Richard Aldington on the eve of his journey to Margate, Lausanne, and the completion of the poem, Eliot writes, "I am satisfied, since being here, that my 'nerves' are a very mild affair, due not to overwork but to an aboulie and emotional derangement which has been a lifelong affliction. Nothing wrong with my mind" (WLFS, xxii). *Aboulie* is a variant of *abulia*, a psychiatric term for the loss or impairment of the ability to decide or act independently. This emotional state pervades and unites the poem, though ironically, for it is a unity of inability, indeterminacy, indecision. Overcompensating, Eliot fills his poem with a clutter of "objective correlatives" for the state of feeling first dramatized by *Hamlet*. Eliot's spelling also significantly recalls his citation of Nerval's "la tour abolie" from "The Disinherited," in which the tower also figures in an Orphic tale that condenses the lover's and the artist's inconsolable fates in a shuttling between two worlds. Orpheus and Eurydice, by way of Hades and Persephone, cast a dark shadow across the mythic revivification of unity presided over by the poet-priest.

According to Eliot, the disinheritance of the modern poets occurred when feeling and intellect split, as they do in the "ordinary" mind. "When a poet's mind is perfectly equipped for its work, it is constantly amalgamating disparate experience; the ordinary man's experience is chaotic, irregular, fragmentary. The latter falls in love, or reads Spinoza, and these two experiences have nothing to do with each other, or with the noise of the typewriter or the smell of cooking: in the mind of the poet these experiences are always forming new wholes" (SE, 247). J. Hillis Miller observes that these "*are* a miscellaneous lot," betraying Eliot's "feeling that experience is in fact chaotic" and harmonized only by "ironic conjunction."[11] This miscellany, however, is no random choice, for it represents just those experiences that *The Waste Land* tries to set in order. In his essays on Leibniz (1916), Eliot's passing references to Spinoza are in the context of debates over the connections between mind and matter or body and soul. "Spinoza represents a definite emotional attitude," he asserts, leaving this attitude undefined, though we may infer a reference again to "Spinoza's naturalism ... his disbelief in free-will and immortality" and the "materialistic epiphenomenalism" of his "view of the relation of mind and body" (KE, 198, 194). Reading Spinoza plunges one into a deterministic "naturalism" that leaves little room for the soul to govern its responses to sensory influences. The doctrines of this heretical, exiled philosopher question the modality of a soul that would transcend, yet still involve, sensation—a doubt Eliot attempts to resolve by recourse to Aristotle and Bradley (KE, 194–95, 205–206). Falling in love and the smell of cooking awaken the natural emotions and senses that lead to these dilemmas. From the "Preludes" to "Burbank with a Baedeker" and "Gerontion," Eliot explores the disturbing effects of sensory life on the orders of consciousness. Of course, it is up to the "noise of the typewriter" to write these feelings into a satisfying accord.

In *The Waste Land*, "whole of feeling" turns out to be an oxymoron since the emotions stirred in the various scenes of sterility, adultery, rape, lust, and purgation are decidedly unwholesome and destructive of harmony or coherence. When we examine the published poem alongside the manuscript drafts, such as the dirges and the portraits of ladies like Fresca and the duchess, we see more clearly than ever that the poem's many voices speak obsessively of the feelings inspired by sex and death, those two main enemies of the fortress of identity. As in Eliot's previous poetry, speakers and readers are made to suffer a morbid acuteness of the senses in scene after scene—the lilacs "breeding ... out of the dead land"; "the brown fog of a winter dawn"; "her strange synthetic perfumes, / Unguent, powdered, or liquid—troubled, confused / And drowned the sense in odours"; "It's them pills I took, to bring it off"; "Silk handkerchiefs, cardboard boxes, cigarette ends / Or other testimony of summer nights"; "White bodies naked on the low damp ground"; "And bats with baby faces in the violet light." Eliot's fragments cohere chiefly in their physicality, in the music of their borrowed sounds and in the kinds of sensual experiences they represent. *The Waste Land*'s "symbols are not mystical, but emotional," wrote I. A. Richards, who called the poem "radically naturalistic."[12] It composes a body, we might say, of sensory and poetic life, if indeed the two can be distinguished. The fragmentation of parts reenacts the *sparagmos* of the physical body of desire, torn by its conflicting responses to the excitements it tries to lift into the wholeness of meaning. Corresponding to these fractures is the poetic *sparagmos* of the body of the literary fathers—"And other withered stumps of time ... told upon the walls"—toward whose sounds and feelings the poet reacts with a neurosis of the poetic libido, so to speak. Philomel's rape and dismemberment are supplemented by their change into "inviolable voice," but that sublation is now "'Jug Jug' to dirty ears." Were we to clean up our response, what would we hear but the painful truth that her voice sings of the violence at its origin? Philomel's change and the metamorphosis of the father in Ariel's song figure the work of art as a transformation of loss into something rich and strange. While it seems to lament our incapacity to realize again such sublimations of the material into the spiritual, Eliot's poem also demonstrates that no "voice" is "inviolable." Even the play of syllables between those two words articulates the work of difference and interpenetration in language, and the location of identity in the rupture between things.

The "dissociation of sensibility" cataloged by Eliot's imagery traces the dissociation of individual senses from each other in the absence of any intellectual *Aufhebung* into a logos. There is a great irony, for example, in Eliot's assertion that "what Tiresias *sees*, in fact, is the substance of the poem." Tiresias' blindness should, according to myth, grant him a vision of the truth. What he "sees" in Eliot's poem is a troping of the primal scene in the mechanical copulation of the typist and the young man carbuncular. The metric, the rhyme scheme, and the ending sight of the "automatic hand" that "puts a record on the gramophone" enforce a feeling of remorseless repetition of a scene "foresuffered" a thousand times in memory and desire. Tiresias endlessly sees the scene of the crime, the origin of his own "blinding" or castration in witnessing the difference between men and women. What Tiresias sees is "substance" itself, physical life (or signifiers) unredeemed by spirit (or a transcendental signified). Eliot's note plays on the philosophic sense of "substance" as essence and tacitly reminds us of its declension into mere matter (see KE, 182–88). In some legends, Tiresias loses his eyes in retaliation for looking upon the naked body of the bathing Athena, goddess of wisdom. In the version from Ovid that Eliot quotes as "of great anthropological interest," we have the tale of the coupling snakes, Tiresias' bisexuality, and his blinding by Hera/Juno for answering that women enjoy sex nine times more than men. Of course, he is also the prophet of the dead in Hades, guide to sailors like Odysseus and Aeneas, and the seer who knows the fatal story of Oedipus. According to Eliot, he is "the most important personage in the poem, uniting all the rest." This unity will not cohere, however; Tiresias figures the mobility of sexual identity and the negative relation of what we see to what we know. To know the body of truth repeats the crime. Tiresias stands for the dissociation of sensibility in "all the rest" and everyone's participation in his pagan version of negative theology. What we see through his eyes is the involvement of transgression in the genesis of the logos. (Eliot's gramma-phone replays the old song recently rewritten by Derrida's grammatology.) A dissociation of sensibility sets in as the new prophet's "inviolable voice" sings out its reading of the writing of the oracular dead.

If we switch from mythological to other allegorical registers or codes of reference, we note that erection and resurrection also figure the *Aufhebung*, or blindness-made-vision, that achieves the "relevé," the raising of the dead or the return of what was invested in a threatening abyss. A castration logic, whereby loss is made the agency or origin of the logos, is the "system" that arranges Eliot's "bits of information." The dissemination of any single lyric speaker amid these babbling tongues seems to denote the final demise of the Romantic subject, but in fact the ventriloquial appropriation of dismembered parts remembered from other authors composes the new poet as an intertextual force. In these acts of loving violence toward the body of tradition, the poet resurfaces not as the origin of the poem but as the poetic principle (principal), the deconstructed genius loci of a textual waste land. The *sparagmos* as theme and method both expresses his dissociation by the daemons inhabiting his poetic landscape and exorcises those daemons by a ritual incorporation of their torn parts. Resemblance, correspondence, and other modes of identification predominate in the "cohesion" of the fragments, and they follow the practice of Lacan's "imaginary," or "mirror stage," discourse. The Father's No, Name, and Law have not been acceded to, the Oedipus complex (as the structure or language of the unconscious) has not dissolved, and a regression to the strategy of narcissism, doubling, identification, competition, and aggression has taken place. *The Waste Land* exhausts, and then will relinquish, the conceptual responses to sexual, philosophical, and poetic indeterminacy already introduced in "Prufrock," "Narcissus," and "Gerontion."

Translating Lacan's terms into poetics, we find that the "specific prematurity of birth," the child's "primordial Discord" and "motor-uncoordination" become the young poet's incoherence. The mirror stage next provides cohesion through speculation. Recognizing his own image in that of others, the subject enters a drama "which manufactures for the subject, caught up in the lure of spatial identification, the succession of fantasies that extends from a fragmented body-image to a form of its totality." Images of the fragmented body recur when the symbolic systems of totalization give way, opening up a return to aggressive rivalry with the other for what both, because of their similarity, desire, so that such images connote at once a violence toward the other and a disintegration of self-identity: "These are the images of castration, mutilation, dismemberment, dislocation, evisceration, devouring, bursting open the body, in short, the *imagos* that I have grouped together under the apparently structural term of *imagos of the fragmented body*." In contrast, "the formation of the *I* is symbolized in dreams by a fortress, or a stadium—its inner arena and enclosure, surrounded by marshes and rubbish-tips, dividing it into two opposed fields of contest where the subject flounders in quest of the lofty, remote inner castle whose form ... symbolizes the id in a quite startling way."[13] The Quester's journey to the Chapel Perilous marks the transition from the *sparagmos* of the God/king to the ritual decipherment of original mysteries, worked out by Eliot in his commentaries on the "Da" of the thunder.

The vocations of the Quester, detective, and critic merge in the attempt to solve once more the riddle of the sphinx or to recapture the sibyl's power to gather the scattering leaves into a logos—a power denied to Dante as he sought to express the vision of the Eternal Light and compared himself to the sibyl. The poem hesitates, like Hamlet, in the face of re-membering, torn between the idea of logos as the recollection of a lost absolute and logos as the emergence, in unauthorized directions, of beings gathered in their difference. The Heideggerian sense comes closer, I think, to Dante's single volume bound by love than Eliot's search for the Word of the Father, as a comparison to the end of "Little Gidding" will suggest. Love, as the call of being, remains open to the life that logocentrism forecloses. What we see with Tiresias throughout the poem is dead people, like scattered leaves, whirled beyond the bounds of love.

For the reader, the question becomes that of whether any interpretative ritual can, or should, reunite the leaves of this *sparagmos* in a transcendental image of harmony. The trace of guilt that marks Oedipus and the Quester suggests that acts of interpretation or divination are also acts of violence, that transgression may not be fully integrated when the truth is finally told. Unless we repeat it word for word, our critical account of the poem must always leave out something, must choose and select to form our solution to its riddle. Reading *The Waste Land* requires an interpretation that will also figure the tension between the desire to totalize and the need to criticize. One figure for the poem, then, is that of a corpus. The various definitions of corpus include 1) a physical body, especially when dead; 2) a structure constituting the main part of an organ; 3) the principal, or capital, as distinguished from the interest, or income, of a fund, estate, investment, or the like; 4) a large collection of writings of a specific kind or on a specific subject. As a critical metaphor, corpus makes the connection between a body of writing and a writing of or about the body. The representations of literature and sexuality in *The Waste Land* join in overdetermined settings, as Eliot draws upon the capital of a certain body of texts for his poetic treatment of failed passions, violent conquests, mechanical copulations, and purgative fires. In the strange logic of condensation, literary potency and sexual potency become a single problem, their result a common issue. The literary surrender of self that negatively produces an authorizing tradition coincides with images of emasculation that negatively body forth a sensation of the sexual sublime. In the metaphor of the corpus we may avoid imposing an a priori discrimination between sexuality and textuality, resist totalizing the poem's vital differences of detail in some metacritical order, and point toward the relations of crisis—between the body and writing, nature and culture, women and men, sons and fathers, talents and traditions—that sound throughout *The Waste Land*.

The critical detective discovers, then, that the corpus itself is a sphinx, an enigmatic collection of texts whose particular puzzle is the bond that joins the animal and the human and by extension the human and the divine. When we look into the corpus of *The Waste Land*, we do not find the identity of its owner, but instead the bric-a-brac from other writers' estates, or from the poet's past texts and memories. And the question those purloined letters pose is most often a variant of the sphinx's: What is man, if he should have such animal desires? What is the logos, that it can raise man's nature to its truth? What is a poet, that he presumes to place himself at such crossroads? The lines that open "The Burial of the Dead" place us before such oracular mysteries.

> April is the cruellest month, breeding
> Lilacs out of the dead land, mixing
> Memory and desire, stirring
> Dull roots with spring rain.

We can sketch with little difficulty the "self-reflexive" allegory of poetic beginnings in this overture. Though Eliot first intended a now-excised Boston night-town scene for his opener, the poem as published fortuitously contrasts with the beginning of Chaucer's *Canterbury Tales*, thus making English poetry new by turning the original celebration of fertility into an ode to dejection. "After great pain, a formal feeling comes," wrote Emily Dickinson, and in Eliot's lines a similar necessity of hurt seems involved in committing his feelings to form. "Winter kept us warm, covering / Earth in forgetful snow," a secure oblivion that seduces and comforts those who do not presume to begin writing again, who do not dare force the moment to its crisis. The meager quantity and the sorrowful content of so much of Eliot's poetry testify, as do his critical statements on daemonic possession, that writing was for him an anguish second only to the "acute discomfort" of feeling like a haunted house. Certainly one of the strongest of the obscure impulses behind *The Waste Land* is Eliot's recurring dread that his poetic springs have run dry. April stands for a new season of poetic creation, "breeding" poems out of the detritus of his literary inheritance and notebook drafts. His memory of past glories (his own and others, for as signs of poetic achievement they come to the same thing) obsesses him, cruelly blocking his desire to engender some new flowering. As a rendition of the Anglican burial service, Eliot's opening inters the corpus of the fathers, buries them to sprout according to his own pronouncements. While it tropes against the poets and metaphors of natural regeneration, it also laments (and so in a sense denies) its own impotence. "Dull roots" characterizes the literary ancestry and the poet's own instrument of creation.

In these lines and throughout the poem, we encounter the same overdetermination of Eliot's rhetoric seen in his critical accounts of poetic genesis. The foregoing poetic allegory already employs terms that lead into an interpretation of the passage as an allegory of sexuality. April denotes the awakening of passion, the surge of desire to break out of the cold forgetfulness of repression. Memories cruelly block the fulfillment of desire, as the dead hand of past experiences—formed by the history of the unconscious—reaches out to obstruct present feelings. Prufrock had invoked the figure of Lazarus, come back from the dead to tell us all, to signify an intercourse he never dares begin. In *The Waste Land*, resurre(re)ction is no "friend to men," since it draws them out of the winter warmth of indifference and into the world of nature, woman, and history. Corresponding with the refinement of the poet's nature by his surrender to the voices of the dead, desire seeks a fiery sublimation that also takes its cue from the figure of Arnaut Daniel, one of Dante's tongues of flame who undergoes a transfiguration into Buddha and Saint Augustine at the end of "The Fire Sermon."

The analysis could be further extended, with appropriate precautions, by invoking the Dantean model, explicated in the letter to Can Grande, of the "polysemous" text so influential in Eliot's method. At the literal level is the poetic exodus from anxiety; at the moral level is the salvation from the death of the soul in lust; at the allegorical level is the soul's ascension from earth to heaven; at the anagogical level is the union of logos and nature in the Corpus Mysticum, or celestial church body, that regathers the saved in the volume of the Word. If there has been a murder here, if author, reader, and Quester join in a single detective adventure, it concerns the discovery of a Corpus Mysticum resolving these various levels in a single thunderous apocalypse that crosses the aporia between nature and the logos.

Eliot's attraction to Catholicism as it emerges in the poem may well turn on the transcendental poetics its theology offers. In contrast to the iconoclasm of Hebrew, Protestant, and Puritan theories of the sign, Catholicism reunites the letter and the spirit, signifier and signified, nature and culture, human and divine in the dogmas of the Incarnation, Passion, and Resurrection. The fertility rituals would be a type to the antitype of the Sacrament, as indeed the Grail legends imply. Following traditional theological exegesis, the waters of *The Waste Land* are both the baptismal river and the blood of the Eucharist. Echoing Dante, these waters mark the entrance to a regenerated Earthly Paradise at the end of purgatory. The first three sections of the poem constitute a kind of preparation of the soul and heart for reception of the Word, adopting from mystic literature their climactic call for a prerequisite purification or celibacy before the final approach to the mystery. The final two sections, written at the last and chiefly at Lausanne, move away from the vegetation ritual schema into two related models—those of the quest and the elegy—to resolve the puzzle. What is achieved thereby is a powerful revision of the precursors as Eliot thinks poetically through the structures of negative theology, but he never finds his Beatrice. The poem leaves us at the edge of purgatory but still far distant from paradise, lacking that loving logos that moved the constellations of Dante and that returns in the brightest moments of the *Quartets*.

Notes

1. J. Hillis Miller, Introduction to Charles Dickens, *Bleak House*, ed. Norman Page (Baltimore, 1971). Eliot taught *Bleak House* in 1916, and in a 1918 letter to his mother he compared his experience with wartime bureaucracy to "a chancery suit—dragging on and on, and always apparently about to end" (WLFS, xv).

2. Grover Smith, *T. S. Eliot's Poetry and Plays: A Study in Sources and Meaning* (2nd ed.; Chicago, 1974), 303; Henry James, "In the Cage," in James, *Eight Tales from the Major Phase*, ed. Morton D. Zabel (New York, 1958), 174.

3. James, "In the Cage," 247.

4. John Hollander, *The Figure of Echo: A Mode of Allusion in Milton and After* (Berkeley, 1981), 104; Ellen Z. Lambert, *Placing Sorrow: A Study of the Pastoral Elegy Convention from Theocritus to Milton* (Chapel Hill, 1976), 155.

5. Eliot later denied the relevance of the phrase's context in Webster. See B. C. Southam, *A Guide to the Selected Poems of T. S. Eliot* (New York, 1968), 79.

6. Smith, *T. S. Eliot's Poetry and Plays*, 81.

7. I refer to James E. Miller, Jr., *T. S. Eliot's Personal Waste Land* (University Park, Pa., 1977), which revives the thesis of John Peter's notorious "A New Interpretation of *The Waste Land*," *Essays in Criticism*, II (July, 1952), suppressed by Eliot and reprinted after his death by the same journal in April, 1969.

8. Quoted in Jay Martin (ed.), *Twentieth Century Views of "The Waste Land"* (Englewood Cliffs, N.J., 1968), 5.

9. Jacques Derrida, *Of Grammatology*, trans. Gayatri Spivak (Baltimore, 1976), 139.

10. William Wallace (trans.), *Hegel's Logic* (Oxford, 1975), 21.

11. J. Hillis Miller, *Poets of Reality* (New York, 1969), 155.

12. I. A. Richards, *Principles of Literary Criticism* (New York, 1928), 292.

13. Jacques Lacan, *Ecrits: A Selection*, trans. Alan Sheridan (New York, 1977), 4, 11, 5. The fragmentation in modern art can also be read according to the theory of reification developed by George Lukács in *History and Class Consciousness*, trans. Rodney Livingstone (Cambridge, Mass., 1971), 83–222. See also Fredric Jameson, *The Political Unconscious: Narrative as a Socially Symbolic Act* (Ithaca, 1981), 206–57.

CLEO McNELLY KEARNS

Eliot, Russell, and Whitman: Realism, Politics, and Literary Persona in The Waste Land

Wyndham Lewis, one of the most penetrating critics of T. S. Eliot's early literary career (and one to whom Eliot's recent biographers should pay more attention), remarked of Eliot that he was "democratic in spite of himself." Eliot, he went on to argue, had "imbibed more than his share of romantically 'radical' values in his tender years," and his classical panache, as Lewis liked to call it, together with his deliberately Gallic pose—"a bit of le dandy as inherited from Baudelaire"—was rather a disguise than a genuine point of view. Radical or no radical, Eliot knew that the contemporary Anglo-Saxon world of arts and letters was "half Marx and half *status quo*," and his early position in aesthetics, if not in politics proper, was more deeply influenced by Bertrand Russell's progressive realism than others who did not know him might suspect. In general, for Lewis, Eliot's position within the world of letters smacked too much of scientism, not to mention a democratization of art fostered by Pound, to be of much comfort to the genuine conservative. Because both Eliot and Pound stressed the need for technique, and attempted to spell out what that technique involved, they reduced art to mechanics, and made it accessible, as Lewis so charmingly puts it, to "anyone certified born of woman, indeed to any son-of-a-bitch" (*Men Without Art*).

Eliot, of course, having more sense, did not go quite so far as Pound in this democratic "manufacture of poets." At least, Lewis notes, Eliot managed

From *The Waste Land*, ed. Harold Bloom. © 1986 by Cleo McNelly Kearns.

to keep from puffing the reputations of *quite* so many losers, and showed nothing like Pound's ability to gather the dubiously "discipular" around him. Nevertheless, Lewis insisted that the separation of belief, personality, and class (and gender) identity from the work of art itself, on which Eliot insisted, cooperated, intentionally or not, with the apparently leftward slide of history. The effective divorce of *The Waste Land* from the belief, the ethos, the social and personal position of its author would make of it, Lewis remarked, his tone dripping acid, a "posthumous ornament," a "feather" in Eliot's cap, a dubious but effective "passport to the communist millennium."

Rightly or wrongly, the judgment of most recent critics about the political implications of Eliot's early career has been quite the reverse of Lewis's. Eliot's separation of issues of personality, personal identity and belief from issues of poetic mastery and strength, far from speeding a leftward slide in history or even a progressive point of view, has seemed to shore up a kind of literary and political conservatism. At the very least, it has prevented critics—or so the argument usually goes—from correcting for "Anglo-Saxony," with its class, race, sexual and even national bias, by paying special attention to work which emanates, biographically and socially, from other sources and points of view. This consensus, not to be lightly dismissed, nevertheless leaves us with an anomaly which critics have always recognized: how could so conservative a view, both in aesthetics and in politics in the larger sense, possibly have produced a text like *The Waste Land*? Whatever cries of elitism and reaction may have risen in the wake of this poem, its initial reception and its continuing impact—not least (as many critical reviews and poems testify) on third-world cultures and on an increasingly literate working class—prevent us from ever completely forgetting its great force as one of the most politically and culturally subversive texts of our century.

Given this anomaly, it may be worth reconsidering Lewis's point of view, or at least attempting to understand a little better the cultural and political matrix that allowed him to put it forth. After all, Lewis had the great advantage not only of knowing Eliot well but of knowing the kinds of conversation—about politics, about art, and no doubt about sex—on which his mind was trained. Whatever rhetorical posturing Lewis himself may have indulged in here, and however hostile he himself was to the portrait he so vividly drew, he was certainly giving us an image very different from the tailored, bowler-hatted Establishment figure we have come to accept as Eliot. To see Eliot's oft-depicted formality as the formality of a dandy rather than that of a Chairman of the Board is revealing, and to further sketch the American democrat under the Gallic poseur is to recast even that image in a new form. Lewis's remarks, polemical as they are, force us to consider at least the possibility that Eliot did indeed have deep and deeply disguised impulses toward radical politics, philosophical realism, and that sexual freedom with which they were often associated in his time, and that these impulses had aesthetic consequences, both in his theory and in his poetry. Ideas, impulses, and directions so different from his official position were, of course, troubling, and Eliot often recognized them indirectly, if at all. Nevertheless, if we look briefly at two important figures in his life, Bertrand Russell and Walt Whitman, and then glance again, equally briefly, at *The Waste Land*, we can trace in Eliot's artistic lineage not only the metaphysical and French symbolist traditions of which he so often spoke, but another, deeper line of descent, one in which the democratic, the sexually open and the philosophically realist views of his greatest mentors take on a new and potentially fruitful life.

Both in Russell's work and in Whitman's, Eliot found a highly mediated, self-reflexive, idealist, and abstract approach to previous texts or philosophical problems challenged and superseded by a new, direct and even sensual apprehension of what we might call, with appropriate caveats and reservations, the "real." In both writers, too, these direct, open, democratically accessible and sense-affirming views were linked with an explicit sexual politics, a politics of "free love," to use the now somewhat dated term, or at least of tremendous sexual affirmation, which Eliot found both disturbing and vital. They were also, and in Eliot's view, less fortunately, allied with an inflated and sometimes sentimental rhetorical style, which was often embarrassingly fatuous or disconcertingly self-revealing, or both. Hence the vogue Eliot himself created for a metaphysical, witty and Gallic poetry, distanced and ironic, even in its treatment of sexuality or of the Eastern traditions was, even as he created it, in part a mask or defense to cover his lifelong agonistic struggle with a very different, even antithetical, style and point of view.

To take the philosophical position first, Russell (and to some extent Santayana as well) represented, for Eliot, a realist position in philosophy, together with a political and sexual point of view which challenged both the Bradleyan idealism of his graduate training and his own conservative instincts. More important, the perspectives opened up by Russell's neorealist philosophy offered the possibility of a new poetics, a poetics of direct sensual apprehension of ideas. Indeed, as Russell frequently testified, his break with idealism and his beginning exploration of a realist point of view had an aesthetic dimension even for the philosophers themselves. When he and Moore suddenly understood, Russell says, that the "meaning of an idea" was "something wholly independent of mind," they both experienced a sense of "emancipation." Though each was later to qualify this view in important ways, the memory of its releasing power did not fade. Importantly for Eliot, Russell's sense of release was occasioned directly by a break with Bradley, who had been his teacher and on whose system he, like Eliot, had formed his first philosophical thought. Later in life, Russell wrote:

> Bradley argued that everything common sense believes in is mere appearance; we reverted to the opposite extreme, and thought that *everything* is real that common sense, uninfluenced by philosophy or theology, supposes real. With a sense of escaping from prison, we allowed ourselves to think that grass is green, that the sun and stars would exist if no one was aware of them, and also that there is a pluralistic timeless world of Platonic ideas. The world, which had been thin and logical, suddenly became rich and varied and solid. Mathematics could be *quite* true, and not merely a stage in a dialectic.

Eliot's most important early critical formulations, the notion of the mind of the poet as a "shred of platinum," the idea of the "objective correlative," even the famous "dissociation of sensibility," can be traced less to his idealist mentors (though there are influences from Royce and Bradley in all of them) than to the new influence of realism. Idealism may have set the terms of his thought, but that drive for a sensual image which would form a direct link to and a necessary invocation of a given train of thought and feeling, that desperate desire to escape from the extreme textuality, the infinite regress, of post-Hegelian idealism, that search for a language which would be "quite true," and not merely a pragmatic tool or a stage in an endless, verbal dialectic, are all motivated by new winds, not old ones. As Santayana so well understood, the new realism could motivate not only a negative rejection of New England Puritanism, or Germanic textuality, but a positive movement as well: a movement toward that "sense of beauty," that aesthetic view of the world, which would be, in its own way, as "rich, and varied and solid" as Russell's. When this movement was allied with the search for a language which would represent it in as precise and compelling a way as a logical symbol or mathematic equation, the combination was heady indeed.

Russell's presence in Eliot's life was itself "rich and varied and solid"—and complex. Russell came to lecture at Harvard in 1914 in Eliot's last year of residence as a graduate student, at a time when that august institution had just lost or was about to lose its giants: Royce and James. The importance of what Russell had to give, both in terms of academic politics and in terms of substance, was not lost on his colleagues, and his presence was courted on every side. Eliot was one of several advanced students presented for his delectation, and he was encouraged to take Russell's course in logic, finding it less than central to his development, but enjoying the sense of "pleasure and power" gained by "manipulating [those] curious little figures." Eliot and some other senior students took advantage of Russell's desire to meet with the brightest young Americans in a tutorial situation, and their ease and confidence before the visitor from abroad, while charming Russell himself, occasioned quite a little flurry among more timid souls. Russell's judgment of Eliot, that he was brilliant, but did not have the temperament of a philosopher, was not an imperceptive one, and their encounter proved the beginning of a vexed but important friendship.

Russell quickly became, much to his own and Eliot's delight, a problematic figure at Harvard. He represented points of view which were new and challenging not only in philosophical but in sexual and political terms as well, and whatever he represented, he did so at maximum force. His aristocratic background and his impeccable credentials made it hard for Cambridge, Massachusetts, to ignore his advanced position on the equality of women and on "free love," and he drew down upon himself a great deal of attention, compounded in equal parts of awe and nerves. If his poetry is any indication, Eliot reveled in Russell's iconoclastic descent into Massachusetts society, and he recorded the resulting comedy of manners in his poem "Mr. Apollinax." The poem was occasioned by a weekend at a house party given by Anglophile academics. Eliot, who attended, associated Russell ever after with a certain faun-like sexuality, with a general stirring of the kinds of desires, fantasies, and images such occasions usually exclude. He enjoyed presenting, in his poem, this troubling sense of a more sexually charged, more alive, less well-repressed world, together with the faint sense of social contretemps which hung in the air. He was vividly struck with Russell's physical appearance (his tiny stature, his pointed ears, his undeniable sexual force) and did not fail to associate these accidents of nature with Russell's philosophical point of view. Both the liberated attitude toward sexuality Russell exemplified and his challenge to the predominant idealism of Harvard's philosophy department were part of what made his position "modern." It was a serious position, and Eliot recognized it as such, in spite of the comedy, and of later reference to Russell as a "priapic" materialist, or in punning terms as a "depressing life-forcer."

"Mr. Apollinax" exemplifies a good deal of that mixture of "stylistic effrontery" and secret fascination with a peculiarly radical and open point of view in Eliot detected by Wyndham Lewis. The poem makes use of Russell's power to stir a number of evocative images, and yet masks the interest of its young writer in these with an overtone of irony, a certain Gallic distance. In presenting images of Russell as an "irresponsible foetus," with laughter "submarine and profound," associated with the "beat of centaur's hoofs," while at the same time mentioning, in wry dismissal, that Professor and Mrs. Channing-Cheetah stimulated only memories of a "slice of lemon, and a bitten macaroon," Eliot was commenting on the power, for poetry, of a certain philosophical, sexual, and political position as well as on the necessity (for him) to frame that position with a certain irony. Russell's later friendship with Eliot and his first wife in London confirmed both these associations and the reservations Eliot was quite right to maintain, and even after they drew apart, Eliot continued to treat both Russell and his point of view with the respect they deserved.

Any disturbing impulses provoked by the party at the Channing-Cheetahs and its aftermath were as nothing, for Eliot, compared with the challenges posed by his reading of the work of Whitman. Russell, after all, was a philosopher, and he offered Eliot no competition whatsoever when it came to his real vocation, the writing of poetry. Whitman, by contrast, was a poet, a great one, and one of Eliot's own line of descent. Antithetical in temperament, taste and technique to Eliot, Whitman shared with him not only a profound engagement with Eastern thought, especially that of the *Bhagavad Gita*, but a transcendental heritage, an interest in realism, and, at least at first, a prophetic sense of vocation as well. For both, too, this early prophetic sense quickly modulated into elegy, as each confronted the collapse of that hope for a new culture through the depredations of modern war. In spite—or perhaps because of—his loose, open, self-revealing style and the risks of content and form he took, Whitman focused for Eliot the tensions he felt between the stance of the American democrat as wisdom poet and universal sage and that of the Gallic aristocrat as metaphysician, dandy and invulnerable wit.

Eliot testified to his ambivalence toward Whitman in terms so reminiscent of Harold Bloom's *Anxiety of Influence* as to be somewhat uncanny, and Bloom's work is perhaps the best theoretical guide both to Eliot's relationship to this precursor and to the way in which it informs *The Waste Land* itself. In a review essay of 1926, for instance, Eliot constructed a classic defense against Whitman's fathering power by comparing him unfavorably to Baudelaire, that *semblable* and *frère*, whose precedent was neither so immediate (taking place as it did in another language) nor so threatening (representing, as it did, at least for Eliot, a classic, heterosexual, and even orthodox point of view). Baudelaire, Eliot argued, understood the great gap, the abyss, between the real and the ideal which yawns especially wide whenever the identity or even the direct connection between the deep self and the outside world is asserted. Whitman did not understand this gap; indeed, he blurred and sentimentalized the line between self and other, perception and truth. Even his much-vaunted sexual frankness, Eliot argued (quite unjustifiably), did not come from courage or honesty but simply from the relatively uncritical insouciance of an assertive nature in a permissive milieu. Whitman had refused, as it were, to "look into the abyss" opened by his own ideas; there was, for him, no "chasm" between the real and the ideal such as opened before the "horrified" eyes of Baudelaire. As a result, Whitman had neither discipline nor the right to speak of it, and he compromised both his material and his own poetic strength ("Whitman and Tennyson"). Eliot rejected the weak stance he associated with Whitman here less for reasons of prudence or prudery than because he simply could not bear to contemplate the kind of vulnerability, both in theory and in practice, Whitman's "blurring of the line" entailed. The possibility that surrender might be reduced to seduction, openness to the world to slavery to sense impressions, and poetic affirmation to the self-inflated rhetoric of what Bloom calls the American Baroque Defeat, was one his own life and thought had brought him to recognize at every turn. To reveal any connection whatever between self and persona was to court the annihilation of both, either by the professorate on the one hand or by the object of one's bewildered desires on the other. The history of this fear and its strong locus in the figure of Whitman was encoded, for Eliot, in the suppressed and very early poem "Ode" from *Ara Vos Prec*. The poem records in cryptic form a moment of intense sexual de-idealization and poetic collapse, haunted on the one side by the submarine laughter of the realist/satyr/ Russell figure we have already seen in "Mr. Apollinax" and on the other by the bubbling of an uninspired Mephitic [female?] river. Between them lies a deadly, misread Whitmanian text, identified by Whitman's own synedoche of the calamus or pond reed.

In general, in his early reaction to Whitman, Eliot shows, as he does in this desperate little verse, more than a touch of phobia—perhaps even homophobia. By declaring, prematurely, the father's impotence, he reveals his own poetic and psychological weakness all the more clearly. It would be wrong, however, to reduce his reactions entirely to the level of repression or even the more self-interested kinds of defensiveness. As he elsewhere testified, Eliot believed that Whitman had identified the ideal and the real too closely and conjoined them too closely, as well, with motives of rhetorical and sexual display. In doing so, Eliot felt, he had put his poetry at risk. To the distrust produced by this risk, Eliot could add his own political suspicion of Whitman's courting of the many, the crowd, what Whitman himself liked to call the "En-mass." When Eliot took refuge beneath the masks of Laforgue, Corbière, and Baudelaire, then, he was defending himself both against the phantoms of fathering omnipotence in Whitman and against legitimate dangers and fears, including fears of that mass culture which sought to reduce them both to caricatures of themselves.

Even as he formulated this defensive stance, however, Eliot was capable of hearing in Whitman another, stronger voice. Again, we can see this more clearly by looking at his changing views of other poets, particularly of Baudelaire. By 1930, Eliot was beginning to see or admit to problems in Baudelaire. Baudelaire had achieved the awareness that no object is equal to human desire, Eliot argued in his essay of that year, but he had not attained to the belief that there exists, beyond the material world, a further object equal to that desire. He had not, that is, as Eliot put it, "learned to look to *death* for what *life* cannot give." Whitman had done precisely this, in his great odes to death. Of Whitman, Eliot elsewhere wrote at about this time: "beneath all the declamations there is another tone, and behind all the illusions there is another vision." For Eliot, that tone and vision surfaced in Whitman's (very American) images of mocking bird and lilac, and he heard them, too, if *The Waste Land* is testimony, in the voice of the hermit thrush, caroling "death's outlet song of life."

Eliot was able fully to admit the greatness of Whitman, however, only after he had to come to terms with his own American identity and achieved that poetic mastery on his own terms which gave him the security to confront his precursor again. The problem was clearly one of influence in the Bloomian sense, and Eliot often put it in just these terms. During the course of an essay called "American Literature and American Language" written in 1953 (in *To Criticize the Critic*) Eliot took up the question of influence explicitly, and he did so, significantly, in the context of a consideration of Whitman, Twain, and Poe. For models to *imitate*, Eliot said, a writer will often go to (usually minor) writers of another country and another language. By contrast, the great writers of the immediate past in his own tradition will function largely as "something definite to rebel against." There is a distinction, however, Eliot went on to argue, between genuine "influence" and the imitation of models or styles. "A true disciple is impressed by what his master has to say," he wrote, "and *consequently* by his way of saying it; an imitator—I might say a borrower—is impressed chiefly by the way his master said it." In this sense, Eliot was an "imitator" or "borrower" from the French, but he was a *disciple* of the Americans, and particularly of Whitman. Furthermore, by his own testimony, his discipleship had to do primarily with "what Whitman had to say" and only consequently with "how he said it."

"What Whitman had to say" involved, as we have seen, both radical democracy and sexual politics, and it also involved, crucially for Eliot, a certain very distinct, cogent and challenging reading of Eastern thought. While he seems to have been innocent of very much direct contact with

Eastern texts, and innocent as well of the kinds of epistemological despair that they raised in both earlier and later orientalists, Whitman had nevertheless achieved, by his maturity, a remarkable, original and culturally prescient understanding of one tendency in the Eastern traditions. That understanding, as recent critics of the relation between American and Hindu thought have increasingly stressed (V. K. Chari, Beongcheon Yu), was highly realist in terms of its Western orientation, rather than representing in a familiar way the philosophical idealism to which Eastern texts are more frequently assimilated in the West. Whitman's importance for Eliot, then, certainly lay in his understanding, inherent in the *Bhagavad Gita*, among other texts, but often overlooked there, of a detached but affirmative relation to sense experience, of an exoteric and culturally open approach to philosophical and religious truth, and of the validity of the active as well as the contemplative life. Eliot was never more Whitman's "disciple" than in his ability to envision in Eastern texts something more compelling, more disturbing and ultimately more liberating than mere denunciations of the world of appearance as pure illusion.

Whitman's realist and affirmative views and Russell's break with idealism had, then, not only great philosophical but great aesthetic and political weight for Eliot. The direction of their thought, however, and the styles in which it was embodied, were antithetical to his temperament and cast of mind. In order to work through these problems, Eliot had first to create a space for himself by the development of an original and opposing style and then to allow the "influence" of his mentors to flow into his own work in a strong, but thoroughly mastered and assimilated way.

One result of this poetic project was *The Waste Land*, a difficult and disturbing poem which has been read, no doubt with some justification, both as the already-dated and highly subjective product of the personal traumas of a bourgeois litterateur and as the most advanced and indeed subversive of modernist texts. To I. A. Richards fell the lot of being first to articulate the latter position, and his terribly modern *Waste Land*, was, no doubt, part of the provocation which made Eliot, in reaction, call it no more than a piece of "rhythmic grumbling." Even as a piece of "rhythmic grumbling," however, *The Waste Land*'s force has not always been lost, even on the discourse of the left. If the poem has not become, as Lewis sardonically predicted, a "passport to the communist millennium," it has at least fulfilled something of Trotsky's 1924 mandate for art. It has, that is, found "the necessary rhythm of words for dark and vague moods"; it has brought "thought and feeling closer"; it has enriched "the spiritual experience of the individual and of the community"; and this it has done "quite independently of whether it appears in a given case under the flag of a 'pure' or of a frankly tendentious art"

("The Formalist School"). We could do worse than to follow Trotsky's lead here, and look to the poem not at all to "incriminate" its author with the thoughts and feelings which he expresses but rather to "ask" to which order of feelings his work corresponds, what are its social and historical coordinates, and above all "what literary heritage has entered into the elaboration of the new form?"

A partial answer to the latter question is certainly found in the remarkable series of allusions to the work of Whitman which inform *The Waste Land*, and are especially marked in its final movement. Together, the heritage of Whitman and that of the Upanishads provide a channel through which a radical, open, democratic, and accessible voice rises in counterpoint and resolution to the closed, metaphysical, and guarded style which appears to dominate Eliot's early work. It is true that these allusions, especially in the case of Whitman, are largely unacknowledged. Eliot's note on the "hermit thrush," whose song is heard in Part V, and whose voice, as we shall see, is so clearly an echo of the same bird who sings in "When Lilacs Last in the Dooryard Bloom'd," directs us not to a previous text, in Whitman or elsewhere, but to the "real" bird of the American Northeast. This suppression of Whitman's name, however, whether unconscious or deliberate, is part of a movement toward direct representation and affirmative feeling which seeks to escape from the infinite regress of textual allusions which seems to pervade the poem and to find the "objective correlative," the conjunction of sound and sense, signified and signifier, knowledge and experience, of which Whitman spoke in different terms, and which he, too, sought to embody.

John Hollander and Harold Bloom have repeatedly drawn attention to the extended and systematic echoes of Whitman in *The Waste Land* (Gauss Lectures, 1981; Figure of Echo). The full impact of these can only be measured, however, by laying "When Lilacs Last in the Dooryard Bloom'd" side by side with Eliot's text. Here, then, are a few of the relevant passages from Whitman, beginning with portions of the opening, moving through the song of the hermit thrush to the lyrical celebration of the American city (of which Eliot's London is a travesty) and ending with the final journey, the poet's last walk along the "long black trail," where he becomes the third of three companions, the other two the "thought of death and the knowledge of death," wending their way to the place of revelation among the "dark cedars and ghostly pines."

When lilacs last in the dooryard bloom'd,
And the great star early droop'd in the western sky in
the night,

I mourn'd, and yet shall mourn with ever-returning
  spring.

In the swamp in secluded recesses,
A shy and hidden bird is warbling a song.

Solitary the thrush,
The hermit withdrawn to himself, avoiding the
  settlements,
Sings by himself a song.

Song of the bleeding throat,
Death's outlet song of life, (for well dear brother I
  know,
If thou wast not granted to sing thou would'st surely
  die.)

Coffin that passes through lanes and streets,
Through day and night with the great cloud
  darkening the land,
With the pomp of the inloop'd flags with the cities
  draped in black,
With the show of the States themselves as of crape-
  veil'd women
  standing,
With processions long and winding and the flambeaus
  of the night,
With the countless torches lit, with the silent sea of
  faces and the
  unbared heads.

—where amid these you journey,
With the tolling tolling bells' perpetual clang,
Here, coffin that slowly passes, I give you my sprig of lilac.

Falling upon them all and among them all, enveloping
  me with the rest
Appear'd the cloud, appear'd the long black trail,
And I knew death, its thought, and the sacred
  knowledge of death.
Then with the knowledge of death as walking one

side of me,
And the thought of death close-walking the other side
of me,
And I in the middle as with companions, and as
holding the hands of companions,
I fled forth to the hiding receiving night that talks not,
Down to the shores of the water, the path by the
swamp in the dimness.
To the solemn shadowy cedars and ghostly pines so
still.
And the singer so shy to the rest receiv'd me,
The gray-brown bird I know receiv'd us comrades
three,
And he sang the carol of death, and a verse for him I
love.

And the voice of my spirit tallied the song of the bird.

I saw battle-corpses, myriads of them,
And the white skeletons of young men, I saw them,
I saw the debris and debris of all the slain soldiers of
the war,
But I saw they were not as was thought,
They themselves were fully at rest, they suffer'd not,
The living remain'd and suffer'd, the mother suffer'd,
And the wife and the child and the musing comrade
suffer'd,
And the armies that remained suffer'd.

Whitman's poem gives us not only the motifs and images of *The Waste Land*, from the lilacs and flowers through the "unreal city" to the disturbing thought of the bodies of dead soldiers, the presence of a double self, a dear brother or semblable, the "murmur of maternal lamentation," the peering faces, and the song of the hermit thrush over the dry bones, but its very tone and pace, the steady andante which makes of both poems a walking meditation. We are not far here from Eliot's themes and tone in Part V:

After the torchlight red on sweaty faces
After the frosty silence in the gardens
After the agony in stony places
The shouting and the crying

Prison and palace and reverberation
Of thunder of spring over distant mountains
He who was living is now dead
We who were living are now dying
With a little patience

Even Whitman's "thought of death" and "knowledge of death," who with him form three companions, seems to herald Eliot's "third who walks always beside you," that ambiguous figure which seems also, like the "singer shy to the rest," half-projection, half-reality, emerging and disappearing into that intermediate zone "where the hermit thrush sings in the pine trees."

What allows Whitman's poetry to flow into Eliot's here is a conjunction not simply of voice but of conscious theme and subconscious psychic preoccupation as well. Both poems move at the boundary between East and West, both approach, with a sense of danger and sacrifice, the great assertion of the identity of the deep self with the divine, fully realized only in and through both a literal and a metaphorical death. For both, that assertion must, if it is to be effective, take place in a material form and have real, physical, and emotional implications. Both are mourning the death of a father figure, with all such mourning implies of violence, ambivalence, self-sacrifice, and pain, and both are seeking a simplicity, a sobriety of expression which will reflect both Wordsworth's "awful power to chasten and subdue" and the equal power to elevate and establish their own poetic identities. Both, furthermore, find that simplicity in sound, in incantation, in chant or "carol" as Whitman calls it, in the intonations of a voice which comes as much from without as from within the egocentric, personal, daily self. At the end, too, both break into great incantations which unclose the eyes and provide a new vision of the dead, no longer threatening to break decaying from the ground, but become, as *The Waste Land* puts it, "dry bones" which "harm no one" because the closed and self-conscious personal self that animated them is at rest.

Eliot's poem, moreover, juxtaposes the "dear brother" of Whitman's "When Lilacs Last in the Dooryard Bloom'd," with the "semblable" and "frère" of Baudelaire's *L'Ennui*. He thus brings into sharp tension his Gallic, metaphysical and antithetical mask and his open, vulnerable plea for a democratic fraternity of poets. Whitman's "dear brother" is, of course, as the poem goes on to make clear, the hermit thrush, whose "song of the bleeding throat" is "death's outlet song of life." The voice of that bird is heard in Eliot's "water-dripping" song, and *The Waste Land* measures the cost of the suppression and subsequent release of this song, which springs from a "bleeding throat," at other points as well. For Eliot, too, song arises from a violation; the "bleeding throat" is matched by the rape of Philomela, metamorphosed into the nightingale, whose voice is "inviolable." Philomela, like Whitman, has learned to "look to death for what life cannot give," and only in contemplating her example—and in "musing on the king my brother's wreck"—can the poem harmonize its "real and its ideal needs." When, however, in its closing lines, *The Waste Land* breaks into the line *quando fiam uti chelidon*, it seems, even at this late and desperate moment, to guard, at least under the disguise of Latin, that pose of classical panache of which Wyndham Lewis had scornfully spoken. This is not the cry of the "democrat in spite of himself" but of the far more careful and controlled *defensor fidei*, the one who has paid, as Lewis put it, "a great deal of curious attention to the sanctions required for the expression of the thinking subject in verse or prose." The content, however, belies the form. "When will I be as the swallow," the verse cries out, linking its cry not only to the song of Philomela, but to Whitman's thrush as well. Whitman's poem looms again here, providing at once a gloss and antiphon to Eliot's, one in which his particular form of defensive self-protection has been utterly forgone. It is toward Eliot, as well as toward the hermit thrush, that Whitman proleptically moves when he calls out in answer to that cry: "For well dear brother I know, / If thou wast not granted to sing thou would'st surely die."

In his relation to Whitman, seen in the context of the thought of Russell, and indeed of the Upanishadic tradition as well, Eliot seeks, before our half-horrified, half-enamoured eyes, to cross the gap or abyss that separates the radical democrat from the Gallic poseur, the sexually free from the sexually contorted or repressed, the poetically accessible and fraternal from the poetically Oedipal and closed, the esoteric and philosophically idealist from the exoteric and realist position. That chasm cannot be easily traversed, and only in recognition of its depth can we make any sense at all of the contradictions in Eliot's work. Eliot's early career, more than that of any other modernist, dramatizes the difficult problem of translation involved when we seek to turn a mental and philosophical image of liberation into the objective reality of political, sexual, and aesthetic release. To have reminded us that such a translation involves prior acts of control, restraint, and sacrifice, and that it must stand up under the acerbic gaze of a Wyndham Lewis as well as under the apparently more benign scrutiny of a Leavis or a Richards, is not the least of Eliot's achievements.

LOUIS MENAND

Problems About Texts

The composition of *The Waste Land* was a famously difficult business. The story of Eliot's troubles is now well enough known to have become, for many readers, part of the experience of the poem.[1] Having been shoring fragments for a long work since his first year in England, Eliot announced his intention to begin putting his poem together in the fall of 1919, but apparently found it almost impossible to proceed. "[E]very evening, he went home to his flat hoping that he could start writing again, and with every confidence that the material was *there* and waiting," he told Conrad Aiken, but "night after night the hope proved illusory: the sharpened pencil lay unused by the untouched sheet of paper. What could be the matter? He didn't know."[2] His writer's block was aggravated by circumstances: the demands of his job at Lloyds Bank, and of the various freelance lecturing assignments he took on to supplement his salary, left him with little energy for poetry; his wife's father became ill, then his wife, then Eliot himself; and a visit from his mother and sister in the summer of 1921 seems to have precipitated a crisis. He took three months' leave from the bank in October 1921, and went first to Margate for a month, then to Lausanne to undergo therapy; and there, working in solitude, he was able to complete a draft of the poem. Pound performed his editorial role in January, and *The Waste Land* seems finally to have been finished in the late spring or early summer of 1922.

Eliot alludes often in his letters during this period to personal troubles—to concern about the state of his marriage, anxiety about his career, recurrent nervous exhaustion, even the fear of mental illness—and it may be, as Ronald Bush has suggested, that the combined traumatic weight of these worries made writing poetry under ordinary conditions impossible by compelling Eliot to confront emotional material that a commitment to literary honesty made nearly intractable.[3] And there seems to have been a purely professional pressure on Eliot as well, the pressure caused by the regular appearance on his desk at *The Egoist* of the chapters of *Ulysses* in manuscript from, which made him feel about his own work, as he explained it to an interviewer many years later, that "[w]hat he was tentatively attempting to do, with the usual false starts and despairs, had already been done, done superbly and, it seemed to him finally, in prose which without being poetic in the older sense, had the intensity and texture of poetry."[4]

But *The Waste Land* must have been difficult to write for another, simpler reason. It was the promised major work of a writer who, in his criticism, had exposed the delusiveness of virtually every conventional prescription for poetical newness. In a period when avant-garde literature seemed a function of theories and manifestos, Eliot was an avant-gardist without a program. Having demonstrated the factitiousness of the traditional building blocks of poetic theory—the definition of what literature is, the epistemological explanation of how literature works, the notion that sincerity is a matter of being true to oneself—Eliot must have found himself with nothing to construct a poem on. Whatever their insight into the way literature is perceived, his prescriptive essays are, from a writer's point of view, entirely impractical: the fourth of the "Reflections on Contemporary Poetry" describes genuine creativity as a business as unpremeditated as falling in love, and "Tradition and the Individual Talent" assigns the poet the whole of the Western tradition as homework but says nothing about how that learning might, in the actual process of composition, be put to use.

"[I]f we are to express ourselves, our variety of thoughts and feelings, on a variety of subjects with inevitable rightness," one of the early essays counsels the modern poet, "we must adapt our manner to the moment with infinite variations."[5] The sentence might have been the model for many of Eliot's early critical prescriptions. It is a formula whose lack of metaphysical content may be satisfying to the skeptic, but whose lack of almost every other sort of content leaves the practitioner somewhat worse off than he was without the advice, for it provokes the question, What is one's manner if it is a thing infinitely adaptable? But let us suppose that this was a question that Eliot, as he sat, a poem in his mind but a blank sheet before him, asked himself at some point. It would not have seemed unfamiliar to him, for it is a particular instance of the general question posed by the extreme ontological relativism of his dissertation: if each thing is entirely a function of its perceived relation to every other thing, what sense does it make for us to speak—as we do speak—of an object's distinctive character? Individuality—the set of qualities that "belong" to the object—is, by the lights of the dissertation, a phantom; it is an accident of the shape ordinary knowledge happens to take, the inexplicable residue that remains after everything else about a thing has been explained, or the unlikeness that is left after all likenesses have been used up. The notion that there are qualities original to the object persists because we have made the decision to treat certain aspects of our experience as discrete. But philosophically these discriminations have no standing; they cannot survive analysis, whose virtue, the dissertation reminds us, "is in showing the destructibility of everything."[6]

This might seem a problem whose working out will be of interest only to metaphysicians and their antagonists; but it is one of those apparently empty philosophical topics that take on life in controversies in which the issues seem quite tangible and the consequences are real enough. The question that Eliot might, in some form or other, have asked himself—What is "mine" about my poem?—is a version of this problem, and it belongs to an important line of nineteenth-century thought. The line is important because it was one of the ways the nineteenth century undertook to defend the status of human endeavor against the implications of scientific determinism, and its consequences mattered because the way the question is answered has an effect on the value that is attributed to art. There is much in Eliot's early writing that can be explained by this nineteenth-century intellectual background; but it is, characteristically, hard to know which side of the issue Eliot wanted to come down on. For if "Tradition and the Individual Talent" seems to lean toward one sort of answer to the question, *The Waste Land* seems to lean in a rather different direction. As is the case with many of the issues that figure in modernist writing, the alternative ways of thinking about the problem can be found articulated in particularly vivid forms in the literature of the 1890s.

Oscar Wilde thought the essay on "Style" the least successful in Pater's *Appreciations*. He considered the subject too theoretical, and felt that Pater did better things when he was engaged with particular works of art. But still, he added, there was something so Paterian about Pater's treatment of his abstract theme that perhaps the essay could be regarded as a success after all: "I think I have been wrong in saying that the subject is too abstract. In Mr. Pater's hands it becomes very real to us indeed."[7]

The ambivalence is typical of Wilde—he always seems willing to be seduced by a pleasing surface—and like so much else in his thought, it was learned from Pater himself. For when it is the writer's unique set of fingerprints we are interested in, it will not matter what he picks up. Pater had made the fingerprints interesting by assigning everything else to determinism, leaving us to choose only the manner in which we submit ourselves to its authority. "Natural laws we shall never modify, embarrass us as they may," advises Pater's essay on Winckelmann; "but there is still something in the nobler or less noble attitude with which we watch their fatal combinations."[8] It is a familiar alliance: aestheticism underwritten by a radical materialism; and "embarrass" is the word that gives the sentence its nineteenth-century flavor. The eighteenth-century empiricist did not consider himself embarrassed by the recognition that he was dependent on imperfect sense data for his knowledge of the world; but Darwin had shamed human-kind by showing it to be descended from the apes.

For a nineteenth-century cultural historian like Pater, Darwinism had a double aspect: it made the job of understanding the past problematic in a new way, but it seemed at the same time to hold out the promise of an extraordinary solution. Evolutionary theory exacerbated the skepticism inherent in the empiricist tradition by suggesting that the men and women of the past were different from ourselves not just in the way the contents of one center of consciousness are different from and ultimately inaccessible to the contents of another, but because those men and women had different physiologies. And the historian who undertook to reconstruct that world of slightly alien creatures was therefore the prisoner not merely of his subjectivity, but of the configuration of his own particular moment in the evolutionary process as well. "Human nature" was no longer a stable paradigm. But in closing off the last window to an objective view of the past—the window afforded by the notion that although its contents may differ, the structure of human consciousness is always the same—Darwinism seemed to make the problem of objectivity disappear. For it suggested that the relation between the historian and the object of his study might now be conceived in a new way: the historian was himself—as a *subject*—the product of the past he was seeking to understand. And his best way of knowing the past was therefore not to try to get outside himself, to aspire to some extrapersonal or ahistorical vantage point, but to remain true to his subjectivity, since that subjectivity was in the end not his own at all, but the property of history itself. "The fancy of a perpetual life, sweeping together ten thousand experiences, is an old one," Pater concludes his famous description of the face of the Mona Lisa; "and modern thought has conceived the idea of humanity as wrought upon by, and summing up in itself, all modes of thought and life. Certainly Lady Lisa might stand as the embodiment of the old fancy, the symbol of the modern idea."[9]

For Pater, the awareness of the determining hand of the past gave the coloring of tragedy to the contemplation of life. In the greatest art, he says, "this entanglement, this network of law, becomes the tragic situation, in which certain groups of noble men and women work out for themselves a supreme *dénouement*."[10] But like any good disciple, Wilde had the courage of his teacher's convictions, and he stripped Darwinism of this Paterian pathos and put it to the essentially comedic service of turning received values upside down, making style (as in his change of mind about Pater's essay) take precedence over substance, artificiality over sincerity, criticism over creation.

Wilde's most ambitious performances in this mode are those imaginary dialogues in *Intentions* (1891), "The Decay of Lying" and "The Critic as Artist," which strike us today as thoroughly Victorian in taste and nearly postmodern in conviction. Gilbert, the protagonist of "The Critic as Artist," has studied Pater's passage on the Mona Lisa carefully. He seems, in fact, to know it by heart: "By revealing to us the absolute mechanism of all action, and so freeing us from the self-imposed and trammelling burden of moral responsibility," he explains to Ernest,

> the scientific principle of Heredity has become, as it were, the warrant for the contemplative life. It has shown us that we are never less free than when we try to act.... It is the only one of the Gods whose real name we know.... And so, it is not our own life that we live, but the lives of the dead, and the soul that dwells within us is no single spiritual entity, making us personal and individual, created for our service, and entering into us for our joy. It is something that has dwelt in fearful places, and in ancient sepulchres has made its abode. It is sick with many maladies, and has memories of curious sins. It is wiser than we are, and its wisdom is bitter. It fills us with impossible desires, and makes us follow what we know we cannot gain.... [T]he imagination is the result of heredity. It is simply concentrated race-experience.[11]

For Wilde, as for Pater, Darwinism made the history of culture hang together in a new way—as a string of subjective moments, each giving meaning to the others by reinterpreting them. It was a conception that turned history into a kind of autobiography. History, like the autobiographical subject, reveals itself only in the process of contemplating itself (so that a Paterian novel like Joyce's *A Portrait of the Artist as a Young Man* [1916] has in this sense, to borrow Gillian Beer's useful phrase, a Darwinian plot). And like the autobiographical subject, history is a whole whose surface is constantly being reinscribed but whose integrity can be empirically tested: we know it to be there because we feel ourselves to be here. Thus the thought of Pater and Wilde exhibits the common characteristic of late-nineteenth-century historicist philosophies: the belief, as Peter Allan Dale has described it, that "the human mind finds its highest expression in the weaving of a vast and continuous system of human culture through time and that the meaning of man in the present can be no more or less than as a participant in that historical culture."[12]

This is a line of thought to which "Tradition and the Individual Talent"—not in spite of, but because of the severity of its strictures on the hypostasization of personality—quite clearly belongs. "No poet, no artist of any art, has his complete meaning alone," runs the familiar passage in Eliot's essay:

> ... The necessity that he shall conform, that he shall cohere, is not one-sided; what happens when a new work of art is created is something that happens simultaneously to all the works of art which preceded it. The existing monuments form an ideal order among themselves, which is modified by the introduction of the new (the really new) work of art among them. The existing order is complete before the new work arrives; for order to persist after the supervention of novelty, the *whole* existing order must be, if ever so slightly, altered; and so the relations, proportions, values of each work of art toward the whole are readjusted; and this is conformity between the old and the new.[13]

It is the modernist edition of the nineteenth-century historicist argument: if we abandon the atomistic conception of subjectivity—the fiction that "personality" is a thing autonomous and coherent enough to express itself—the subject will be revealed to be a nondetachable part of a greater whole, with the capacity to express, and by expressing to remake, something "more valuable"[14] than itself. For by giving up the search for what is original with the poet, Eliot's essay explains, "we shall often find that not only the best, but the most individual parts of his work may be those in which the dead poets, his ancestors, assert their immortality most vigorously."[15]

Sitting at his desk with a blank sheet before him, Eliot must thus have felt that in order to write a poem about the experience of contemporary life, he would have to write a poem that took in everything. And *The Waste Land* is indeed a literary work that seems to regard the present moment—as it is experienced by the individual subject—as a reinscription of the whole of the cultural past, and the cultural past as though it were the autobiography of a single consciousness. Or so, at least, the notes to the poem suggest. "Tiresias," explains the note to line 218,

> although a mere spectator and not indeed a "character," is yet the most important personage in the poem, uniting all the rest. Just as the one-eyed merchant, seller of currants, melts into the Phoenician Sailor, and the latter is not wholly distinct from Ferdinand Prince of Naples, so all the women are one woman, and the two sexes meet in Tiresias. What Tiresias *sees*, in fact, is the substance of the poem.[16]

And the "one woman" of which all the women in the poem are said to be types seems very like a version of Pater's emblem for the evolutionary history of consciousness summed up in the expression of a single face, La Gioconda. Eliot's symbol of perpetual life appears first in the epigraph as the ancient Sybil who cannot die, and again, perhaps, in "The Burial of the Dead" as "Belladonna, the Lady of the Rocks" ("She is older than the rocks among which she sits ..." runs Pater's description).[17] She is the woman in "The Game of Chess," surrounded by "her strange synthetic perfumes" and on whose dressing-room walls hang the "withered stumps of time"—the artistic record of the mythical past ("... and all this has been to her but as the sound of lyres and flutes, and lives only in the delicacy with which it has moulded the changing lineaments, and tinged the eyelids and the hands"). And she appears, finally, in "The Fire Sermon," where she draws "her long black hair out tight," while

> bats with baby faces in the violet light
> Whistled, and beat their wings
> And crawled head downward down a blackened wall

("... like the vampire, she has been dead many times, and learned the secrets of the grave").[18]

But *The Waste Land* makes a strange gloss on "Tradition and the Individual Talent," for it seems infected with a doubt not addressed by the essay, but implicit in the intellectual tradition to which the essay belongs. The doubt stems from the assault the historicist thesis, in the name of subjectivity, makes on the integrity of the individual subject: for after everything in the poem that belongs to the tradition has been subtracted, what sort of value can be claimed for what is left? Pater called the remainder "style," and he made it the signal—in fact, the single—virtue of the literary object; but in Eliot's essay, all the emphasis is directed the other way. The writer who, in obedience to "Tradition and the Individual Talent"'s "programme for the *métier* of poetry,"[19] undertakes to produce the "really new" work of art, is given no place to look for its origins; the program is distinctly inhospitable to such notions as the Paterian "inner vision." And the suspicion thus arises that newness is nothing more than a kind of accident, a mistake that could not, in the end, be avoided. The manner in which *The Waste Land* dramatizes this doubt derives from the critique of the historicist defense of culture, a critique to which Eliot himself, in his brief career as a philosopher, made a relevant contribution.

Wilde's thought, unlike Pater's, leaned in the direction of Utopianism, and he saw in the acceptance of an extreme materialism the chance to make a number of false issues about literary values go away. To begin with, materialism seemed to him to solve the problem of artistic content. For if ethical standards, on a deterministic view like Gilbert's, are simply things thrown out and then swallowed up again by the evolutionary flux, we no longer need to trouble ourselves about making our response to a work of art answerable to the moral fashions of our time, since the content of one statement is as good as the content of another. There are only differences in the forms the statements take, and those differences must be what matters. "From time to time the world cries out against some charming artistic poet, because, to use its hackneyed and silly phrase, he has 'nothing to say,'" Gilbert declares. "But if he had something to say, he would probably say it, and the result would be tedious. It is just because he has no new message, that he can do beautiful work."[20] All the poet's material is given culturally (as all the components of personality are given genetically), but the shape into which that received information is molded will always be unique (just as each person carries off his assigned role in the evolutionary program differently). The form of an artistic statement can therefore be treated as a behavioral gesture: an attitude, a style, a pose—something that does not require us to engage in pointless debate over its meaning or moral intentions, as my way of walking is expressive but has no message to deliver.

Emptying out the content seems to liberate the notion of interpretation as well, since if it makes no sense to speak of originality of conception, it is pointless to draw a distinction between creation and criticism. Not only does objectivity become a problem to be solved by being ignored, but it is in fact, says Gilbert, the critic's "duty" to misinterpret: "To give an accurate description of what has never occurred is not merely the proper occupation of the historian, but the inalienable privilege of any man of parts and culture."[21] For it is of a series of misinterpretations that history is made. When we look for a reality in the past that we might describe, we find only the descriptions others have made; and our understanding of those prior descriptions will scarcely be objective, since the organ of our understanding is itself one of the things they have created ("the imagination is ... simply concentrated race-experience"). Because it never affirmeth, art is the best record of our misreadings: "The fact is," explains Vivian in "The Decay of Lying," "that we look back on the ages entirely through the medium of Art, and Art, very fortunately, has never once told us the truth."[22] And the critic will therefore want the same freedom to make a new thing out of his failure to achieve an accurate representation of the object of his attention as the artist has traditionally been granted.

In extending the implications of Pater's thought, Wilde was, of course, continuing the work that has been taken up anew by each generation of aesthetic theorists in modern times—the task of adapting the values of art to a new phase of the progressive disenchantment of the world. The strategy Wilde had learned from Pater was a radical one. He did not try to oppose aesthetic values to scientific ones, to force his contemporaries to choose among competing *Weltanschuuangen*; he made his argument for the superiority of the language of art turn precisely on an acceptance of the most advanced scientific view of things. He made science underwrite an argument for its own inadequacy. But it was a risky business, and it required, as we have seen, extreme measures. For like any formalist ideology, aestheticism invites the complaint that in order to preserve art's special status, it effectively gets rid of everything that makes art matter to most people. In rescuing art from the threat of determinism, Wilde not only felt himself obliged to jettison the notion of valid interpretation, the notion that we can have an understanding of a work of art that corresponds to the artist's intention and to the understandings of other people; he had to subvert or abandon the values of content, representation, and originality as well. It was Wilde's contention that art was well rid of these things, that it only made itself richer by handing them over to the enemy, but he had embarked on a line of reasoning that has no natural stopping place. For if the matter of our expressions is not ours, why is the manner?

It was in fact the belief of some of Wilde's contemporaries that *every* aesthetic value, even the value of style, is reducible, without remainder, to a scientific explanation. "The mysterious gift of inspiration, essential to all literary and artistic genius," explained J. F. Nisbet in *The Insanity of Genius* (1891), "is evidently nothing but the automatic activity of the nerve-cells of the brain—a phase of that morbid condition which finds its highest expression in insanity."[23] Nisbet described the method of his book as the assertion of "the principle of a fatalism in the lives of great men," and he proposed, by replacing the mystical notion of the brain as spirit with the scientific notion of the brain as matter, to account for every attribute of extraordinary behavior physiologically. It is in the structure of the brain, he announced, that "the solution of such problems as reason, judgment, imagination, and inspiration is to be sought," and he proceeded to give a material explanation not only of inspiration, but of such elements of style as rhyme and meter (a "special susceptibility of the motor as well as of the auditory centres and their connections"), assonance, imagery, puns, wit, clarity, and the mot juste.[24]

Nisbet's book belongs to the phenomenon Allon White has described as the rise of symptomatic reading, the method of treating literature as the record of a state of affairs which, by definition, the writer cannot manipulate—as the symptom of the writer's historical situation, or of his unconscious impulses, or of his neurological health.[25] Because everything has been given over to determining forces, what the writer intended to say—even what he intended to say about his unconscious impulses or the conditions of his time—cannot count; it is what he could not help saying, what he has said in spite of himself, that is his meaning. Symptomatic reading is the practical critical response to the notion of art as behavior: my way of walking will tell you something about me only as long as it remains unpremeditated; if I deliberately change its style, what will be revealing will be not the new manner of walking itself, but the fact of my having chosen to adopt it.

Symptomatic reading is a way of setting up the game so that the critic will always be one move ahead of the writer (though White has shown how the modern writer, by adopting the literary strategy of obscurity, took revenge on his interpreters). Its most celebrated practitioner in Wilde's day was Max Nordau, whose *Degeneration* (1892) is still in some ways the summa of all the attacks that have ever been made on modernism in art. "[T]he application of the term 'degenerates' to the originators of all the *fin-de-siècle* movements in art and literature," Nordau maintained, "is ... no baseless conceit, but a fact." And he offered what amounted to an improvement on Nisbet's method: he did not need, he argued, "to measure the cranium of an author" to prove his assertion, for he had available the literary work itself, whose attributes could be analyzed as one would analyze the symptoms—Nordau called them the stigmata—of the diseased person.[26]

Nisbet had classed the artist with the lunatic; Nordau, taking his cue from Cesare Lombroso's physiological studies of the "born criminal," classed him with the sociopath. And, ascribing to the popular speeded-up Darwinism of the time,[27] he explained genetically inscribed sociopathic tendencies by environmental change. Modern life—bigger cities, faster railways, a greater rate and volume of economic activity—added up to a "vastly increased number of sense impressions and organic reactions, and therefore of perceptions, judgments, and motor impulses." But civilized humanity, Nordau argued, "had no time to adapt itself to its changed conditions of life.... It grew fatigued and exhausted, and this fatigue and exhaustion showed themselves in the first generation, under the form of acquired hysteria; in the second, as hereditary hysteria." Nordau meant his diagnosis literally: "railway-spine" and "railway-brain" (the consequences of "the constant vibrations undergone in railway travelling") had brought about an actual physiological alteration—first directly, and then through genetic transmission—in the organ of perception.[28] Thus an Impressionist painting, for example, was not the product of a conscious effort to adapt artistic form to the subject matter of modern life; it was an accurate representation of the optical image produced by a nervous system in the process of devolution:

> The degenerate artist who suffers from *nystagmus*, or trembling of the eyeball, will, in fact, perceive the phenomena of nature trembling, restless, devoid of firm outline, and, if he is a conscientious painter, *will* give us pictures reminding us of the mode practised by the draughtsmen of the *Fliegende Blätter* when they represent a wet dog shaking himself vigorously.[29]

And by the same token, the poses of the aesthete, precisely because they differ from the behavior of the normal person, are the symptoms of a deviation that calls for a psychological diagnosis:

> The predilection for strange costume is a pathological aberration of a racial instinct.... When ... an Oscar Wilde goes about in "aesthetic costume" among gazing Philistines, exciting either their ridicule or their wrath, it is no indication of independence of character, but rather from a purely anti-socialistic, egomaniacal recklessness and hysterical longing to make a sensation....[30]

The artist who subscribes to Wilde's position has no good way of defending himself against this sort of critical treatment, since although he can, according to the Wildean view of artistic content, say what he likes, he has effectively relinquished control over what he means. *Degeneration* is the nightmare version of late-nineteenth-century aestheticism; it is the danger Wilde was flirting with when he enlisted scientific determinism in his defense of art. Pater and Wilde had undertaken to preserve the status of art under a materialist dispensation by assigning value to whatever it is that gives a thing its distinctive form, that makes it what it is and not another thing. The work of art is the type of the distinctive object; its style is the sign of its uniqueness, and the evidence of the artist's triumph—in the aggregate, of humanity's triumph—over impersonal process. Nordau responded, in effect, by pointing out that materialism leaves no room for an independent intention, so that whatever distinguishes a thing from the norm is analyzable as the symptom of an evolutionary aberration. To claim that the history of culture, taken as a series of misinterpretations, is coherent on grounds that it is the evolutionary record of the subject is to claim that a list of errors adds up to the truth. Participation in culture cannot be the meaning of human life, because culture is purely reflexive; it adds nothing to what is there: "every work of art," says Nordau, "always comprises in itself truth and reality in so far as, if it does not reflect the external world, it surely reflects the mental life of the artist."[31] In Nordau's version of Darwinian historicism, wholeness becomes totality: the evolutionary law covers every case, and reduces everything to its terms. Nordau, like Nisbet, explained the distinctive act physiologically for the simple reason that on his view it could not be accounted for in any other way. He thus made the artist the victim of his own individuality, of the very quality the aesthete had hoped would save him.

The 1890s is the missing chapter in many versions of the history of literary modernism, in part because all the issues in its cultural controversies appear to be overdrawn, so that it is not easy to know just how seriously to take them. If Nordau's position seems absurd, Wilde's seems deliberately calculated to provoke absurdity. But however self-consciously extravagant it may have been, the aestheticist valorization of style had a significant role in the formation of the ideology of modern art, and the problem Nordau's argument makes for it is a real one.

Nor is it the only difficulty that can be pointed to. In December 1913, T. S. Eliot read a paper on a problem in comparative anthropology to Josiah Royce's graduate seminar at Harvard. Eliot's particular examples were Jane Harrison's *Themis: A Study of the Social Origins of Greek Religion* (1912) and Frazer's *Golden Bough*, and his argument was that the efforts of those writers to describe religious ritual scientifically were misconceived, and could lead to no conclusive results.[32] The problem, Eliot maintained, was not merely the traditional epistemological problem of uncertainty, the problem of having no way of knowing when our knowing is objectively true. We assume, of course, that the scientist's interpretations will interfere with the facts of the phenomenon he is trying to provide an account of, that those interpretations will disappear into the data and emerge in the analysis as "descriptions." But this difficulty is exacerbated in the case of a social phenomenon such as a religious ritual by the circumstance that the person who performs the ritual will have his own interpretation of its meaning, and this interpretation will be an additional fact to be described. For unless the description of an action takes account of the meaning it has for the actor, Eliot argued, it treats behavior as "mere mechanism."[33]

But when we look to the internal meaning of an action, we find ourselves confronting a further problem, the problem that the individual participant's interpretation of a ritual cannot be taken as definitive, that it will be an interpretation "probably not in accordance with the facts of [the ritual's] origin."[34] Because a religious ritual is a social activity, its meaning cannot be the meaning given to it by one of the participants (an "[i]nterpretation which the individual makes is not made by the group," as Eliot put it, "and hence [is] not the cause"[35]). And since a ritual is, furthermore, an activity that has a history, it cannot even be, at any given moment, the sum of all the meanings given to it by all the participants; for each time the ritual is performed, it will mean something different, the interpretations of each new generation constituting a reinterpretation of a phenomenon which is already defined in part by the interpretations of the previous group, and so forth backward in time. "Interpretation is thus ever a new problem added to increase the difficulty of the old," Eliot concluded; and the comparative study of religions, he noted, was a subject "especially good to bring this out, for here interpretation has succeeded interpretation, not because the older opinions were refuted, but because the point of view has changed."[36]

Royce commented on Eliot's paper by suggesting that in everyday life we might solve problems of interpretation by asking questions until a mutual understanding was reached. But Eliot did not see how this proposal met the case, and he replied by asking Royce: "Is there no essential distinction between a social statement in language which asks for interpretation and a something not intended as a sign?"[37] It is a nice question, for the answer would seem to be that there is a distinction, since we make it all the time, but that there is nothing essential about it, since a thing is a sign when it is treated as one and not a sign when it is not, as when you suddenly interpret my habit of raising my eyebrows as skepticism. But even on these relative terms, the distinction has a consequence for our understanding. The point of Eliot's response to Royce is that once something is regarded as behavior, interpretation becomes not merely a problem (as Royce had hope to leave the matter) but problematic. The meaning of a statement that was intended to have a meaning can be ascertained, if only in a rough and ready way, as when I ask if this is what you meant by something you said, and you say yes. But the meaning of behavior is indeterminate: my interpretation of my way of walking is not definitive; it is just one more piece of the puzzle, and one that cannot now be left out. But it was precisely by thinking of art as like a way of walking that Wilde had hoped to avoid the goose chase after meanings.

All the difficulties with the late-nineteenth-century idea of style seem to be summed up in *The Waste Land*. It is, to begin with, a poem that includes an interpretation—and one "probably not in accordance with the facts of its origin"—as part of *the poem*, and it is therefore a poem that makes a problem of its meaning precisely by virtue of its apparent (and apparently inadequate) effort to explain itself. We cannot understand the poem without knowing what it meant to its author, but we must also assume that what the poem meant to its author will not be its meaning. The notes to *The Waste Land* are, by the logic of Eliot's philosophical critique of interpretation, simply another riddle—and not a separate one—to be solved. They are, we might say, the poem's way of treating itself as a reflex, a "something not intended as a sign," a gesture whose full significance it is impossible, by virtue of the nature of gestures, for the gesturer to explain.[38]

And the structure of the poem—a text followed by an explanation—is a reproduction of a pattern that, as the notes themselves emphasize, is repeated in miniature many times inside the poem itself, where cultural expressions are transformed, by the mechanics of allusion, into cultural gestures. For each time a literary phrase or a cultural motif its transposed into a new context—and the borrowed motifs in *The Waste Land* are shown to have themselves been borrowed by a succession of cultures[39]—it is reinterpreted, its previous meaning becoming incorporated by distortion into a new meaning suitable to a new use. So that the work of Frazer and Weston is relevant both because it presents the history of religion as a series of appropriations and reinscriptions of cultural motifs, and because it is itself an unreliable reinterpretation of the phenomena it attempts to describe. The poem (as A. Walton Litz argued some time ago) is, in other words, not about spiritual dryness so much as it is about the ways in which spiritual dryness has been *perceived*.[40] And the relation of the notes to the poem proper seems further emblematic of the relation of the work as a whole to the cultural tradition it is a commentary on. *The Waste Land* is presented as a contemporary reading of the Western tradition, which (unlike the "ideal order" of "Tradition and the Individual Talent") is treated as a sequence of gestures whose original meaning is unknown, but which every new text that is added to it makes a bad guess at.

The author of the notes seems to class himself with the cultural anthropologists whose work he cites. He reads the poem as a coherent expression of the spiritual condition of the social group in which it was produced. But the author of the *poem*, we might say, does not enjoy this luxury of detachment. He seems, in fact, determined to confound, even at the cost of his own sense of coherence, the kind of interpretive knowingness displayed by the author of the notes. The author of the poem classes himself with the diseased characters of his own work—the clairvoyante with a cold, the woman whose nerves are bad, the king whose insanity may or may not be feigned. He cannot distinguish what he intends to reveal about himself from what he cannot help revealing: he would like to believe that his poem is expressive of some general reality, but he fears that it is only the symptom of a private disorder. For when he looks to the culture around him, everything appears only as a reflection of his own breakdown: characters and objects metamorphose up and down the evolutionary scale; races and religions lose their purity ("Bin gar keine Russin, stamm' aus Litauen, echt deutsch"); an adulterated "To His Coy Mistress" describes the tryst between Sweeney and Mrs. Porter, and a fragmented *Tempest* frames the liaison of the typist and the young man carbuncular; "London bridge is falling down." The poem itself, as a literary object, seems an imitation of this vision of degeneration: nothing in it can be said to point to the poet, since none of its stylistic features is continuous, and it has no phrases or images that cannot be suspected of—where they are not in fact identified as—belonging to someone else. *The Waste Land* appears to be a poem designed to make trouble for the conceptual mechanics not just of ordinary reading (for what poem does not try to disrupt those mechanics?) but of *literary* reading. For insofar as reading a piece of writing as literature is understood to mean reading it for its style, Eliot's poem eludes a literary grasp.

But the composition of *The Waste Land* was not a reflex, of course, and Eliot was not trying to produce a text determined entirely by submission to outer circumstance and inner compulsion; he was trying, I think, to write a poem that would be "his own." And for such an intention, "style," as the late nineteenth century conceived it, would have restricted what was his in his poem precisely by drawing a line between what could and could not be helped. For, as we have seen, in preserving something in the work of art the artist can truly call his own, Wilde and Pater handed over nearly everything to external forces—to the given. But by renouncing as an illusion the very value aestheticism had rescued from the flux, Eliot's poem seems to have won an even greater authority. For it was the common argument of *The Waste Land*'s early champions—Wilson (1922), Richards (1925), Leavis (1932)—that the poem was held together not by its meaning, or by its author's beliefs, or by metaphysics, but by the unity of a single, coherent authorial presence.[41] If we want to account for this perception of a work that appears so radically decentered—and to do so by saying something more specific to the case than that *The Waste Land* is a poem that takes advantage of the universal habit of reading by which we infer an author for every text—we might suggest that insofar as style had become a problematic literary value, *The Waste Land* was a poem that succeeded by presenting itself as a symptom. For the result of this strategy is that since nothing in *The Waste Land* (except the notes, of course, whose self-consciously "authorial" manner only makes the symptomatic character of the rest appear more striking) is more "Eliot's" than anything else, everything in *The Waste Land* is Eliot's. Eliot appears nowhere, but his fingerprints are on everything. And this gives him a victory over hermeneutics as well, for there is no level of reading of Eliot's poem at which it is possible to say that we have reached a meaning that might not have been put there by Eliot himself.

This view of *The Waste Land* belongs to the school that takes the poem to be a work of "decreation," as Frank Kermode has called it, or a "roadway to nowhere," in Eloise Knapp Hay's more recent phrase;[42] it differs from the school that takes the poem to be a signpost pointing toward "a further stage in [Eliot's] development," or an account of "the trials of a life in the process of becoming exemplary."[43] If the poem was indeed intended as a kind of deliberate dead end, an explosion of the nineteenth-century metaphysics of style leaving nothing in its place, this ambition was perhaps one of the things Eliot learned from Joyce. *Ulysses,* Eliot told Virginia Woolf in a famous conversation, "destroyed the whole of the 19th century. It left Joyce with nothing to write another book on. It showed up the futility of all the English styles.... [T]here was no 'great conception': that was not Joyce's intention.... Joyce did completely what he meant to do."[44] An essay Eliot published in the *Nouvelle Revue Française* a few months after this conversation gives us a better idea of the nature of the accomplishment he had in mind: "The influence of [the style of] Walter Pater," he says there,

> ... culminates and disappears, I believe, in the work of James Joyce.... In *Ulysses* this influence, like the influence of Ibsen and every other influence to which Mr. Joyce has submitted, is reduced to zero. It is my opinion that *Ulysses* is not so distinctly a precursor of a new epoch as it is a gigantic culmination of an old. In this book Joyce has arrived at a very singular and perhaps unique literary distinction: the distinction of having, not in a negative but a very positive sense, no style at all. I mean that every sentence Mr. Joyce writes is peculiarly and absolutely his own; that his work is not a pastiche; but that nevertheless, it has none of the marks by which a "style" may be distinguished.

> Mr. Joyce's work puts an end to the tradition of Walter Pater, as it puts an end to a great many other things....[45]

We are likely to feel that traditions are not so easily killed off as the modernists supposed, that they live on long after their metaphysics have been demolished. But this strange life of the buried past is one of the things *The Waste Land*—and its tradition—are all about.

The notion that cultural history is the product of a series of errors, that the new appears as the result of a misinterpretation of what is received, is articulated in Eliot's paper on ritual and seems to inform the structure of *The Waste Land*; but it is left dangling, as we have noted, in "Tradition and the Individual Talent." Eliot appears to have been concerned almost immediately after the publication of *The Waste Land* to withdraw "Tradition and the Individual Talent"'s apparent invitation to subjectivism. An interpretation, he announced in "The Function of Criticism" (October 1923), "is only legitimate when it is not an interpretation at all, but merely putting the reader in possession of facts which he would otherwise have missed." And its goal, thus conceived, lies entirely outside the historicist hermeneutical system: it is the "possibility of arriving at something outside of ourselves, which may provisionally be called truth."[46]

But this "official" view of the editor of *The Criterion* is sometimes subverted, in unobtrusive places, in Eliot's later writings. His introduction to his mother's dramatic poem *Savonarola* (1926), for instance, is rather weak on the importance of the positivistic "sense of fact" endorsed by "The Function of Criticism":

> [A] work of historical fiction is much more a document on its own time than on the time portrayed. Equally relative, because equally passed through the sieve of our interpretation, but enabling us to extend and solidify this interpretation of the past which is its meaning, its sense, for us. By comparing the period described in *Romola* as we know that period, with George Eliot's interpretation of it, we can supplement our knowledge (which is itself an interpretation and relative) of the mind and of the epoch of George Eliot. But unless George Eliot's novel gave a faithful presentation of Romola's time to George Eliot's contemporaries, it would have little to say to us about George Eliot's time.[47]

And in his introduction to G. Wilson Knight's *Wheel of Fire* (1930), Eliot seems to have been seduced even farther away from an objectivist position by the allurements of a theory of explicitly *bad* interpretation:

> [O]ur impulse to interpret a work of art ... is exactly as imperative and fundamental as our impulse to interpret the universe by metaphysics.... And Bradley's apothegm that "metaphysics is the finding of bad reasons for what we believe upon instinct; but to find these reasons is no less an instinct," applies as precisely to the interpretation of poetry.
>
> ... [I]t occurs to me as possible that there may be an essential part of error in all interpretation, without which it would not be interpretation at all.... The work of Shakespeare is like life itself something to be lived through. If we lived it completely we should need no interpretation; but on our plane of appearances our interpretations themselves are a part of our living.[48]

We have Eliot's final thoughts on this problem only at third hand, from Joseph Summers's report of a conversation with F. O. Matthiessen in 1950. Eliot, according to Matthiessen, had

> thought of writing a book to be entitled "The Fruitfulness of Misunderstanding." The central idea was that many of the significant changes in poetry have occurred when a writer who is attempting to imitate another or others, through misunderstanding of his model or models creates inadvertently something new. The specific cases Eliot intended to develop ... were Coleridge's misunderstanding of German philosophers, Poe's misunderstanding of Coleridge, Baudelaire's and the French *symbolistes*' misunderstanding of Poe, and Eliot's own misunderstanding of the French writers.[49]

This is a lovely piece of self-directed irony, and it exhibits a fatalism even a determinist might admire, since it manages to tie Eliot, by an incredible run of bad luck, to the very tradition he had devoted most of his career to distinguishing himself from.

Notes

1. The fullest biographical account of the writing of *The Waste Land* is the one provided by Valerie Eliot in the introduction to her edition of *The Waste Land: A Facsimile and Transcript of the Original Drafts* (New York: Harcourt Brace Jovanovich, 1971), pp.

ix–xxix. Lyndall Gordon provides a detailed study of the evolution of the manuscript in *Eliot's Early Years* (Oxford: Oxford University Press, 1977), pp. 86–109, 143–46.

2. Conrad Aiken, "An Anatomy of Melancholy," in *T. S. Eliot: The Man and His Work*, ed. Allen Tate (New York: Dell, 1966), p. 195.

3. See Ronald Bush, *T. S. Eliot: A Study in Character and Style* (New York: Oxford University Press, 1984), pp. 67–72.

4. Anthony Cronin, "A Conversation with T. S. Eliot About the Connection Between *Ulysses* and *The Waste Land*," *The Irish Times*, 16 June 1971, p. 10. The conversation took place in the late 1950s.

5. "Whether Rostand Had Something About Him," *The Athenaeum*, 25 July 1919, p. 665. Eliot was commenting on his sense that the effort to avoid rhetoric had become a rhetoric itself.

6. *Knowledge and Experience in the Philosophy of F. H. Bradley* (London: Faber and Faber, 1964), p. 157. Eliot's dissertation is discussed herein in chapter two.

7. Oscar Wilde, "Mr. Pater's Last Volume," in *The Artist as Critic: Critical Writings of Oscar Wilde*, ed. Richard Ellmann (New York: Random House, 1969), p. 231. Wilde's review first appeared in *Speaker*, 1 (22 March 1890), 319–20.

8. Walter Pater, *The Renaissance: Studies in Art and Poetry*, ed. Donald L. Hill (Berkeley and Los Angeles: University of California Press, 1980), p. 185.

9. Pater, p. 99. For a discussion of Pater s relation to late-nineteenth-century historicism and the development of modern hermeneutics—to the thought of Dilthey, Croce, and Meinecke—see Peter Allan Dale, *The Victorian Critic and the Idea of History: Carlyle, Arnold, Pater* (Cambridge, Mass., and London: Harvard University Press, 1977), pp. 171–205. The co-presence in Pater's writing of two conceptions of the subject—one continuous with outer circumstance (*The Renaissance*), the other a core of individuality radically distinct from everything outside it ("Style")—is noted herein in chapter three, where Pater's troubles with the latter model are discussed.

10. Pater, p. 185.

11. Oscar Wilde, "The Critic as Artist," in *The Artist as Critic*, pp. 382–84.

12. Dale, p. 204.

13. *The Sacred Wood: Essays on Poetry and Criticism*, 2d ed. (London: Methuen, 1928), pp. 49–50. This is the edition cited below.

14. *The Sacred Wood*, pp. 52–53.

15. *The Sacred Wood*, p. 48.

16. Quotations from *The Waste Land* are from the Boni and Liveright edition (1922), reprinted at the end of *The Waste Land: A Facsimile and Transcript of the Original Drafts*, ed. Valerie Eliot.

17. Grover Smith makes this identification in "T. S. Eliot's Lady of the Rocks," *Notes and Queries*, 194 (19 March 1949), 123–25. "The Madonna of the Rocks" is the title given to another Leonardo portrait.

18. Pater, p. 99. Crawling down a wall head first is a habit of vampires, one exhibited by the hero of Bram Stoker's popular *Dracula* (1897). In an earlier version of this passage in *The Waste Land*, the woman gives way first to a vampire, then to a man who wishes not to be reborn, and finally to something like the "diver in deep seas" of Pater's description (see *The Waste Land* facsimile, pp. 113–15).

19. *The Sacred Wood*, p. 52.

20. Wilde, *The Artist as Critic*, p. 398.

21. Wilde, *The Artist as Critic*, pp. 359, 349.

22. Wilde, *The Artist as Critic*, p. 316.

23. J. F. Nisbet, *The Insanity of Genius and the General Inequality of Human Faculty Physiologically Considered*, 6th ed. (New York: Scribner's, 1912), p. 263.

24. Nisbet, pp. xvii, 254, 279; on the elements of literary style, see pp. 254–300.

25. See Allon White, *The Uses of Obscurity: The Fiction of Early Modernism* (London, Boston, and Henley: Routledge and Kegan Paul, 1981), esp. pp. 1–9. White uses the advent of symptomatic reading (the phrase, as he notes, is borrowed from Althusser) to account for some of the salient characteristics of modernist writing, notably the difficulty it presents to its readers. I am indebted, in this chapter, to his demonstration of the movement's importance.

26. Max Nordau, *Degeneration*, trans. from the 2d German ed. (1895; rpt. New York: Howard Fertig, 1968), p. 17. This is the standard English translation; new editions appeared in 1898, 1913, and 1920.

27. The tendency, that is, to treat the changes that according to evolutionary theory require millennia to produce as though they could happen over the course of a few generations. Ruskin's "The Storm-Cloud of the Nineteenth Century" (1884) is an especially dramatic example of the coloring the Darwinian metaphor could give to the social criticism of modern life. The notion that modernist style was a response to changes in the structure of human consciousness (as opposed, say, to changes in beliefs or social arrangements) belongs to this version of popular Darwinism; it was, of course, an important feature of twentieth-century literary ideology. Virginia Woolf's explanation that "human character changed" in 1910 is a hyperbolic, possibly parodic instance of the mode. Eliot's theory of the dissociation of sensibility (like Ruskin's and Nordau's, and unlike Woolf's, a *de*volutionary account) is discussed as a contribution to this manner of accounting for cultural change in chapter six herein.

28. Nordau, pp. 42, 40, 41.

29. Nordau, p. 27.

30. Nordau; pp. 318–19.

31. Nordau, p. 336.

32. The manuscript of Eliot's paper—usually referred to as "The Interpretation of Primitive Ritual"—is in the Hayward Bequest in the King's College Library, Cambridge. Eliot describes the paper briefly but usefully (and gives it its title) in his introduction to Charlotte Eliot's *Savonarola: A Dramatic Poem* (London: R. Cobden-Sanderson, n.d. [1926]), p. viii. Substantial selections are quoted in Piers Gray, *T. S. Eliot's Intellectual and Poetic Development 1909–1922* (Sussex: Harvester Press, 1982), pp. 108–42. A summary of the paper and the seminar discussion that followed appears in *Josiah Royce's Seminar, 1913–1914: As Recorded in the Notebooks of Harry T. Costello*, ed. Grover Smith (New Brunswick, N.J.: Rutgers University Press, 1963), pp. 72–87. I have generally quoted from Costello's version of Eliot's paper (which Gray reports to be faithful to the substance of the manuscript); quotations of Eliot's remarks to Royce are, of course, from the same source.

33. *Josiah Royce's Seminar*, p. 85. Eliot seems to have been willing, for the purposes of this argument, to regard interpretation in natural science as a nonproblem: "[T]here is a difference," he explained, "between natural and social evolution in that in the former we are able practically to neglect all values that are internal to the process, and consider the process from the point of view of *our* value, wh[ich] is for our purposes conceived of as outside the process.... While to some extent in a social progress, and to a very great extent in religious progress, the internal values are part of the external description" (quoted in Gray, p. 115). But he took a more radical view in his dissertation, where he argued that an external object of any kind is an insupportable abstraction: "in order to conceive the development of the world, in the science of geology, let us say, we have to present it as it

would have looked had we, with *our* bodies and our nervous systems, been there to see it. [But] [t]o say that the world was as we describe it, a million years ago, is a statement which overlooks the development of mind" (*Knowledge and Experience*, p. 22). The nature of a rock, that is, depends on the nature of the mind that observes it; we can assume that rocks were different things a million years ago because we assume that minds were different as well.

34. *Josiah Royce's Seminar*, p. 78.

35. *Josiah Royce's Seminar*, p. 76.

36. *Josiah Royce's Seminar*, p. 78.

37. *Josiah Royce's Seminar*, p. 77.

38. It is part of the tradition of *Waste Land* hermeneutics to regard the notes as more or less incidental to the poem proper, and therefore as bits of text that can be treated selectively—some notes may be considered more applicable than others, at the discretion of the commentator—and at face value, as meaning what they say in a way the rest of the poem is assumed not to. (Thus, for instance, the poem has been reprinted in various anthologies, including *The Norton Anthology of English Literature*, with editorial annotations of some lines interspersed among Eliot's own notes.) It is true, of course, that *The Waste Land* was first published without the notes, which Eliot added for the book edition; but they appeared together in every subsequent reprinting. The relevance of Eliot's graduate paper on interpretation alone, not to mention the larger intellectual background I have sketched in, seems enough to justify an approach that considers the notes as part of the poem; but even if Eliot did intend the notes to be straightforward elucidations of the meaning, or some part of the meaning, of his poem, on what hermeneutical grounds can they be considered differently from the rest of the text?

It might be noted that when Arnold Bennett asked Eliot, in 1924, whether the notes to *The Waste Land* were "a skit," Eliot answered that "they were serious, and not more of a skit than some things in the poem itself" (*The Journals of Arnold Bennett*, ed. Newman Flower [London: Cassell, 1933], III, 52; entry for 10 September 1924). For Eliot's own comments on the circumstances of publication that led to the production of the notes, see "The Frontiers of Criticism" (1956), in *On Poetry and Poets* (New York: Farrar, Straus and Cudahy, 1957), pp. 121–22. It is natural (on my view of the poem) that Eliot should generally have disparaged the explanatory (as opposed to the literary) significance of the notes—they are, in any case, fairly self-disparaging as they stand—since their interpretive inadequacy is precisely their point.

39. The conflation, for instance, of the iconography of the Tarot pack, the symbolic figures of Frazer's vegetation rites, and the mythology of Christianity (highlighted by the note to line 46).

40. See A. Walton Litz, "*The Waste Land* Fifty Years After," in *Eliot in His Time*, ed. Litz (Princeton: Princeton University Press, 1973), p. 7.

41. See Edmund Wilson, Jr., "The Poetry of Drouth," *The Dial*, 73 (December 1922), 611–16 ("the very images and the sound of the words—even when we do not know precisely why he has chosen them—are charged with a strange poignancy which seems to bring us into the heart of the singer" [p. 616]); I. A. Richards, *Principles of Literary Criticism*, 2d ed. (1925; rpt. New York and London: Harcourt Brace Jovanovich, n.d.), pp. 289–95 ("the poem still remains to be read.... But that is not difficult to those who still know how to give their feelings precedence to their thoughts, who can accept and unify an experience without trying to catch it in an intellectual net or to squeeze out a doctrine.... The ideas [in Eliot's poetry] ... combine into a coherent whole of feeling and attitude" [pp. 292–3]); F. R. Leavis, *New Bearings in English Poetry* (London: Chatto and Windus, 1932), pp.

90–113 ("the unity of *The Waste Land* is no more 'metaphysical' than it is narrative or dramatic.... The unity the poem aims at is that of an inclusive consciousness" [p. 103]).

42. See Frank Kermode, "A Babylonish Dialect," in *T. S. Eliot: The Man and His Work*, ed. Tate, p. 240; and Eloise Knapp Hay, *T. S. Eliot's Negative Way* (Cambridge, Mass., and London: Harvard University Press, 1982), p. 48.

43. See A. D. Moody, *Thomas Stearns Eliot: Poet* (Cambridge: Cambridge University Press, 1979), p. 79; and Gordon, *Eliot's Early Years*, p. 110.

44. Virginia Woolf, *The Diary of Virginia Woolf*, ed. Anne Olivier Bell, II (New York and London: Harcourt Brace Jovanovich, 1978), 203. Entry for 26 September 1922.

45. "Contemporary English Prose," *Vanity Fair*, 20 (July 1923), 51. First published, in French, in *Nouvelle Revue Française*, 19 (1 December 1922), pp. 751–56; it was solicited for *Vanity Fair* by the magazine's young managing editor, Edmund Wilson (see Wilson, *Letters on Literature and Politics 1912–1972*, ed. Elena Wilson [New York: Farrar, Straus and Giroux, 1977], p. 103).

46. "The Function of Criticism," *The Criterion*, 2 (October 1923), 40–41, 42.

47. Introduction to *Savonarola*, p. vii.

48. Introduction to *The Wheel of Fire: Essays in Interpretation of Shakespeare's Sombre Tragedies*, by G. Wilson Knight (London: Oxford University Press, 1930), pp. xv–xvi, xix.

49. Joseph H. Summers, *The Heirs of Donne and Johnson* (New York and London: Oxford University Press, 1970), p. 129.

JAMES LONGENBACH

The Waste Land:
Beyond the Frontier

"And of course the only real truth is the whole truth" (KE, 163). This sentence is one of the most telling that Eliot ever wrote. Not only does it epitomize his ideas about the nature of tenable criteria for truth, but it reveals how self-evident he considered those criteria to be; the "of course" is particularly telling. Furthermore, this sentence, and Eliot's general dependence upon the idea of wholeness and the "systematic" nature of truth, reveal his strong reliance upon nineteenth-century traditions in both philosophy and poetry.

Hegel provided the *locus classicus* of this tradition when he wrote in the *Phenomenology of Mind* that the "truth is the whole. The whole, however, is merely the essential nature reaching its completeness through the process of its own development."[1] In nineteenth-century German philosophy, this emphasis upon the wholeness of truth gave rise to the "hermeneutic circle," given its most famous articulation by Schleiermacher, and reformulated by Eliot in his essay on "The 'Pensees' of Pascal" (1931): "We cannot quite understand any of the parts, fragmentary as they are, without some understanding of the whole" (SE, 368). Understanding is a dialectic between the part and the whole, and we cannot understand any individual part without some prior knowledge of the whole.

From *Modernist Poetics of History: Pound, Eliot, and the Sense of the Past.*

The same emphasis on the priority of wholeness lies behind Coleridge's famous formulation of the symbol: in contrast to allegory, a symbol

> is characterized by a translucence of the Special in the Individual or of the General in the Especial or of the Universal in the General. Above all by the translucence of the Eternal through and in the Temporal. It always partakes of the Reality which it renders intelligible; and while it enunciates the whole, abides itself as a living part of that Unity, of which it is the representative.[2]

Eliot is an inheritor of this Romantic desire to embody "the whole truth" when he praises the wide scope of Pound's *Cantos*. In his own work, *The Waste Land* stands as an even more striking offspring of this tradition.

Poems such as "The Death of the Duchess" or "Gerontion" express only the negative side of Eliot's philosophy. Trapped within limited points of view, the speakers of these poems fail miserably. From the very moment of its publication *The Waste Land* has also been read as a poem of failure, a poem of fragments that articulates a painful nostalgia for a wholeness that is no longer possible. Surely the poem does crystallize, both formally and thematically, around the line, "These fragments I have shored against my ruins" (CPP, 50); but Eliot himself emphasized in 1923 that "*The Waste Land* is intended to form a *whole*."[3] The emphasis upon fragmentation is made possible by Eliot's belief that truth is wholeness; the very idea of a fragment implies the idea of a unified whole of which it is a part.

In his *Romanticism and the Forms of Ruin* Thomas McFarland makes this point with characteristic elegance. Subliminal in all Romantic poetry's emphasis upon fragmentation, writes McFarland, is the question,

> how can a fragment be identified as a fragment unless there is also the conception of a whole from which it is broken off? ... In truth, notwithstanding the massive testimony of the Romantic era to incompleteness, fragmentation, and ruin, that era was almost equally preoccupied with at least the idea of the whole. "The common end of all *narrative*," says Coleridge, "nay, of *all*, Poems is to convert *a series* into a *Whole*."[4]

Eliot inherited the problem of making a long poem out of a sequence of shorter ones from his Romantic predecessors. And like Coleridge and Wordsworth, Eliot depended upon the idea of wholeness as much as the idea of fragmentation. McFarland also points out that more than the construction of poems depended upon this Romantic yearning for wholeness: not only poetic wholeness but metaphysical wholeness, "the sense of eternal power and of a divine spark," was inseparable "from incompleteness, fragmentation, and ruin."[5] The same can be said for Eliot. As he pushed himself beyond the limited strategies of "The Death of the Duchess" and "Gerontion," his desire to compose a long poem became coequal with his yearning for "the whole truth." The search for poetic wholeness and metaphysical wholeness became one. In "Tradition and the Individual Talent" Eliot proposed to stop "at the frontier of metaphysics or mysticism" (SW, 59), but in composing *The Waste Land* he became a pilgrim in that uncharted territory.

After *The Waste Land* was completed Eliot offered one much-abused key to the pattern of wholeness in the poem. In "*Ulysses*, Order, and Myth" he outlined the "mythical method" of Joyce's work, and his readers were quick to sense the importance of the method for *The Waste Land*:

> In using the myth, in manipulating a continuous parallel between contemporaneity and antiquity, Mr. Joyce is pursuing a method which others must pursue after him. They will not be imitators, any more than the scientist who uses the discoveries of an Einstein in pursuing his own; independent, further investigations. It is simply a way of controlling, of ordering, of giving a shape and a significance to the immense panorama of futility and anarchy which is contemporary history. It is a method already adumbrated by Mr. Yeats, and of the need for which I believe Mr. Yeats to have been the first contemporary to be conscious. It is a method for which the horoscope is auspicious. Psychology (such as it is, and whether our reaction to it be comic or serious), ethnology, and *The Golden Bough* have concurred to make possible what was impossible even a few years ago. Instead of narrative method, we may now use the mythical method.[6]

This passage has encouraged, on the one hand, New Critical readings of *The Waste Land* that impose a spurious grail legend plot on the poem; on the other hand it has provoked readings that require us to read the "mythical method" as some kind of ironic deception.[7]

Neither of these views will do. The relationship of "*Ulysses*, Order, and Myth" to *The Waste Land* is problematic. The essay is a part of what Ronald Bush has called the "revised literary program" Eliot undertook after the completion of *The Waste Land*: "After many years of vacillating between a drive to represent his inner life and a drive to order it, he now was willing to let the balance tip toward the 'intellect' and toward 'classicism.'"[8] The "mythical method" had virtually nothing to do with the composition of Eliot's first long poem; rather, it represents his attempt to impose an order on a body of work that he desperately wanted to leave behind him. The "mythical method" has much more to do with the revised literary program of the 1926 Clark Lectures and *The Hollow Men*. To investigate the whole truth of *The Waste Land* we must turn to the concerns Eliot held during the actual gestation period of the poem. A fair place to begin, once again, is with Bradley.

While Eliot's shorter poems are spoken by personae who cannot develop their perceptions of the world into a "system," *The Waste Land* is an attempt to present an interpretation of historical knowledge from a "systematic" point of view. Although he does not capitalize upon Eliot's use of the "systematic" nature of truth in his discussion of *The Waste Land*, Michael Levenson has shown how Eliot's emphasis upon the importance of transcending individual points of view for a vision of wholeness became one of the structural principles of the poem.[9] In his dissertation, Eliot's discussion of transcendence emphasizes the irrationality and painfulness of the process:

> for the life of a soul does not consist in the contemplation of one consistent world but in the painful task of unifying (to a greater or less extent) jarring and incompatible ones, and passing, when possible, from two or more discordant viewpoints to a higher which shall somehow include and transmute them. (KE, 147–148)

This passage is central to Eliot's critique of Bradley's concept of the Absolute (the ultimate synthesis of all diversity, difference, and contradiction). In "Leibniz' Monads and Bradley's Finite Centres," published in the *Monist* in 1916, Eliot points out that Bradley's Absolute "responds only to an imaginary demand of thought, and satisfies only an imaginary demand of feeling. Pretending to be something which makes finite centres cohere, it turns out to be merely the assertion that they do" (KE, 202). Instead of Bradley's Absolute, Eliot proposes his own theory of the unification of points of view: "if one recognizes two points of view which are quite irreconcilable and yet melt into each other, this theory [of the Absolute] is quite superfluous." In his dissertation Eliot was thinking along the same lines when he wrote that "the pre-established harmony [of the Absolute] is unnecessary if we recognize that the monads [of individual experience] are not wholly distinct" (KE, 206, 147). Because individual points of view are not completely distinct, the painful task of unification becomes possible without relying on the easy consolations of the Absolute.

As Levenson points out, Eliot's note about Tiresias's function in *The Waste Land* echoes these passages from his philosophical writing about the possibility of transcending and combining individual points of view. Since all the personages of *The Waste Land* are "*not wholly distinct*" from each other, they "*melt into*" each other and converge in the presiding consciousness of Tiresias:

> Tiresias, although a mere spectator and not indeed a "character," is yet the most important personage in the poem, uniting all the rest. Just as the one-eyed merchant, seller of currants, *melts into* the Phoenician Sailor, and the latter is *not wholly distinct* from Ferdinand of Naples, so all the women are one woman, and the two sexes meet in Tiresias. (CPP, 52; my emphasis)

Eliot employs the same phrase ("melts into") once again when he describes the unification of the two lovers in *Romeo and Juliet*: Shakespeare "shows his lovers melting into incoherent unconsciousness of their isolated selves, shows the human soul in the process of forgetting itself" (SW, 83). This "painful task of unifying" builds bridges between individual consciousnesses as one mind "melts into" the other, overcoming the solipsistic condition of the finite center.

It is important to see that this process of the unification of points of view is different from what Eliot's teacher, Josiah Royce; meant by the growth of a "Community of Interpretation." As we have seen, Royce stressed that in the formation of such a community, the interpreting mind and the interpreted mind "would remain distinct.... There would be no melting together, no blending, no mystic blur, and no lapse into mere intuition." In contrast to Royce, Eliot insists that a "melting together" of minds is precisely what takes place. While Royce maintains that the "distinctions of the persons ... is as essential to a Community of Interpretation as is the common task" in which these persons engage, Eliot presents a more overtly mystical theory of the way in which individuals come to understand one another.[10] From Eliot's point of view, no real understanding takes place in Royce's "Community of Interpretation"; individuals must subject themselves to the painful task of melting into one another in order for a true unity to be achieved.

This rationally inexplicable process of the combination of points of view is one way in which Eliot approaches "the whole truth" in *The Waste Land*. An earlier poem, "Dans le Restaurant," portrays this painful task of unification quite dramatically. A waiter approaches the speaker of the poem and tells him a sordid little story about a thwarted sexual experience he had as a child:

> Mais alors, vieux lubrique, à cet âge ...
> "Monsieur, le fait est dur.
> Il est venu, nous peloter, un gros chien;
> Moi j'avais peur, je l'ai quitée à mi-chemin.
> C'est dommage."
> Mais alors, tu as ton voutour!
>
> Va t'en te décrotter les rides du visage:
> Tiens, ma fourchette, décrasse-toi le crâne.
> De quel droit payes-tu des expériences comme moi?
> Tiens, voilà dix sous, pour la salle-de-bains. (CPP, 32)

The speaker of the poem becomes outraged as he realizes that his own experiences are not unique; the tidy borders of his consciousness are threatened as the consciousness of the waiter "melts into" his own and the painful task of unifying begins. In the final stanza of the poem, which Eliot himself translated from the French to make the "Death by Water" lyric in *The Waste Land*, the speaker undergoes an even more dramatic transformation as he is metamorphosed into Phlebas the Phoenician. Slowly, this process of the unification of points of view builds from an individual consciousness to a universal mind that encompasses the whole truth.

"Dans le Restaurant" was an important poem in Eliot's own transition from poems that present only a limited point of view to *The Waste Land*, the culmination of his attempt to formulate a "system." Throughout *The Waste Land* the process of transcending individual points of view—the creation of a "system"—becomes far more intricate: there, Phlebas the Phoenician from "Dans le Restaurant" melts into the one-eyed merchant and Ferdinand of Naples—and each of these personages is not wholly distinct from the presiding consciousness of Tiresias.

Eliot also used allusions to enact this movement toward wholeness. In "A Note on Ezra Pound" he compared Pound's use of allusion with Joyce's, calling Joyce "another very learned literary artist, [who] uses allusions suddenly and with great speed, part of the effect being the extent of the vista opened to the imagination by the very lightest touch."[11] This is the effect

Eliot sought in his own use of allusion. "Cousin Nancy" begins as a satire of New England manners:

> Miss Nancy Ellicott
> Strode across the hills and broke them,
> Rode across the hills and broke them—
> The barren New England hills—
> Riding to hounds
> Over the cow-pasture.

But the poem ends with an allusion to Meredith's "Lucifer in Starlight," which, as Eliot wrote of Joyce's allusions, occurs "suddenly and with great speed" and "by the very lightest touch" expands "the vista opened to the imagination":

> Upon the glazen shelves kept watch
> Matthew and Waldo, guardians of the faith,
> The army of unalterable law. (CPP, 17–18)

"The army of unalterable law," a line taken from Meredith's poem about the fallen Lucifer's attempt to reclaim the heavens, expands the vista of "Cousin Nancy" by comparing Arnold and Emerson with Milton's God and the modern Cousin Nancy with the rebellious Satan. The final line of the poem enacts a sudden movement toward "the whole truth." The last stanza of "Sweeney Among the Nightingales" creates a similar effect: pivoting on the change in tense of the verb to "sing," these lines suddenly compare the degenerate Sweeney's predicament with Agamemnon's, radically expanding the historical significance of the poem:

> The host with someone indistinct
> Converses at the door apart,
> The nightingales are singing near
> The Convent of the Sacred Heart,
>
> And sang within the blood wood
> When Agamemnon cried aloud,
> And let their liquid siftings fall
> To stain the stiff dishonoured shroud. (CPP, 36)

In *The Waste Land* Eliot employs allusions in the same way, adding reference to reference in order to build the most comprehensive point of view possible. The opening lines of "The Fire Sermon" are perhaps the most concentrated in the entire poem:

> The river's tent is broken: the last fingers of leaf
> Clutch and sink into the wet bank. The wind
> Crosses the brown land, unheard. The nymphs are departed.
> Sweet Thames, run softly, till I end my song.
> The river bears no empty bottles, sandwich papers,
> Silk handkerchiefs, cardboard boxes, cigarette ends
> Or other testimony of summer nights. The nymphs are departed.
> And their friends, the loitering heirs of city directors;
> Departed, have left no addresses.
> By the waters of Leman I sat down and wept ...
> Sweet Thames, run softly till I end my song,
> Sweet Thames, run softly, for I speak not loud or long.
> But at my back in a cold blast I hear
> The rattle of bones, and chuckle spread from ear to ear.
> A rat crept softly through the vegetation
> Dragging its slimy belly on the bank
> While I was fishing in the dull canal
> On a winter evening round behind the gashouse
> Musing on the king my father's death before him.
> White bodies naked on the low damp ground
> And bones cast in a little low dry garret,
> Rattled by the rat's foot only, year to year.
> But at my back from time to time I hear
> The sound of horns and motors, which shall bring
> Sweeney to Mrs. Porter in the spring.
> O the moon shone bright on Mrs. Porter
> And her daughter
> They wash their feet in soda water
> *Et O ces voix d'enfants, chantant dans la coupole!* (CPP, 42–43)

While in "The Death of the Duchess" the speaker falls into the "trap of interpretation" because he cannot perceive *The Duchess of Malfi* within the context of a whole and coherent "system," these lines from *The Waste Land* reveal the construction of such a "system," building up a palimpsest of historical references to Spenser, Marvell, Shakespeare, Verlaine, and ancient vegetation rituals—all of which are synthesized into the reality of the present. Unlike "The Death of the Duchess" or "Gerontion," there is no evidence of a self-deceiving interpreter speaking these lines. The speakers of the shorter poems are content to remain locked in their limited interpretations of the world; they do not attempt the task of unifying. In *The Waste Land*, on the other hand, so many individual consciousnesses are unified that the voice intoning the poem often seems to be the voice of history itself, an expression of the "entire past" woven into the texture of the present.

The voices in *The Waste Land* are thus both past and present, both personal and universal, both autobiographical and historical—distinctions that, like Dilthey, Eliot collapses. Dilthey writes that in autobiography "we approach the roots of all historical comprehension.... It alone makes historical insight possible."[12] Eliot makes tile same point in "Modern Tendencies in Poetry," an essay published a few months after "Tradition and the Individual Talent," which appears to be a casual rewriting of the more famous manifesto. In "Modern Tendencies in Poetry" Eliot writes much more clearly about the nature of personality in poetry, establishing that a lack of personality is as detrimental as an excess: a scientist "submerges himself in what he has to do, [and] forgets himself" but in the work of a great scientist, there is still "a cachet of the man all over it." A strong sense of personality is just as important for the historian or the poet. Like Dilthey, Eliot insists that we cannot know the past except through our personal interests; if our personal present ceased to be important, the past would cease to exist.

> If you imagine yourselves suddenly deprived of your personal present, of all possibility of action, reduced in consciousness to the memories of everything up to the present, these memories, this existence which would be merely the totality of memories, would be meaningless and flat, even if it *could* continue to exist. If suddenly all power of producing more poetry were withdrawn from the race, if we knew that for poetry we should have to turn always to what already existed, I think that past poetry would become meaningless. For the capacity of appreciating poetry is inseparable from the power of producing it, it is poets themselves who can best appreciate poetry. Life is always turned toward creation; the present only, keeps the past alive.[13]

This dictum is embodied in *The Waste Land*, a poem both richly historical and painfully autobiographical. In the passage quoted above from "The Fire Sermon," some readers may combine the references to Spenser's "Prothalamion," Marvell's "To His Coy Mistress" and the ballad of Mrs. Porter into a portrait of Eliot's sense of his own failed marriage; others may read these allusions as the attempt of the "constantly amalgamating" (SE,

247) mind to construct a city's history of isolation and betrayal. But neither of these readings cancels out the other. As Eliot's own historicism reveals, each reading makes the other possible. Autobiography and history are merged in the "painful task of unifying," and the poem expresses a point of view that is at once individual and capable of encompassing what Eliot thought of as the "entire past."

In the final movement of *The Waste Land*, Eliot invokes the voice of the entire past even more successfully in the mystical rumblings of the thunder. "What the Thunder Said," in fact, is written in a style strikingly different from that of "The Fire Sermon" (though placed third in the sequence, "The Fire Sermon" was the first movement of the poem Eliot drafted while "What the Thunder Said" was the last).[14] In the later stages of composition, Eliot became dissatisfied with the mosaic-like style he had perfected in "The Fire Sermon," and in the "water dripping song" he began to experiment with the freer, more incantatory style that would carry him through *The Hollow Men* to the *Four Quartets*. Eliot's comments on Pound's early *Cantos* suggest the reasons for his rejection of his own earlier style: when he compared Joyce's use of allusion with Pound's, he disparaged the "deliberateness" of *Three Cantos*, preferring Joyce's epiphanic effects to what amounted to a "rag-bag of Mr. Pound's reading in various languages."[15] Eliot feared that his long poem would become the same thing—a "rag-bag" of fragments rather than a "system" that is somehow greater than the sum of its parts. He also realized that it was beyond the capability of a merely human consciousness to create this vision of wholeness. When Eliot criticized Bradley's solipsistic vision of experience, remarking that he divided human knowledge so resolutely into distinct finite centers that the world "is only by an act of faith unified" (KE, 202), he identified the very thing required to articulate a vision of "the whole truth." It is finally not rational process but an irrational *faith in* the possibility of wholeness that makes Eliot's world cohere.

Eliot learned this lesson from Dante. In the final essay of *The Sacred Wood* (a book that rests upon the "systematic" nature of truth in its judgments of both criticism and poetry) he presented *the Divine Comedy* as the most comprehensive expression of a "system" ever attempted. The poem

> is an ordered scale of human emotions. Not, necessarily, *all* human emotions; and in any case all the emotions are limited, and also extended in significance by their place in the scheme.
>
> But Dante's is the most comprehensive, and the most *ordered* presentation of emotions that has ever been made. (SW, 168)

This description of the *Divine Comedy* reiterates the two essential ingredients of a "system": wholeness and coherence. At the end of the essay, Eliot states that there is one additional ingredient that makes Dante's "system" superior to that of any modern poet: the intensity and reality of its *vision*.

When Eliot reshaped this essay on Dante for inclusion in *The Sacred Wood*, he added an introduction in which he quoted a paragraph from Paul Valéry's introduction to Lucien Fabre's *Connaissance de la Déese* (1920). Eliot was not familiar with Valéry's entire essay, but he read an excerpt that was quoted in Charles du Bos's "Letters from Paris" in the *Athenaeum*:[16]

> La philosophie, et même la morale tendirent à fuir les oeuvres pour se placer dans les réflexions qui les précèdent.... Parler aujourd'hui de poésie philosophique (fût-ce en invoquant Alfred de Vigney, Leconte de Lisle, et quelques autres), c'est naivement confondre des conditions et des applications de l'esprit incompatibles entre elles. N'est-ce pas oublier que le but de celui qui spécule est de fixer ou de créer une notion—c'est-à-dire un *pouvoir* et un *instrument de pouvoir*, cependant que le poète moderne essaie de produire en nous un *état* et de porter cet état exceptionnel au point d'une jouissance parfaite. (SW, 159)

Valéry is a straw man in Eliot's argument. While making his respect for Valéry's work clear, Eliot comments that "if Mr. Valéry is in error in his complete exorcism of 'philosophy,' perhaps the basis of the error is his apparently commendatory interpretation of the effort of the modern poet, namely, that the latter endeavours 'to produce in us a *state*'" (SW, 160). At the end of the essay, Eliot returns to Valéry when he points out that the aim of Dante's poetry is not to produce a state in the reader but to "state a vision." That vision, insists Eliot, is something real, something seen by the poet:

> Dante helps us to provide a criticism of M. Valéry's "modern poet" who attempts "to produce in us a *state*. "A state, in itself, is nothing whatever.
>
> M. Valéry's account is quite in harmony with pragmatic doctrine, and with the tendencies of such a work as William James's *Varieties of Religious Experience*, The mystical experience is supposed to be valuable because it is a pleasant state of unique intensity. But the true mystic is not satisfied merely by feeling, he must pretend at least that he *sees*, and the absorption into the divine is only the necessary, if paradoxical, limit of this

> contemplation. The poet does not aim to excite—that is not even a test of his success—but to set something down. (SW, 170)

Eliot's invocation of theories of mysticism and vision should not be taken lightly here; between 1908 and 1914 he read extensively in mystical literature and took copious notes from many books, including the chapter on "Mysticism" in James's *Varieties of Religious Experience*. Eliot associates James's psychological explanation of mystical states with Valéry's theory of modern poetry; in contrast, he associates Dante's work with what he calls the "true mystic"—one who actually sees and records his vision. In Evelyn Underhill's *Mysticism* (1911), a book he read and annotated particularly closely, Eliot underlined this passage:

> Visionary experience is—or at least may be—the outward sign of a real experience. It is a picture which the mind constructs, it is true, from raw materials already at its disposal: as the artist constructs his picture with canvas and paint.[17]

This passage describes the orientation of the "true mystic," and it bears a significant resemblance to Pound's conception of visionary experience. In "Psychology and Troubadours" Pound wrote that the visions of true mystics are "for them *real*" (SR, 92). Eliot must have had Pound's ideas about mysticism in mind (in addition to Underhill's) when he rewrote his essay on Dante: when he quoted these lines from the first canto of the *Paradiso* as an example of Dante's visionary intensity,

> Nel suo aspetto tal dentro mi fei,
> qual si fé Glauco net gustar de l'erba
> che 'l fé consorto in mar de li altri dèi.
>
> [Gazing upon her I became within me such as Glaucus became on tasting of the grass that made him sea-fellow of the other gods],[18]

he added a footnote that reads "See E. Pound, *The Spirit of Romance*" (SW, 169). In *The Spirit of Romance* Pound also quotes these lines about Glaucus's transformation and comments that "nowhere is the nature of the mystic ecstasy so well described" (SR, 141). By tasting the magical grass, Glaucus is transformed into a sea-creature; his visionary experience is tangible and real.

Dante's power to perceive and transcribe visionary experience in concrete terms is what makes his "system," his "*ordered* presentation of emotions," so successful. Modern poets, says Eliot, have lost this ability, and as Valéry suggests, strive instead to produce some sort of ill-defined state in the reader. Even when modern poets "confine themselves to what they had perceived," says Eliot, "they produce for us, usually, only odds and ends of still life and stage properties: but that does not imply so much that the method of Dante is obsolete, as that our vision is perhaps comparatively restricted." Dante's visionary capabilities are in no way restricted, and he is able to present a vision that is "nearly complete" (SW, 171, 170).

The visionary ability Eliot describes in this essay on Dante underlies a conception of myth that is far more important for *The Waste Land* than the one outlined in "*Ulysses*, Order, and Myth." While he was actually working on *The Waste Land* Eliot described myth in "The Romantic Englishman" (1921) as life seen "in the light of imagination": myth is "a point of view, transmuted to importance; it is made by the transformation of the actual by imaginative genius."[19] This more supple conception of myth has much more to do with *The Waste Land* than any "continuous parallel between contemporaneity and antiquity." Eliot's approach to "the whole truth" depends—as he believed Dante's "system" of the *Divine Comedy* did—upon this ability to transform the actual into the mythical.

Eliot's ambition was to be a poet such as Dante, of course, and not the type of the modern poet described by Valéry or William James; and it is essential to recognize the role of transcendental vision in Eliot's presentation of a "system" in *The Waste Land*. While I have demonstrated how Tiresias functions in the poem to suggest a point of view that is constantly amalgamating limited points of view to approach a vision of wholeness, it is just as important to see that Tiresias functions as the "true mystic" Eliot describes in his essay on Dante. From the evidence of *The Waste Land* manuscript, it is clear that "The Fire Sermon" crystallized around these lines (ultimately deleted) that introduced the presiding consciousness of Tiresias. After a prophetic description of the inhabitants of London as "phantasmal gnomes" who know neither how to think nor how to feel, Tiresias is presented as one of the few human minds capable of sensing the meaning hidden in this meager existence. He sees these limited lives as part of a much larger whole:

> Some minds, aberrant from the normal equipoise
> (London, your people is bound upon the wheel!)
> Record the motions of these pavement toys
> And trace the cryptogram that may be curled
> Within these faint perceptions of the noise,
> Of the movement, and the lights!
>
> Not here, O Glaucon, but in another world. (WLF, 31)

Pound persuaded Eliot to cut these lines, suggesting that the "phantasmal gnomes" reminded him of the benevolent elves of Palmer Cox's "Brownie" poems for children (WLF, 31, 127). The passage nevertheless reveals how Tiresias was to function not only as the "most important personage in the poem" but as an observing consciousness who can penetrate the everyday world of Sunday outings and closed carriages to "trace the cryptogram" of a higher reality—transforming that everyday reality into a visionary world of myth. Most of London's inhabitants, like the modern poets Eliot rejects in his essay on Dante, see nothing beyond "the normal equipoise." But there are a few who do not burrow "in brick and stone and steel" but are able to perceive their fragmentary, materialistic condition as part of a much larger whole. These few, like Dante, like Tiresias, can see into another world. Glaucon, invoked in the final line of this passage, is one of the speakers in Plato's *Republic*. When he asks Socrates if the ideal city can be found on earth, Socrates replies, "perhaps there is a pattern of it laid up in heaven for him who wishes to contemplate it and so beholding to constitute himself its citizen" (WLF, 128).

Only with this kind of visionary power can one transcend the "normal equipoise" and perceive the "systematic" interconnectedness of all things, earthly and ethereal, past and present. When Eliot defined myth as the product of "the transformation of the actual by imaginative genius," he was remembering his discussions of the hallucinatory consciousness in his dissertation:

> It is not true that the ideas of a great poet are in any sense arbitrary: certainly in the sense in which imagination is capricious, the ideas of a lunatic or an imbecile are more "imaginative" than those of a poet. In really great imaginative work the connections are felt to be bound by as logical necessity as any connections to be found anywhere; the apparent irrelevance is due to the fact that terms are used with more or other than their normal meaning, and to those who do not thoroughly penetrate their significance the relation between the aesthetic expansion and the objects expressed is not visible. (KE, 75)

The truly imaginative work, says Eliot, is the result of penetrating the normal terms of reality to discover a deeper and consequently fantastic and often obscure meaning. In his 1919 essay on "Beyle and Balzac" he explains that the fantastical "aura" of many of Balzac's works was not the result of a truly imaginative consciousness; "it is an atmosphere thrown upon reality direct from the personality of the writer." Contrasting Balzac with Dostoevsky, Eliot explains that Dostoevsky's "most successful; most imaginative 'flights'" are

> projections, continuations, of the actual, the observed: the final scene of the "Idiot," the hallucinations at the beginning of the same book and in "Crime and Punishment," even (what is more questionable) the interview of Ivan Karamazov with the Devil—Dostoevsky's point of departure is always a human brain in a human environment, and the "aura" is simply the continuation of the quotidian experience of the brain into seldom explored extremities of torture. Because most people are too unconscious of their own suffering to suffer much, this continuation appears fantastic.[20]

To push "quotidian experience of the brain into seldom explored extremities of torture" was Eliot's goal in *The Waste Land*. Throughout the poem the gaze of Tiresias acts as a metaphor for the visionary gaze of the inspired poet, transforming reality into myth. The well-known "Unreal City" passage enacts just the imaginative process Eliot admired in Dostoevsky. It begins by painting a scene that could be purely naturalistic:

> Under the brown fog of a winter dawn,
> A crowd flowed over London Bridge, so many,
> I had not thought death had undone so many. (CPP, 39)

Only if the reader recognizes the reference to the third canto of the *Inferno* would he suspect that any other world but modern London were being invoked; Eliot even remarks in a note that this crowd crossing London Bridge is a "phenomenon which I have often noticed" (CPP, 51). The lines that follow are scrupulously accurate in their depiction of London's geography (were London Bridge still in place one could cross it and pass St. Mary Woolnoth at the corner of King William and Lombard Streets): at the same time the lines begin to invoke another world:

> Sighs, short and infrequent were exhaled,
> And each man fixed his eyes before his feet.
> Flowed up the hill and down King William Street
> To where Saint Mary Woolnoth kept the hours
> With a dead sound on the final stroke of nine. (CPP, 39)

Yet even when the ghostly Stetson appears, the scene continues to be depicted in purely naturalistic terms. With the word "Mylae," a battle in the Punic Wars, we suspect that we have entered a different level of reality—one in which the boundaries between the past and the present have been severed. The corpse that has been planted in the garden in place of the expected seed or bulb confirms the suspicion. By the end of the passage we are deep inside the "seldom explored extremities of torture" of the mind:

> There I saw one I knew, and stopped him, crying "Stetson!
> "You who were with me in the ships at Mylae!
> "That corpse you planted last year in your garden,
> "Has it begun to sprout? Will it bloom this year?
> "Or has the sudden frost disturbed its bed?
> "Oh keep the Dog far hence, that's friend to men,
> "Or with his nails he'll dig it up again!
> "You! Hypocrite lecteur!—mon semblable,—mon frère!" (CPP, 39)

This is, as the speaker of the opening passages of the poem promised he would show, "something different from either / Your shadow at morning striding behind you / Or your shadow at evening rising to meet you" (CPP, 38). Yet the ghostly Stetson remains closely linked to the reality of everyday London.

Like the ghosts of Pound's *Three Cantos* Stetson is a ghost "patched with histories." He is simultaneously a fourteenth-century Florentine condemned to limbo in Dante's hell, a third-century B.C. Greek who fought at Mylae, one of the "spectres" of Baudelaire's "Les Sept Viellards" who "en plein jour raccroche le passant!" [in broad daylight accosts the passer-by], and a soldier who witnessed the crucifixion at the final stroke of nine. And while the multiple allusions in the passage establish Stetson's historical identities, he is simultaneously a modern Londoner, a soldier who has returned from the Great War—the event that turned Europe into a wasted landscape of corpses and ghosts. These lines are the equivalent in Eliot's work to Pater's *La Gioconda* or Yeats's "The Secret Rose"; they incorporate the "entire" past into an intense consciousness of the present.

Eliot had little faith in the individual's ability to achieve this kind of transcendent vision of "the whole truth" on his own. Most people are restricted to the narrow vision of "Gerontion," and their understanding of history is consequently limited, their ability to interpret restricted to their knowledge of their own consciousness. Only the inspired interpreter (such as Dante or Tiresias) can attain a vision of "the whole truth" and escape the inevitable "trap of interpretation." While Eliot recognized that any statement about the world is necessarily an imperfect interpretation, he nevertheless confessed in less guarded moment's that he felt himself able to transcend those limitations and feel the presence of the past with visionary intensity. In the fourth segment of "Reflections on Contemporary Poetry" (1919) he explained this mystical ability to know the past: the poet's ultimate experience is to

> possess this secret knowledge, this intimacy, with the dead man, that after few or many years or centuries you should have appeared, with this indubitable claim to distinction; who can penetrate at once the thick and dusty circumlocutions about his reputation, can call yourself alone his friend.... We may not be great lovers; but if we had a genuine affair with a real poet of any degree we have acquired a monitor to avert us when we are not in love. Indirectly, there are other acquisitions: our friendship gives us an introduction to the society in which our friend moved; we learn its origins and its endings; we are broadened. We do not imitate, we are changed; and our work is the work of the changed man; we have not borrowed, we have been quickened, and we become bearers of a tradition.[21]

When Eliot suggests that an actor should transmit rather than interpret his lines, he has this visionary sense of the past in mind. A poet may know "the origins and endings" of the past if he is able to transcend the limitations of rational interpretation. For Eliot, the creation of a "systematic" point of view depends on this ability.

Like Pound, Eliot alternated between a wildly poetic sense of the past and a sternly skeptical critique of historical knowledge. And because his skepticism was more rigorous than Pound's, his infrequent eruptions of visionary fervor appear all the more outrageous. Once we understand this tension in Eliot's work, the often contradictory comments Eliot offers about the nature of interpretation throughout his entire career become far more explicable. We have seen that in his dissertation (1916) Eliot writes that any "assertion about the *world* ... will inevitably be an interpretation" (KE, 165). Yet in his 1919 review of *The Duchess of Malfi* he maintains that "there is no such thing as the interpretation of poetry; poetry can only be transmitted."[22] This same contradiction is evident in his critical writings from the 1930s. In a 1936 lecture on Yeats the skeptical Eliot says that "a 'perfect understanding' of a foreign literature or of an earlier period of our own, is an unattainable ideal: sometimes the way in which it is *mis*-understood is the important thing."[23] Yet in his introduction to G. Wilson Knight's *The Wheel of Fire* (1930) Eliot maintains that a reader of poetry should avoid interpretation and "limit his criticism of poetry to the appreciation of vocabulary and syntax, the analysis of line, metric and cadence; to stick as closely to the more trustworthy senses as possible."[24]

Here Eliot's circumvention of the "trap of interpretation" sounds more like a phenomenological reduction than a visionary sense of the past, yet the mysticism inherent in this position becomes clearer later in the essay. Eliot admits that a "restless demon in us drives us also to 'interpret' whether we will or not" but then cautions that "if one was as great a poet as Shakespeare, and was also his 'spiritual heir,' one would feel no need to interpret him; interpretation is necessary perhaps only in so far as one is passive, not creative, oneself."[25] Here Eliot reveals the same faith in a rationally inexplicable immediacy between two authors that he exhibited in his 1919 essay on contemporary poetry. In the dull rounds of everyday life, interpretation and its imperfections are inevitable. But if a poet discovers himself to be the "spiritual heir" of a dead poet, the intervening centuries fall away and (as Eliot phrased it in 1919) he achieves an "intimacy with the dead man" and becomes a "bearer of a tradition." He does not interpret but lives the past. In "Thinking in Verse: A Survey of Seventeenth-Century Poetry" (1930) Eliot even suggested that a historian could adopt the method of mystical meditation and become "so steeped in Greek history as to see Thermopylae as he has seen events in his own life."[26] The speaker of "Gerontion" does not have this power; he was not at the "hot gates" (Eliot's literal translation of "Thermopylae"). The visionary consciousness of *The Waste Land*, on the other hand, meets with the soldiers from the ships at Mylae as he meets the common pedestrian. He has had the "genuine affair" with the past; he has glimpsed the "whole truth." More often than not, these transcendent moments remained part of a buried life that the skeptical Eliot only hinted at in public.

Today, this Romantic ideal of transcending the vagaries of interpretation for an immediate experience of the past seems alien to us, but Eliot was not alone in expressing his desire to do so. In the nineteenth century Schleiermacher maintained that the "divinatory [method of hermeneutics] is that in which one transforms oneself into the other person in order to grasp his individuality directly." Schleiermacher emphasized this divinatory method more and more in his later work, yet like Eliot, he vacillated between this transcendental impulse and a more skeptical critique of understanding. Paul Ricoeur has noticed that this tension marks the entire history of hermeneutic thought:

> Schleiermacher's hermeneutical programme thus carried a double mark: *Romantic* by its appeal to a living relation with the process of creation, *critical* by its wish to elaborate the universally valid rules of understanding. Perhaps hermeneutics is forever marked by this double filiation—Romantic and critical, critical and Romantic. The proposal to struggle against misunderstanding in the name of the famous adage "there is hermeneutics where there is misunderstanding" is critical; the proposal "to understanding an author as well as and even better than he understands himself" is Romantic.[27]

We can see how Eliot's desire for a mystical knowledge of the past places him in a Romantic tradition, and occasionally Eliot made statements that reveal that he sensed this himself. In 1916 he reviewed John Theodore Merz's *Religion and Science* for the *International Journal of Ethics*, and in 1918 he reviewed it again for the *Monist*. The two reviews are nearly identical, but in the *Monist* Eliot adds a new paragraph in which he states that "Mr. Merz knows his Schleiermacher" and an even more telling concluding sentence: "The account of description, explanation, and interpretation is the best part of the book."[28] Turning to Merz's account of interpretation, it is easy to see what Eliot found so attractive. Like Eliot, Merz believed that the only truth is the "whole truth": "Every description or explanation remains, however, incomplete; to become complete it should really comprise the whole universe, allotting to every special thing or event its exact location in space and time." For Merz as for Eliot, interpretation may only approach truth by expanding its point of view to encompass a coherent "system." And like Eliot, Merz believed that such "completeness is unattainable to the human mind." There is one way, however, in which Merz thought the human mind might grasp the "whole truth":

> The manifold features of existence, the endless variety of colour, shape, sound, in their never-ending change, must in some way or other "contract into a span," so that they may be grasped by the human eye or the human intellect; and this contracted image or symbol must give the impression of completeness, of indicating, suggesting, or embracing a totality: in the highest sense the totality of everything—the Universe, the All. The human mind possesses two very different means of achieving this. The first is abstract thought, the second the creation of the artist.[29]

This is precisely the power that Eliot attributed to Dante, the "true mystic." While Eliot thought that Bradley's skepticism denied him the consolations of the Absolute, he found that this unified whole could be made available by the visionary artist (Dante, Tiresias, Eliot himself) who presents the image of "the totality of everything—the Universe, the All" in his art.

An account of the visionary powers Eliot perceived in Dante and attempted to locate in Tiresias's consciousness in *The Waste Land* is lacking from his description of the ideal poet in "Tradition and the Individual Talent." These powers lay beyond the "frontier of metaphysics or mysticism," and Eliot's description of the "system" of tradition relies on the more explicable process of the unification of points of view: one's knowledge of the "whole truth" of "the whole of the literature of Europe from Homer" is built up slowly, piece by piece, with "great labour" (SW, 49).

By the time Eliot wrote "Tradition and the Individual Talent" (1919) he had been discussing the importance of tradition (especially in connection with Pound's work) for several years. His first extended explanation of tradition came in the third installment of "Reflections on Contemporary Poetry," published two years before his most famous essay:

> Each of us, even the most gifted, can find room in his brain for hardly more than two or three new ideas, or ideas so perfectly assimilated as to be original; for an idea is a speciality, and no one has time for more than a few. With these, or with one, say, hexagonal or octagonal idea, each sets to work and industriously and obliviously begins building cells; not rebelling against the square or the circle, but occasionally coming into collision with some other Bee which has rectangular or circular ideas. All the ideas, beliefs, modes of feeling and behaviour which we have not time or inclination to investigate for ourselves we take second-hand and sometimes call Tradition.

This paragraph provides a neat metaphorical description of the process of the unification of points of view, the building of a "system" out of inherited and acquired bits of knowledge. At the end of this paragraph, however, Eliot adds a curious footnote:

> For an authoritative condemnation of theories attaching extreme importance to tradition as a criterion of truth, see Pope Gregory XVI's encyclical *Singulari nos* (July 15, 1834), and the Vatican Council canon of 1870, *Si quis dixerit ... anathema sit.*[30]

The influence of Pound, Bradley, and Dante on Eliot's conception of tradition is predictable enough, but this rather cryptic note seems to imply that Eliot's theory owes something to rather more esoteric—if more orthodox—sources. This footnote, in fact, is a cryptogram to Eliot's journey beyond the frontier of metaphysics or mysticism, and it is possible to follow that journey step by step.

Eliot's conversion to the Anglican church did not occur until 1927, but as Lyndall Gordon has shown, Eliot was attracted to the church for many years and came close to conversion in 1916. He was, as he wrote of himself in "Eeldrop and Appleplex," enormously learned in theology ("a sceptic with a taste for mysticism"), and between 1916 and 1919, when he reviewed extensively for the *International Journal of Ethics*, almost all his reviews were of books on scholastic philosophy. The reading list for his 1916 extension lecture on "The Return to the Catholic Church" reveals an even more widely ranging knowledge of contemporary theology.[31]

Despite this background knowledge, however, Eliot's reference in "Reflections on Contemporary Poetry" to obscure texts of Catholic theology, the *Singulari nos* of Gregory XVI and the papal canons issued by the first Vatican council, have an aura of "bogus scholarship"—the phrase he used to describe the notes to *The Waste Land* (OPP, 121). The *Singulari nos*, for instance, has never been translated into English in its entirety, and it is difficult to believe that Eliot would have read it. Both of the texts to which Eliot refers are indeed authoritative condemnations "of theories attaching extreme importance to tradition as a criterion for truth," but they condemn a special conception of tradition. In Catholic theology "traditionalism" refers very specifically to a heretical philosophy developed by Louis de Bonald (1754–1840) and popularized throughout the nineteenth century. Eliot was not only familiar with the philosophy of "traditionalism," but his references to the church's condemnations of its doctrines are lifted from the works of scholastic theology he was reviewing for the *International Journal of Ethics*.

A month before the third segment of "Reflections on Contemporary Poetry" appeared in the *Egoist*, Eliot reviewed the first volume of Cardinal Mercier's *Manual of Modern Scholastic Philosophy* for the *International Journal of Ethics*. In this review he remarked that "no student of contemporary philosophy can afford to neglect the neo-scholastic movement since 1879."[32] Neither could a student of "traditionalism" afford to neglect Cardinal Mercier's *Manual of Modern Scholastic Philosophy*. A succinct account of the philosophy appears in the chapter on "criteriology," the study of various criteria for truth:

> *Traditionalism.*—The most well-known representatives of this system, de Bonald and La Mennais, in order the better to refute

> the arguments of rationalism against religion, laid down the principle that the human reason is incapable by itself of attaining to a certain knowledge in matters metaphysical, religious or moral. They maintained that these truths must have been originally revealed by God to humanity, and that this primitive revelation has been handed down by tradition either through *social teaching* (so de Bonald) or by the *general reason* that is the basis of the beliefs admitted by all mankind (so La Mennais).
>
> The last motive of certitude in these matters is thus an *act of faith* in divine revelation. Indeed if we follow the general implication of the arguments brought forward by the traditionalists we find that in its last analysis *all certitude rests on an act of faith*.[33]

This is a fair and accurate account of "traditionalism." Faced with the sordid conclusions of the French Revolution, de Bonald set out in his *La Législation primitive* (1802) and his *Recherches philosophiques sur les premiers objects de nos connaissances morales* (1818) to build a philosophy that would not rely upon human reason; the errors of human reason had poisoned the ideals of the revolution and caused the political and social chaos surrounding him. Directing his argument against Rousseau (a strategy that would have pleased any pupil of Irving Babbitt), de Bonald maintained that the individual is not capable of determining truth on his own. Truth is available only as a revelation from God. These revelations were made available to primitive man and have been transmitted to modern times by the process of tradition. According to "traditionalist" doctrine, as Mercier states, all certitude rests "on an act of faith" and on the maintenance of the knowledge derived from this primitive act of faith by the process of tradition.

Neither of the Papal condemnations of "traditionalism" that Eliot cites in his footnote are mentioned in Mercier's *Manual of Modern Scholastic Philosophy*, but the *Si quis dixerit* is cited in another book Eliot reviewed at around the same time: Peter Coffey's *Epistemology* (1917). In the first volume of this treatise, Coffey offers a brief sketch of "traditionalism": for some people, truth is "above the power of the human mind to have discovered without revelation," and their assent to these truths is "an assent of *Faith* in the strictest sense." In opposition to this doctrine Coffey cites the Vatican Council canon, *Si quis dixerit*:

> The Vatican Council defined that the existence of God can *be known for certain* from the facts of experience by the natural light of human reason: "Si quis dixerit Deum unum ac verum,

> Creatorum ac Dominum nostrum, per ea quae facta sunt naturali rationis humanae lumine certo cognosci nos posse, anathema sit.[34]

The text of this canon, which Coffey does not translate, means: "If anyone says that the one true God, our Creator and Lord, cannot be shown with certainty by the natural light of human reason by means of the things that are made, let him be anathema."[35] This statement, says Coffey, "condemns the view that this evidence [the facts of experience] is of itself, and without such supernatural aid as that of revelation, insufficient to exclude reasonable doubt and so produce certain knowledge."[36] Since Eliot refers to the *Si quis dixerit* as a condemnation of his own theory of tradition, it seems logical that he knew—however much he hesitated to admit it—that his own theory was based upon the importance of supernatural aid. Even the inspired poet would have difficulty attaining a knowledge of "the whole truth" on his own.

As we have seen, Eliot was dissatisfied with Bradley's account of the Absolute because it "responds only to an imaginary demand of thought, and satisfies only an imaginary demand of feeling. Pretending to be something which makes finite centres cohere, it turns out to be merely the assertion that they do" (KE, 202). Because Bradley locked the individual so securely in his "finite center" or point of view, Eliot found his leap to the whole truth untenable. "Bradley's universe," he wrote in "Leibniz' Monads and Bradley's Finite Centres," while "actual only in finite centres, is only by an act of faith unified" (KE, 202). Given Bradley's rigorous skepticism, this act of faith is not possible. But in the philosophy of "traditionalism," where all certitude rests upon an act of faith, the idea of the Absolute becomes tenable. For Eliot, Bradley's philosophy led "to something which, according to your temperament, will be resignation or despair."[37] In "traditionalism," which takes the responsibility for enacting "the painful task of unifying" away from the individual by offering divine assistance the whole truth becomes available once more. Comparing Leibniz' monads to Bradley's finite centers, Eliot commented that in Bradley's work (despite the rigorous skepticism) he was "not sure that the ultimate puzzle is any more frankly faced, or that divine intervention plays any smaller part" (KE, 207). Divine intervention plays no smaller part in Eliot's own theories of tradition and the unification of points of view.

The Latin texts that Eliot cites in his footnote in "Reflections on Contemporary Poetry" are condemnations of an excessive dependence upon supernatural aid: by citing them as a condemnation of his own theory, Eliot pointed the way toward "the frontier of metaphysics or mysticism." He crossed that frontier most daringly in "What the Thunder Said," the final movement of *The Waste Land*. In this part of the poem, the doctrine of divine revelation, which is central to "traditionalism," provided him with another way of approaching the whole truth. Eliot himself felt that the new incantatory voice of "What the Thunder Said" came from some place beyond the parameters of his own mind. In his essay on "The 'Pensees' of Pascal" (1931), Eliot ventured a description of mystical experience that he later confessed was derived from his own experience of writing the last movement of *The Waste Land*:

> What can only be called mystical experience happens to many men who do not become mystics.... it is a commonplace that some forms of illness are extremely favorable, not only to religious illumination, but to artistic and literary composition. A piece of writing meditated, apparently without progress, for months or years, may suddenly take shape and word; and in this state long passages may be produced which require little or no retouch.... You may call it communion with the Divine, or you may call it a temporary crystalization of mind. (SE, 357–358)

While Eliot felt that the writing of "What the Thunder Said" involved some sort of mystical experience, the process of revelation plays an even more important part in the very structure of this part of *The Waste Land*. Eliot wrote to Bertrand Russell that "What the Thunder Said" is "not only the best part [of *The Waste Land*], but the only part that justifies the whole, at all" (WLF, 129). The "whole" was just what Eliot was after in "What the Thunder Said"—not only formally, as a satisfying conclusion to a long poem, but also ideologically, as an expression of spiritual wholeness. In the "fable of the meaning of the Thunder" (CPP, 54), as he calls it in his notes, Eliot shows how a primitive revelation of "the whole truth" (the thunderous "DA") is disseminated, by the process of tradition, throughout history. As Eliot presents it, this process bears a significant resemblance to de Bonald's "traditionalism." In his discussion of "traditionalism" in *A Manual of Modern Scholastic Philosophy* Mercier explains how de Bonald believed that language itself is based upon the reality of divine revelation:

> The necessity of an initial revelation, according to de Bonald, is based on the fact of language. He argues thus:—Man possesses language. But man could not have invented it; for to do so the power of thought is necessary, and man is incapable of thinking without inwardly formulating words, according to the celebrated dictum of Rousseau: "Man must think his word before he can

> speak his thought." Therefore to invent language man must first have been in possession of words—which is self-contradictory. He concludes, then, that man received language from without, and this he could have done only from God. Hence did human reason commence to think only by an act of faith in the divine word which revealed at once both language and its meaning. And consequently, every certain assent of the mind must rest ultimately on an act of faith in a primitive revelation.[38]

According to de Bonald's reasoning, man could not have invented language because language is anterior to thought and at the same time thought is necessary to formulate language. The only way out of this closed circle is to postulate the theory of the divine origins of language.[39] The primitive revelation, incarnate in language, is disseminated through time by the process of "social teaching" and by the continuities of language itself. These mechanisms of tradition make divine knowledge available in the present—providing that faith and divine favor are maintained. Without this supernatural aid, history becomes the story of mankind's corruption and decline.

Throughout the nineteenth century de Bonald's theory of the divine origins of language remained important for thinkers who opposed Darwin's theory of evolution and Robert Chambers's hotly disputed hypothesis (put forth in *Vestiges of the Natural History of Creation* [1844]) that animals possessed a primitive kind of sign language that was refined by human beings. Conservative thinkers such as Max Müller and Julius Charles Hare used de Bonald's language-origin theory to undermine these materialistic accounts of man's progress and to emphasize the necessity of a divine presence in the world.[40]

Eliot was attracted to the theory for much the same reason. As Ronald Schuchard has demonstrated, Eliot had by 1916 already begun to oppose the scientific skepticism of his age by formulating a theological world-view based upon the Hulmian doctrine of original sin.[41] "Traditionalism" provided him with an alternative to the decidedly anti-mystical doctrine of Unitarianism, the religion in which he was raised; he grew dissatisfied with the intellectual and puritanical rationalism of Unitarianism, becoming convinced of the necessity of revelation.[42] And while Hugh Kenner has suggested that Eliot's use of the "fable of the meaning of the Thunder" in *The Waste Land* owes something to Romantic theories of the origin of language and "invokes some two centuries' philological effort to recover the deepest memories of the tribe,"[43] Eliot's attraction to "traditionalism" reveals the Romantic origins of his art even more clearly.

In his notes to *The Waste Land* Eliot explains that "Datta, dayadhvam, damyata" means "Give, sympathize, control" and that this "fable of the meaning of the Thunder is found in the *Brihadaranyaka-Upanishad*" (CPP, 54). He then directs the reader to Paul Duessen's German translation of the Upanishad; but Eliot probably first read the parable in an English translation by his Harvard Sanskrit professor, Charles Lanman:

> Three kinds of children of Prajā-pati, Lord of Children, lived as Brahman-students with Prajā-pati their father: the gods, human beings, the demons.—Living with him as Brahman-students, the gods spake, "Teach us, Exalted One."—Unto them he spake this one syllable Da. "Have ye understood?"—"We have understood," thus they spake, "it was dā́myata, control yourselves, that thou saidest unto us."—"Yes," spake he, "ye have understood."
>
> Then spake to him human beings, "Teach us, Exalted One."—Unto them he spake that selfsame syllable Da. "Have ye understood?"—"We have understood," thus they spake, "it was dattá, give, that thou saidest unto us."—"Yes," spake he, "ye have understood."
>
> Then spake to him the demons, "Teach us, Exalted One."—Unto them he spake that selfsame syllable Da. "Have ye understood?"—"We have understood," thus they spake, "it was dáyadhvam, be compassionate, that thou saidest unto us."—"Yes," spake he, "ye have understood."
>
> This it is which that voice of god repeats, the thunder, when it rolls "Da Da Da," that is dā́myata dattá dáyadhvam. Therefore these three must be learned, self-control, giving, compassion.

Lanman remarked of this passage, "a bit of the oldest Indo-European narrative prose," that it "gives to some of the cardinal virtues the sanction of divine revelation."[44] As in de Bonald's "traditionalist" theory of the origin of language, the divine revelation of knowledge is revealed in the gift of language ("DA"), and its meaning is then disseminated by the process of social teaching. Although divine knowledge is interpreted differently by different peoples, it nevertheless remains absolutely true. The "trap of interpretation" has been avoided.

This crossing of the "traditionalist" theory of the origin of language with Indian wisdom literature is not haphazard. Beginning with Herder's *Ueber den Ursprung der Sprache* (1772) the idea of India as the cradle of all human knowledge and of Sanskrit as the origin of all human languages became a commonplace in Romantic philology. In *Ueber die Sprache und Weisheit der Indier* (1808), perhaps the most influential text for the development of Sanskrit studies in the nineteenth century, Friedrich von Schlegel calls Sanskrit the *Ursprache*, the common source of all languages; he intimates that its origins are divine: "the Indian is almost entirely a philosophical or rather a religious language.... it has no variable or arbitrary combination of abstractions, but is formed on a permanent system, in which the deep symbolic signification of words and expressions reciprocally explain, elucidate, and support each other."[45]

Eliot's use of the parable of the thunder in *The Waste Land* shows a clear affinity with this Romantic tradition of Sanskrit philology. The thunder's utterance of the syllable "DA" is the closest that Eliot comes to an expression of "the whole truth." It is the moment of primitive revelation on which de Bonald believed all certitude rests; it is the origin of language and tradition. As the Sanskrit fable of the thunder suggests, Eliot believed that this primitive knowledge was not available to modern man in its original form; as it is passed on to different peoples, the expression of divine wisdom necessarily changes. In "The Beating of a Drum" (1923), a review of W.O.E. Oesterley's *The Sacred Dance*, Eliot criticizes Oesterley for "formulating intelligible reasons for the primitive dancer's dancing." Like Pound and Yeats, Eliot faced the problem of an "irrevocable past" and suggested that meaning necessarily changes over time because of the process of interpretation:

> An unoccupied person, finding a drum, may be seized with a desire to beat it; but unless he is an imbecile he will be unable to continue beating it, and thereby satisfying a need (rather than a "desire"), without finding a reason for so doing. The reason may be the long continued drought. The next generation or the next civilization will find a more plausible reason for beating a drum. Shakespeare and Racine—or rather the developments which led up to them—each found his own reason. The reasons may be divided into tragedy and comedy. We still have similar reasons, but we have lost the drum.[46]

Eliot believed that the artist must keep in touch with these primitive energies, but he knew that the very process of tradition by which they come down to us distorts their original meaning. In his review of Wyndham Lewis's *Tarr* (1918) he wrote that "the artist ... is more *primitive*, as well as more civilized, than his contemporaries, his experience is deeper than civilization, and he only uses the phenomena of civilization in expressing it.

Primitive instincts and the acquired habits of ages are confounded in the ordinary man. In the work of Mr. Lewis we recognize the thought of the cave-man."[47] While Lewis is in touch with primitive energies, he cannot present primitive man in his original state; *Tarr* reveals the shape these energies take in the twentieth century.

A year after his review of *Tarr* Eliot remembered the qualities he admired in Lewis, combined them with his admiration for Pound's wide-ranging knowledge, Bradley's emphasis on the "systematic" point of view, and de Bonald's "traditionalist" theory of primitive revelation, and presented a refined program for poetry:

> The maxim, Return to the sources, is a good one. More intelligibly put, it is that the poet should know everything that has been accomplished in poetry (accomplished, not merely produced) since its beginnings—in order to know what he is doing himself. He should be aware of all the metamorphoses of poetry that illustrate the stratifications of history that cover savagery.[48]

I have already quoted this passage from Eliot's review of an anthology of North American Indian songs and chants to illustrate the "stratifications of history" he builds up in the opening of "The Fire Sermon" or the "Unreal City" passage in "The Burial of the Dead. "Juxtaposed with Eliot's interest in "traditionalism" and his use of the fable of the thunder in "What the Thunder Said," the significance of Eliot's desire to present "the stratifications of history that cover savagery" becomes even clearer:

> The jungle crouched, humped in silence.
> Then spoke the thunder
> DA
> *Datta*: what have we given?
> My friend, blood shaking my heart
> The awful daring of a moment's surrender
> Which an age of prudence can never retract
> By this, and this only, we have existed
> Which is not to be found in our obituaries
> Or in memories draped by the beneficent spider
> Or under seals broken by the lean solicitor
> In our empty rooms
> DA
> *Dayadhvam*: I have heard the key

Turn in the door once and turn once only
We think of the key, each in his prison
Thinking of the key, each confirms a prison
Only at nightfall, aethereal rumours
Revive for a moment a broken Coriolanus
DA
Damyata: The boat responded
Gaily, to the hand expert with sail and oar
The sea was calm, your heart would have responded
Gaily, when invited, beating obedient
To controlling hands. (CPP, 49–50)

These lines are usually read as an expression of Eliot's perception of the reduction of possibilities in his modern world; within the prison of consciousness, man does not seem capable of giving or sympathizing. The only rays of hope shine through the gloom in the "awful daring of the moment's surrender" (which makes giving seem as horrible as not giving) and "your heart [which] would have responded / Gaily, when invited, beating obedient / To controlling hands" (though this is no more than a supposition). While these lines express a vision of man's solipsistic existence, however, the structure of the passage undermines that vision. Even as Eliot writes that every person "in his prison / Thinking of the key, ... confirms a prison," and quotes Bradley to support this description of the prison-house of consciousness, the structure of the passages shows (just as Bradley wanted to show) that each of us can transcend that limited consciousness. (Eliot's citation of Bradley at this point, in fact, has always seemed problematic because it ignores the central thrust of his philosophy: the necessity of transcending individual consciousnesses for the condition of the Absolute.)[49] Based on the fable of the thunder in which sacred knowledge is interpreted in three different ways, this passage reveals the process of tradition operating successfully. The continuities of past and present, heaven and earth, are demonstrated in the act of interpretation. From "DA," the moment of what de Bonald would have called primitive revelation; through the three Sanskrit interpretations of these words, the passage affirms historical continuity; it illustrates what Eliot called "the stratifications of history that cover savagery." At the end of the poem, the proliferation of tongues, the fragments shored against ruin, must be seen as emanating from the thunderous "DA." Fragments they are, but fragments with a common origin, fragments within a tradition that begins with a moment of revelation.

Eliot's emphasis of historical continuity in *The Waste Land* reveals the positive side of a poem rooted in psychological and cultural disarray. When he added the notes to the poem, however, Eliot pointed out that one of the three themes of "What the Thunder Said" is "the present decay of eastern Europe" (CPP, 53). Like his account of the "mythical method," this retrospective comment has helped to lead more than one generation of readers to perceive the poem as a statement of cultural despair. Yet the provenience of that remark can help us to see that Eliot's attitude toward history was far more ambiguous. In a note to lines that introduce the voice of the thunder and harken back to the "Unreal City" passage in "The Burial of the Dead," Eliot directs his readers to a few sentences from Hermann Hesse's *Blick in· Chaos*. Although he quotes from the original German, Eliot almost certainly first encountered these sentences in English when a translation of one of the essays in Hesse's book ("Die Brüder Karamasoff oder der Untergang Europas"—"The Brothers Karamazov--The Downfall of Europe") was published in the July 1922 issue of the *Dial*. It is easy to see why Eliot found Hesse's discussion of Dostoevsky so attractive. Hesse's treatment of the visionary consciousness in *The Brothers Karamazov* is quite similar to Eliot's own treatment of the topic in his essay on "Beyle and Balzac" (1919). And in the following paragraph (which ends with the three sentences Eliot quotes in German in the notes to *The Waste Land*) Hesse offers a perfect description of the dilapidated yet visionary state of mind in which Eliot admitted he had written "What the Thunder Said":

> I said Dostoevsky is not a poet, or he is only a poet in a secondary sense. I called him a prophet. It is difficult to say exactly what a prophet means. It seems to me something like this. A prophet is a sick man, like Dostoevsky, who was an epileptic. A prophet is the sort of sick man who has lost the sound sense of taking care of himself, the sense which is the saving of the efficient citizen. It would not do if there were many such, for the world would go to pieces This sort of sick man, be he called Dostoevsky or Karamazov, has that strange, occult, godlike faculty, the possibility of which the Asiatic venerates in every maniac. He is a seer and an oracle. A people, a period, a country, a continent has fashioned out of its corpus an organ, a sensory instrument of infinite sensitiveness, a very rare and delicate organ.... Every man has visions, every man has fantasies, every man has dreams. And every vision, every dream, every idea and thought of a man, on the road from the unconscious to the conscious, can have a thousand different meanings, of which every one can be right. But the appearances and visions of the seer and the prophet are not his own. The nightmare of visions

> which oppresses him does not warn him of a personal illness, of a personal death, but of the illness, the death of that corpus whose sensory organ he is. This corpus can be a family, a clan, a people, or it can be all mankind. In the soul of Dostoevsky a certain sickness and sensitiveness to suffering in the bosom of mankind which is otherwise called hysteria, found at once its means of expression and its barometer. Mankind is now on the point of realizing this. Already half Europe, at all events half Eastern Europe, is on the road to Chaos. In a state of drunken illusion she is reeling into the abyss and, as she reels, she sings a drunken hymn such as Dmitri Karamazov sang. The insulted citizen laughs that song to scorn, the saint and seer hear it with tears.

When Eliot returned to London from his treatment with Dr. Vittoz in Lausanne, he read this paragraph and saw a correlative for his own experience of finishing *The Waste Land*. He too had been the victim of an illness that gave him "that strange, occult, godlike faculty" to intuit a continent's "nightmare of visions." Hesse wrote that in Dostoevsky's *The Brothers Karamazov* "the unconscious of a whole continent and age has made of itself poetry in the nightmare of a single, prophetic dreamer," and concluded that no other work "has ever set forth with more lucid clearness the communication of a human being with his own unconscious self."[50] No work, we might add, until *The Waste Land*, Eliot's deepest descent into "the poet's inner world of nightmare" (SE, 166).

When Hesse wrote that Dostoevsky depicted Europe "on the road to chaos," he meant something far more complicated than this simply pessimistic line implies. In fact, he believed that this movement toward chaos "discloses the rich possibilities of the New Life."

> This downfall is a return home to the mother, a turning back to Asia, to the source, to the "*Faustischen Muttern*" and will necessarily lead, like every death on earth, to a new birth.
>
> We contemporaries see a "downfall" in these events in the same way as the aged who, compelled to leave the home they love, mourn a loss to them irreparable while the young think only of the future, care only for what is new.

These sentences provide a worthy description of the sensibility Eliot depicted in "Gerontion": an old man whose perspective on the world is so limited that he necessarily sees historical change as the augury of apocalypse. In contrast, the parable of the thunder in *The Waste Land* presents "a turning back to Asia, to the source," and its portrait of "the present decay of eastern Europe" is as ambiguous as Hesse's analysis of Dostoevsky and the history of the modern world:

> But quite another question is how we are to regard this Downfall. Here we are at the parting of the ways. Those who cling definitely to the past, those who venerate time-honoured cultural forms, the Knights of a treasured morality, must seek to delay this Downfall and will mourn it inconsolably when it passes. For them the Downfall is the End; for the others, it is the Beginning. For the first, Dostoevsky is a criminal, for the others a Saint. For the one party Europe and its soul constitute an entity once and for all, foreordained, inviolate, a thing fixed and immutable. For the other it is a becoming, a mutable, ever-changing thing.[51]

In *The Waste Land*, history is a mutable, ever-changing thing. Eliot's use of the parable of the thunder reveals that he tried to depict what may appear as "the present decay of eastern Europe" in the context of a long tradition that leads us back to the very origins of language. Even the modern world of the "Unreal City" is part of the "whole truth," a moment resting on the accumulation of the "entire past." Only the inspired poet, Hesse and Eliot agreed, can see beyond the chaos to the "possibilities of the New Life" that it portends.

When Eliot drafted the final lines of *The Waste Land*, the poem's most famous line did not read "These fragments I have shored against my ruins" but "These fragments I have spelt into my ruins" (WLF, 81). The change to "shored against" is consonant with Eliot's final revisions of the poem: the selection of the title, the addition of the notes, and later on, the description of the "mythical method." These textual revisions and critical pronouncements constitute the first interpretation of *The Waste Land*, and it led a generation of readers (in Eliot's phrase) to see "their own illusion of being disillusioned" in the poem (SE, 324). To think of Eliot spelling the fragments of the past into his present ruins rather than shoring them against his ruins makes it easier to see the poem as an attempt to express wholeness (whether personal, historical, or spiritual). Exfoliating from the thunderous and meaningless "DA," *The Waste Land* spells the entire history of language into the texture of modern English. The final lines of the poem move from Sanskrit to Latin, Provençal, French, and back to the mystical origins of language and tradition in the Sanskrit "Shantih"—"The Peace which passeth understanding." This use of the parable of the thunder embodies the lesson of "The Three Provincialities," an essay on the fate of English language and literature that Eliot published in the same year as *The Waste Land*:

> Whatever words a writer employs, he benefits by knowing as much as possible of the history of these words, of the *uses to which they have already been applied*. Such knowledge facilitates his task of giving to the word a new life and to the language a new idiom. The essential of tradition is in this; in getting as much as possible of the whole weight of history of the language behind the word.[52]

The Waste Land reveals such a tradition operating successfully, yet the success is only partial. Even with the divine assistance Eliot believed was necessary to realize "the whole truth," he knew that his attempt to express this whole must ultimately fail. Like Pound's *Cantos*, *The Waste Land* vacillates between the assurance of transcendental vision and a skepticism that threatens to obliterate the possibility of knowledge altogether. Yet like Pound, Eliot might have written that "it coheres all right / even if my notes do not cohere" (114/797). *The Waste Land* presents a divided sensibility very much like that of Pater's *Renaissance*: while describing the prison of consciousness, both works depend upon the idea of an eternal mind that makes the entire past available in the present. After *The Waste Land* Eliot would never again attempt to write a poem so thickened by historical reference. *The Waste Land* remains the ultimate "poem including history" produced in the twentieth century, and if Yeats was right to present Pater's *La Gioconda* as the first "modern" poem, then *The Waste Land* may well be the last.

Notes

1. G. W. F. Hegel, *The Phenomenology of Mind*, trans. J. B. Baillie (New York: Harper & Row, 1967), p. 81.

2. Samuel Taylor Coleridge, *Lay Sermons*, ed. R. J. White (Princeton: Princeton Univ. Press, 1972), p. 30.

3. Quoted in Robert Langbaum, "New Modes of Characterization in *The Waste Land*," in A. Walton Litz, ed., *Eliot in His Time* (Princeton: Princeton Univ. Press, 1973), p. 96; my emphasis.

4. Thomas McFarland, *Romanticism and the Forms of Ruin: Wordsworth, Coleridge, and Modalities of Fragmentation* (Princeton: Princeton Univ. Press, 1981), pp. 50–51.

5. McFarland, p. 15.

6. T. S. Eliot, "*Ulysses*, Order, and Myth" (1923); rpt. In *The Selected Prose of T. S. Eliot*, ed. Frank Kermode (London: Faber & Faber, 1975), pp. 177–178.

7. See A. Walton Litz, "*The Waste Land* Fifty Years After," in *Eliot in His Time*, pp. 3–22, for an examination of the use and misuse of the "mythical method" in Eliot criticism.

8. Bush, *T. S. Eliot*, p. 82.

9. See Levenson, pp. 186–189.

10. Royce, *Problem of Christianity*, 2:210, 236.

11. Eliot, "A Note on Ezra Pound," p. 6.

12. Dilthey, *Selected Writings*, p. 215.

13. T. S. Eliot, "Modern Tendencies in Poetry," *Shama'a* 1 (April 1920): 12. This essay was originally delivered as one of a series of five lectures, beginning in October 1919. See Donald Gallup, *T. S. Eliot: A Bibliography* (London: Faber & Faber, 1969). p. 206.

14. For an account of the chronology of the composition of *The Waste Land*, see Hugh Kenner, "The Urban Apocalypse," in *Eliot in His Time*, pp. 23–50. For an examination of the stylistic transformation of "What the Thunder Said," see Bush, *T. S. Eliot*, pp. 67–78.

15. Eliot, "A Note on Ezra Pound," p. 6.

16. See Charles du Bos, "Letters from Paris IV.—On the Symbolist Movement in French Poetry," *Athenaeum* 4708 (23 June 1920): 126. For an account of the way Eliot revised his essays for inclusion in *The Sacred Wood*, see Linda M. Shires, "T. S. Eliot's Early Criticism and the Making of *The Sacred Wood*," *Prose Studies* 5 (1982): 229–238.

17. Evelyn Underhill, *Mysticism* (1911; rpt. New York: E. P. Dutton, 1961), p. 271. See also Gordon, Eliot's *Early Years*, p. 60. As Eliot approached his conversion his thoughts about mysticism became more complex and divided. Several of his 1926 Clark Lectures are concerned with the development of a taxonomy of different kinds of mysticism. One of these unpublished lectures has appeared in a French translation: "Deux attitudes mystiques: Dante et Donne," *Chroniques* 3 (1927): 149–173.

18. Dante, *The Divine Comedy: Paradiso*, trans. Singleton, pp. 6–7.

19. T. S. Eliot, "The Romantic Englishman, the Comic Spirit, and the Function of Criticism," *Tyro* 1 (Spring 1921): 4.

20. T. S. Eliot, "Beyle and Balzac," *Athenaeum* 4648 (30 May 1919): 392.

21. Eliot, "Reflections on Contemporary Poetry [IV]," p. 39.

22. Eliot, "'The Duchess of Malfi' at the Lyric," p. 39.

23. Eliot, "Tradition and the Practice of Poetry," p. 878.

24. T. S. Eliot, Introduction to *The Wheel of Fire* by G. Wilson Knight (London: Oxford Univ. Press 1930), pp. xvi–xvii.

25. Ibid., pp. xvii–xviii.

26. T. S. Eliot, "Thinking in Verse: A Survey of Early Seventeenth-Century Poetry," *Listener* 3 (12 March 1930): 443.

27. Friedrich Schleiermacher, *Hermeneutik*, ed. Heinz Kimmerle (Heidelberg: Carl Winter, 1959), p. 109; translation in Palmer, p. 90. Paul Ricoeur, *Hermeneutics and the Human Sciences*, ed. and trans. John B. Thompson (New York: Cambridge Univ. Press, 1982), p. 46. Ricoeur quotes from Schleiermacher, *Hermeneutik und Kritik*, vol. 7 of *Sämmtliche Werke*, ed. F. Lucke (Berlin: G. Reimer, 1938), secs. 15–16 and *Hermeneutik*, p. 56.

28. T. S. Eliot, "[A review of] *Religion and Science* by John Theodore Merz," *Monist* 28 (April 1918): 319, 320. This unsigned review, along with seven others, has been identified by Elizabeth R. Earners and Alan M. Cohn in "Some Early Reviews by T. S. Eliot (Addenda to Gallup)," *Papers of the Bibliographical Society of America* 70 (1976): 420–424.

29. John Theodore Merz, *Religion and Science: A Philosophical Essay* (London: William Blackwood & Sons, 1915), pp. 113–114.

30. T. S. Eliot, "Reflections on Contemporary Poetry [III]," *Egoist* 4 (November 1917): 151.

31. See Ronald Schuchard, "T. S. Eliot as Extension Lecturer, 1916–1919," *Review of English Studies* 25 (1974): 167.

32. T. S. Eliot, "[A review of] *A Manual of Modern Scholastic Philosophy* by Cardinal Mercier et al.," *International Journal of Ethics* 28 (October 1917): 137.

33. Cardinal Mercier et al., *A Manual of Modern Scholastic Philosophy*, 3rd English ed., ed. and trans. T. L. Parker and S. A. Parker (London: Kegan Paul, Trench, Trubner & Co., 1928), 1:363.

34. P. Coffey, *Epistemology or the Theory of Knowledge* (London: Longmans, Green, & Co., 1917), 1:54–55.

35. I quote this translation from the book in which Eliot probably read it: Paul Sabatier, *Modernism*, trans. C. A. Miles (New York: Charles Scribner's Sons, 1908), p. 238. This translation of the *Si quis dixerit* as well as a passage translated from Pope Gregory XVI's *Singulari nos* would have been known to Eliot, and it is possible to reconstruct rather closely the steps Eliot took to locate these attacks of "traditionalism." After quoting the *Si quis dixerit* in *Epistemology*, Coffey refers to the "*Moto proprio* of Pope Pius X against the errors of Modernism" (p. 55). Like "traditionalism," "modernism" refers to a specific heretical doctrine in Catholic theology; the word became a commonplace in theology by 1900, twenty years before it became a commonplace in literary history. Eliot was even more learned in "modernism" than "traditionalism," and in his reading list for his 1916 extension lecture on "The Return to the Catholic Church" he defined it as "a compromise between the point of view of historical criticism—inherited from Renan—and orthodoxy" (Schuchard, p. 167). Although the church perceived "modernism" as a completely unacceptable challenge to its authority, the movement is more correctly understood, as Eliot says, as an effort to adapt orthodox Catholicism to the discoveries of modern scientific and historical methods. In the reading list for his lecture, Eliot included Sabatier's *Modernism*, a sympathetic account of the movement, which included a translation of Pope Plus X's *Pascendi Gregis*, a proclamation condemning modernist doctrine.

When he read Coffey's comment on "modernism" in *Epistemology*, Eliot must have pulled his own copy of Sabatier's *Modernism* from his shelf: in its translation of Pope Pius's *Pascendi Gregis* are passages from Gregory XVI's *Singulari nos* and the Vatican Council canon, *Si quis dixerit* (which Coffey had quoted in Latin). I have already quoted the translation of the *Si quis dixerit*; here is the passage Eliot would have known from the *Singulari vos* (the other text to which he refers his readers in "Reflections on Contemporary Poetry" for an "authoritative condemnation of theories attaching extreme importance to tradition as a criterion for truth"):

> They are seen to be the way of a blind and unchecked passion for novelty, thinking not at all of finding some solid foundation of truth, but despising the holy and apostolic traditions, they embrace other and vain, futile, uncertain doctrines, unapproved by the Church, on which, in the height of their vanity, they think they can base and maintain truth itself. (Sabatier, p. 252)

This statement seems more like a condemnation of theories of truth that do not pay enough attention to tradition. Eliot could present it as the opposite because he knew that the *Singulari nos* was a condemnation of "traditionalism," which from the perspective of orthodox Catholicism was highly antitraditional. Interestingly enough, Eliot associates his own description of tradition with heretical "traditionalism" rather than the orthodox traditions of the church.

36. Coffey, p. 55.

37. T. S. Eliot, "A Prediction in Regard to Three English Authors," p. 29. Compare Eliot's analysis of Bradley's ultimate reliance on faith to William James's analysis of the mysticism latent in absolute idealism in general: "I cannot help suspecting that the palpable weak places in the intellectual reasonings they use are protected from their own criticism by a mystical feeling that, logic or no logic, absolute Oneness must somehow at any cost be true.... The theory of the Absolute, in particular, has had to be an article of faith" (*Pragmatism*, ed. Frederick H. Burkhardt [Cambridge: Harvard Univ. Press, 1975), pp. 76, 78). Both James and Eliot saw this latent reliance on faith as a flaw in idealist logic, but Eliot also saw that a philosophy that openly relied upon faith (such as "traditionalism") made the idea of absolute oneness possible in a way that Bradley's idealism finally did not.

38. Mercier, p. 364.

39. See Louis de Bonald, *La Législation primitive* (Paris: A. Le Clere, 1817), 1:81.

40. See Hans Aarsleff, *The Study of Language in England 1780–1860* (Minneapolis: Univ. of Minnesota Press, 1983), pp. 223–229.

41. See Ronald Schuchard, "Eliot and Hulme in 1916: Toward a Revaluation of Eliot's Critical and Spiritual Development," *PMLA* 88 (1973): 1091–1092.

42. See T. S. Eliot's contribution to *Revelation*, ed. John Baillie and Hugh Martin (London: Faber & Faber, 1937), pp. 1–39.

43. Kenner, *Pound Era*, p. 110.

44. Charles R. Lanman, "Hindu Law and Custom as to Gifts," in *Anniversary Papers by Colleagues and Pupils of George Lyman Kittredge* (Boston: Ginn & Co., 1913), p. 1.

45. Frederick von Schlegel, *The Aesthetic and Miscellaneous Works of Frederick von Schlegel*, trans. E. J. Millington (London: Henry G. Bohn, 1849), p. 457. For a discussion of Herder, Schlegel, and nineteenth-century Sanskrit studies, see Aarsleff, pp. 147–159.

46. Eliot, "Beating of a Drum," p. 12.

47. T. S. Eliot, "Tarr," *Egoist* 5 (September 1918): 106. My discussion of the importance of the "primitive" in Eliot's work is indebted to two essays by William Harmon: "T. S. Eliot, Anthropologist and Primitive," *American Anthropologist* 78 (1976): 797–811; "T. S. Eliot's Raids on the Inarticulate," *PMLA* 91 (1976): 450–459.

48. Eliot, "War-paint and Feathers," p. 1036.

49. See Richard Wollheim, "Eliot and F. H. Bradley," in Graham Martin, ed., *Eliot in Perspective* (London: Macmillan, 1970), pp. 185–186. In "Leibniz' Monads and Bradley's Finite Centres" (1916) Eliot quotes the same passage from Bradley's *Appearance and Reality* that he quotes in his notes to *The Waste Land* (KE, 203); he does so, as Wollheim points out, "to illustrate not Bradley's solipsism but rather his ambiguity or ambivalence on the subject of 'the common world.'"

50. Hermann Hesse, "The Brothers Karamazov—The Downfall of Europe," trans. Stephen Hudson, *Dial* 72 (June 1922): 618, 616, 615. In the notes to *The Waste Land* Eliot quotes from the original German version of Hesse's essay, "Die Brüder Karamasoff oder der Untergang Europas," in *Blick ins Chaos* (Bern: Verlag Seldwyla, 1920).

51. Hesse, pp. 614, 609, 611.

52. T. S. Eliot, "The Three Provincialities," *Tyro* 2 (Spring 1922): 13.

WAYNE KOESTENBAUM

The Waste Land: *T. S. Eliot's and Ezra Pound's Collaboration on Hysteria*

It is a curious fact of intellectual history that psychoanalysis was born as a collaboration between two men—Josef Breuer's and Sigmund Freud's *Studies on Hysteria* (1895). The "talking cure" itself grew out of a collaborative relation between Josef Breuer and his patient, Anna O., and so Freud's and Breuer's partnership echoes the psychoanalytic collaboration between doctor and hysteric. Another portrait of hysteria over which two men brooded came forth in England in 1921–22, *The Waste Land*; its manuscript reveals that this supposedly impersonal icon of New Criticism has connections with Eliot's own mental breakdown, and that Ezra Pound's work on the poem transformed it from a "sprawling chaos" into something hard and powerfully disjunctive.[1]

Despite its sibylline discontinuities, *The Waste Land* was taken up as a monument of male modernist propaganda. Joyce wrote that it "ended the idea of poetry for ladies," and Pound commented that "Eliot's *Waste Land* is I think the justification of the 'movement,' of our modern experiment, since 1900."[2] Critics have often sought a male protagonist in the poem, and identified this quest figure with the male reader. In 1934, I. A. Richards described the obstacles this quester faces: "Even the most careful and responsive reader must reread and do hard work before the poem forms itself clearly and unambiguously in his mind.... And it is easy to fail in this

From *Twentieth Century Literature* 34, no. 2 (Summer 1988): 113–139.

undertaking."[3] Delmore Schwartz, in 1945, described Eliot's protagonist—and Eliot himself—as an "international hero," and D. C. Fowler, in 1953, called the poem's protagonist "both hero and king."[4] The poem's heroic readers, whom John Crowe Ransom, in 1966, called "those sturdy people who studied *The Waste Land*," formed a brotherhood of critics who, in Ransom's words, "were tough-minded as they were competent, and when they succeeded they were elated like professional sportsmen over their triumphs."[5]

This sportsman-reader of Eliot's heroic poem has until recently obscured the affinities between the discourse of high male modernism and the discourse of hysteria. Hysteria's ruptures, discontinuities, and absences are similar to the "pre-Oedipal semiotic babble"[6] which Julia Kristeva sees as characteristic of experimental literature. If "for at least a century, the literary avant-garde ... has been introducing ruptures, blank spaces, and holes into language," and if "the moment of rupture and negativity" is feminine, then Eliot's semiotic *Waste Land* has pronounced affiliations with the discourse of the female hysteric.[7]

Hysteria is a disturbance in language; and the very word hysteria has marked it as an affliction of women.[8] In Breuer's and Freud's *Studies on Hysteria*, where the hysterics are all women, female speech is both the illness and the cure: (disordered) talking is the sickness cured by talking. Anna O.'s illness consisted in

> a deep-going functional disorganization of speech. It first became noticeable that she was at a loss to find words.... Later she lost her command of grammar and syntax; she no longer conjugated verbs, and eventually she used only infinitives, for the most part incorrectly formed from weak past participles; and she omitted both the definite and indefinite article. In the process of time she became almost completely deprived of words. She put them together laboriously out of four or five languages and became almost unintelligible.... At times when she was at her best and most free, she talked French and Italian.[9]

Hysterical discontinuities of speech like Anna O.'s, however, offer openings for analytic entrances; the hysteric's riddles cry out for a collaborator's interpretation. Freud considered the female hysteric as an oracle to be shared with his male collaborator and his male reader, for he refers to a patient as "our oracle" (*SH*, p. 276).[10] By interpreting this enigma, Freud becomes a midwife who helps draw sense out of hysteria's "narrow cleft":

> The whole spatially-extended mass of psychogenic material is in this way drawn through a narrow cleft and thus arrives in consciousness cut up, at it were, into pieces or strips. It is the psychoanalyst's business to put these together once more into the organization which he presumes to have existed. (*SH*, p. 291)

If the analyst is a midwife, then the hysteric is a woman in symbolic labor, like Anna O., whose analysis terminated in a hysterical pregnancy. However, when Freud describes the talking cure as a collaboration, he refers to the hysteric as a "he":

> By explaining things to [the patient] ... by giving *him* information about the marvellous world of psychical processes into which we ourselves only gained insight by such analyses, we make *him himself* into a *collaborator*, induce *him* to regard *himself* with the objective interest of an investigator.... (*SH*, p. 282. Emphasis mine.)

Freud's hysterics were, in fact, women, but in order to imagine them as comrades in scientific inquiry, he must think of them as men. By collaborating with his female hysterics, Freud transforms them into male co-investigators; by helping the hysteric talk away her "disturbances of speech," he translates her symptoms of female distress back into masculine language.

Because the manuscript of *The Waste Land* resembles hysterical discourse—a "private theater" of fantasy like Anna O.'s, a female language which Pound, like a psychoanalyst, appropriated and renovated—I will use Breuer's and Freud's collaboration on female hysteria as a paradigm for Pound's and Eliot's collaboration. The collaborative renewal of the poem involves a male relation toward hysterical speech: Pound and Eliot can bond as men because they perceive the discontinuous text to be female. The manuscript, like Vivien, Eliot's "mad" wife, is a female hysteric with whom Pound and Eliot form a triangle. I will argue that the manuscript of *The Waste Land* embodied a desire for Pound's curative arrival; Eliot's act of handing over his "chaotic" poem to another man exists as a gesture intrinsic to the poem, and prior to his actually giving it to Pound.

In the years preceding *The Waste Land*, Eliot was preoccupied with nerves—his own and his wife's; together, they suffered from vague and variously diagnosed emotional and somatic disorders.[11] The progression of his nervousness led to therapeutic retreats to Margate and to Lausanne in 1921, and to the composition of *The Waste Land*: it is now widely understood that Eliot's own mental breakdown was a condition of the poem's composition. Hysteria is a legitimate term for Eliot's affliction; male hysteria—sanctioned as "shell shock" during World War I—certainly existed.[12] Eliot indicates his familiarity with the diagnosis of hysteria in "Sweeney Erect," in which an "epileptic on the bed / Curves backward, clutching at her sides"; Eliot wryly observes, "hysteria / Might easily be misunderstood."[13]

Eliot's most explicit confrontation with hysteria, however, is his prose poem, "Hysteria."[14] Confronting the disease in a woman, Eliot finds it in himself, for the female hysteric is only uncertainly external to the male "I" who observes her: "As she laughed I was aware of becoming involved in her laughter and being part of it...." Lost "in the dark caverns of her throat," he has entered her language, her mouth, a vagina dentata with "unseen muscles" and a row of teeth like "accidental stars." To separate himself from the hysteric, Eliot invokes an "elderly waiter"—a paternal spirit guide, like Pound. But even the waiter is not safe from hysteria: hands "trembling," he gives voice to Eliot's own paralysis in a stutter, like the speech tics of Freud's patient, Frau Emmy von N. (*SH*, pp. 48–105). The waiter repeats, "If the lady and gentleman wish to take their tea in the garden...." The waiter is no help, and Eliot must confront hysteria alone: "I decided that if the shaking of her breasts could be stopped, some of the fragments of the afternoon might be collected, and I concentrated my attention with careful subtlety to that end." Eliot—overcareful, anxious, and hysterical—will fail; he cannot cure hysteria without another man's collaboration. The shaking breasts are the subject he wishes to capture in his poem, and the symbol of his emotional state as he attempts to write that poem. Any movement Eliot makes, single-handedly, toward cohesion, will be tainted by the sympathetic vibrations that the shaking breasts set off in his stuttering language.

Although Eliot had this long poem on his mind as early as 1919,[15] he found himself, like Anna O., "almost completely deprived of words." Feeling that he had "dried up completely," he wrote poems in French to outwit his paralysis—a sort of hysterical conversion from one tongue to another, like Anna O. speaking English because she was suddenly unable to speak her native German (*L*, p. 80). Conrad Aiken related that although every evening Eliot "went home to his flat hoping that he could start writing again ... night after night the hope proved illusory: the sharpened pencil lay unused by the untouched sheet of paper."[16] In 1918, Eliot's doctor ordered him not to write any prose for six months; at Margate, the work he did on *The Waste Land* was against the advice of his doctor, who, according to Eliot, ordered him "to go away at once ... not exert my mind at all and follow his strict rules for every hour of the day."[17] Prohibition against fatiguing brain-work was the cure that women writers like Alice James, Virginia Woolf, and Charlotte Perkins Gilman endured: the doctors treated Eliot, too, like a female hysteric. Eliot's emotional paralysis, in fact, corresponds to the female hysteric's literal paralysis: in 1918, he wrote that "the experiences I have been through have been paralyzing" (*F*, p. xv). In addition, he complained of "an aboulie and emotional derangement which has been a lifelong affliction" (*F*, p. xxii): abulia was a hysterical symptom which Freud's patient, Emmy von N., exhibited. Because the hysteric, in her classic formulation, is invariably female, there is something feminine about Eliot's paralyzed and barren condition as he was contemplating and composing *The Waste Land*. Using the discourse of female hysteria, Eliot invoked the aid of a male analyst.

Conrad Aiken, in fact, believed that an "intrusion" by a psychiatrist catalyzed the composition of *The Waste Land*. A friend of Aiken asked a psychiatrist about Eliot's writing block, and the psychiatrist pronounced that Eliot "thinks he's God." Aiken wrote: "When I told Eliot ... he was literally speechless with rage. The *intrusion*, quite simply, was one that was intolerable."[18] Yet Aiken believed that this strong male figure's "intrusion"—which intensified Eliot's hysterical speechlessness—fertilized his imagination and freed him to write *The Waste Land*. At Lausanne, under the care of Dr. Vittoz, Eliot enjoyed further intrusions, for this doctor performed a laying-on-of-hands similar to the "pressure technique" Freud describes in *Studies on Hysteria*; Freud pressed his hand to the patient's forehead and commanded her to remember what she had repressed.[19] Under the hand of Vittoz, Eliot became as oracular as that patient who, under Freud's hand, fell into a trance and saw "curious signs looking rather like Sanskrit" (*SH*, p. 277). Eliot, too, saw curious Sanskrit signs—*Da*, *Datta*, *Dayadhvam*, and *Shantih*; while under Vittoz' care, Eliot wrote the body of "What the Thunder Said," lines he considered the best in the poem (*F*, p. 129). He was able to compose these lines, paradoxically, *because* of his illness, for, in his essay on Pascal, he wrote that "it is a commonplace that some forms of illness are extremely favorable, not only to religious illumination, but to artistic and literary composition."[20] Eliot's state of grace-through-illness resembles Anna O.'s *condition seconde*, her auto-hypnotic *absence*, "which may well be likened to a dream in view of its wealth of imaginative products and hallucinations, its large gaps of memory and the lack of inhibition and control in its associations" (*SH*, p. 45). Eliot believed that illness could inspire: he was fond of Housman's comment, "I have seldom written poetry unless I was rather out of health," and, in *The Use of Poetry and the Use of Criticism*, he wrote that "ill-health, debility, or anaemia, may ... produce an efflux of poetry in a way approaching the condition of automatic writing."[21] For Eliot, poetic composition was a cathartic birth, like Anna O.'s hysterical childbirth, or the "talking cure" itself: the poet, Eliot believed, "is going to all that trouble, not to communicate with anyone, but to gain relief from acute discomfort," for he "is oppressed by a burden which he must bring to birth in order to bring relief."[22]

Hysteria, in Eliot's prose poem, was a pathology of femininity with which he felt an uneasy sympathy. T. S. and Vivien Eliot spent their marriage sharing this pathology; in 1919, for example, while Vivien complained of migraine, swollen face, tiredness, and depression, Eliot was depressed, bedridden, and exhausted (*L*, p. 94). Vivien's mother feared that her daughter had inherited "moral insanity," one feature of which was her "irregular and over-frequent menstrual cycle"; on the other hand, a doctor told Eliot, "Mr. Eliot, you have the thinnest blood I've ever tested" (*L*, pp. 62–66). Thin-blooded Eliot obliquely associated Vivien's "over-frequent" bleeding with his own less frequent poetry: when Aiken praised Eliot's 1925 *Poems*, he responded "with a printed page torn out of *The Midwives' Gazette*, on which he had underlined in ink" a description of vaginal discharge: "*Blood—mucous—shreds of mucous—purulent offensive discharge.*"[23] The strange conjunction of Vivien's blood, Eliot's use of *The Midwives' Gazette* to characterize his own poetry, his statement that the poet is "oppressed by a burden which he must bring to birth," and Pound's role as midwife of *The Waste Land*, reveal that women, blood, and birth were central to Eliot's poetry, and imply that Vivien embodied the hysteria that *The Waste Land* both suffers and portrays.

Eliot's alliance with Vivien was more than symbolic: she was part of his work. He asked her to accompany him to Margate, where she wrote letters for him; as he worked on *The Waste Land*, "her approval was his prime consideration" (*L*, p. 114). In therapy at Lausanne, his aim was to get well enough to "be able to take some of the burden off Vivien who had had to do so much of the 'thinking' for him in the past" (*L*, p. 150). She found *The Waste Land*'s publication painful, since the poem was so tied to her. "As to Tom's *mind*, I am his mind," she wrote (*L*, pp. 129, 150). Mysteriously confined to an asylum in 1938, she died, still confined, in 1947. It is telling that the two midwives of Eliot's poem of hysteria spent long years in asylums—Vivien at Northumberland House, Pound at St. Elizabeth's. Eliot turned his hysteria into an institution, *The Waste Land*, while Vivien suffered a more literal institutionalization.

The most conspicuous midwife of *The Waste Land* was Ezra Pound, who had a decisive effect on Eliot's life and work. In 1915, Pound stimulated him to begin writing after a lapse of three years, and encouraged him to settle in England and marry Vivien (*L*, p. 150). In personal as well as in poetic matters, Eliot depended on Pound's blunt mediation and superior strength.

Two days after Eliot's marriage, Pound wrote to Eliot's father: "Your son asks me to write this letter, I think he expects me to send you some sort of apologia for the literary life in particular."[24] Eliot's literary life and conjugal life were equally unacceptable to his father, who had not been told of the marriage to Vivien. Indeed, by writing to Eliot's father without speaking of Vivien or of the wedding, Pound poses as a suitor for Eliot's hand in literary marriage, as Eliot embarks on a life led under Pound's wing.

Pound, in fact, was the only person in whom Eliot confided his marital problems (*L*, p. 97).[25] Such confidences facilitated the men's exchange of poetic powers. In an essay on Wordsworth and Coleridge, Eliot describes how male poets influence each other through the mediation of a shared woman:

> This reciprocal influence [of Wordsworth and Coleridge] would hardly have been possible to such a degree without another influence which held the two men together, and affected both of them more deeply than either knew, the influence of a great woman. No woman has ever played so important a part in the lives of two poets at once—I mean their poetic lives—as did Dorothy Wordsworth.[26]

By qualifying "the lives of two poets" with an aside—"I mean their poetic lives"—Eliot indicates that the distinction between life and poetry was not, for him, absolute, and that the woman whom two poets share is a body analogous to the body of poetic work they forge together. Writing to Pound in 1915, Eliot enclosed two poems about formidable women: "Portrait of a Lady," and the still unpublished "Suppressed Complex," about a woman in bed—either asleep or hysterically paralyzed.[27] Discussing "Portrait of a Lady," Eliot makes no distinction between the poem—which he calls the Lady—and the lady who inspired the poem. If a poem about a lady, and a lady herself, were the same, then when Eliot asks Pound to burn "Suppressed Complex" after reading it, he is asking Pound to burn the woman that the poem represents. Eliot sends Pound poems about hysterical or problematic femininity because he can depend on Pound to exorcise the male poet's own identification with the hysterical woman he purports merely to describe.

Given Pound's perceived power over hysteria, it is not surprising that Vivien Eliot should turn to him for advice, and as a go-between in her troubled relations with her husband. In letters, she begs Pound to urge Eliot to rescue her from The Stanboroughs, a hydrotherapy institution, and thanks Pound for his medical attentions; she confesses to Pound her powers as a medium, her ability to fall into trances.[28] Pound's attentions to Vivien's hysteria and to *The Waste Land*'s hysteria are related editorial events, for when Eliot went to Lausanne to be treated by Vittoz, he left his wife in Pound's care—along with, the evidence suggests, the manuscript of *The Waste Land*.[29] Eliot disburdened himself of two hysterical presences—the poem and the wife; he saw Pound as the one who could make both right.

Pound's and Eliot's homosocial literary relations were shadowed by a sometimes disguised misogyny—specifically, a dislike of women writers.[30] In a letter of 1915, Eliot comments disparagingly on how women have taken over literature; in a letter of 1917, he refers to a literary gathering marred by the presence of too many women, and suggests that the men meet separately. Contemporary life, he complains, has become too feminine. In another letter of 1917, he mocks Edith Sitwell (finding the word "shit" in her name), and remarks on the scarcity of gifted women.[31] But a more vituperative misogyny is unleashed in John Quinn's letters to Ezra Pound. John Quinn, a lawyer and agent, helped mastermind the practical and financial aspects of Eliot's literary career; in recognition of those efforts, Eliot gave Quinn the original manuscript of *The Waste Land* after the poem had been published. Though no *miglior fabbro*, Quinn, like Pound, was a man with whom Eliot felt compelled to share his manuscript. Quinn, Pound, and Eliot were close friends; Pound, in fact, introduced Quinn to Eliot. In Quinn's letters to Pound, misogyny is so much the rule, and not the exception, that these attitudes probably served as common ground for the three friends. Eliot's recourse to the phrase "purulent offensive discharge"—the clipping from *The Midwives' Gazette* which Eliot sent Aiken—shares a motive with Quinn's fulminations to Pound about the two women who edited the *Little Review*:

> Without being personal, I think of female literary excrement; washy urinacious menstruations; with the mental stink but without the physical hardihood of the natural skunk ... a feeling of stale urine exuded in the place of the cream of the jest.
>
> Putrid ignorance, imbecile brazenness, banal pretense—that make the sight of a squatting bitch dachshund pouring a sheet of urine into a ditch a poetic, if not a pitiful, sight.
>
> These people seem to sweat urine and probably urinate sweat.
>
> I don't mind the aberrations of a woman who has some openness and elasticity of mind ... but, by God! I don't like the thought of women who seem to exude as well as bathe in piss, if not drink it, or each other's.[32]

These are the sentiments about literary women that distinguish the man whom Eliot gave, in gratitude, his manuscript of *The Waste Land*. Did Eliot and Pound share these sentiments, or merely tolerate them in Quinn? Describing female literary activity as "excrement," and obsessively focusing on a woman's urine, strengthens Quinn's male bond to Pound, and, possibly, to Eliot: the conviction that a woman's urine, excrement, or blood are substances connected to her literary products underlies the omitted Fresca passages from "The Fire Sermon": Quinn's execrations tap the same prejudices as Eliot's description of Fresca's "good old hearty female stench," her reading of *Clarissa* while she produces her "needful stool," or even the typist's "dirty camisoles and stays." Quinn expresses a lascivious hatred that, in muted form, structures Eliot's desire to have a second man launder and bless his *Waste Land*.

Pound and Eliot indulged together in a bawdiness like their friend Quinn's. Eliot wrote (still unpublished) poems with references to penises and sphincters—parts of an epic, "King Bolo and His Great Black Queen"—and incorporated the verses into his letters to Pound (*L*, p. 52). Pound wrote counterparts to Eliot's "King Bolo" verses: in the letter to Eliot in which Pound suggests revisions to *The Waste Land*, Pound includes a series of comic verses, describing himself as midwife, and Eliot as mother, of *The Waste Land*. Unfortunately, Paige expurgated the poem in his *Selected Letters of Ezra Pound*.[33] I will quote the entire poem; the lines that Paige omitted, until now unpublished, I enclose in brackets.

SAGE HOMME

These are the Poems of Eliot
By the Uranian Muse begot;
A Man their Mother was,
A Muse their sire.

How did the printed Infancies result
From Nuptials thus doubly difficult?

If you must needs enquire
Know diligent Reader

That on each Occasion
Ezra performed the caesarean Operation.

E.P.

//////////////.

Cauls and grave clothes he brings,
Fortune's outrageous stings,
About which odour clings,
    Of putrifaction,
Bleichstein's dank rotting clothes
Affect the dainty nose,
He speaks of common woes
    Deploring action.

He writes of A.B.C.s.
And flaxseed poultices,
Observing fate's hard decrees
    Sans satisfaction;
Breeding of animals,
Humans and cannibals,
But above all else of smells
    Without attraction

Vates cum fistula

E.P.

[E.P. hopeless and unhelped

Enthroned in the marmorean skies
His verse omits realities,
Angelic hands with mother of pearl
Retouch the strapping servant girl,

The barman is to blinded him
Silenus bubbling at the brim, (or burbling)
The glasses turn to chalices
Is his fumbling analysis
And holy hosts of hellenists
Have numbed and honied his cervic cysts,
Despite his hebrew eulogists.

Balls and balls and balls again
Can not touch his fellow men.
His foaming and abundant cream
Has coated his world. The coat of a dream;
Or say that the upjut of his sperm
Has rendered his senses pachyderm.

Grudge not the oyster his stiff saliva
Envy not the diligent diver. et in aeternitate]

The first verses revealed that Pound was the midwife of *The Waste Land*, and that Eliot was the mother, but left ambiguous how Eliot had been impregnated. Impregnation depends on sperm that the expurgated verses supply: "His foaming and abundant cream / Has coated his world." Receptive Eliot takes in Pound's sperm, for E.P., the "blinded him" who, merely masturbatory, cannot "touch his fellow men," is the source of this upjutting "cream." Pound, Eliot's male muse, is the Sire of *The Waste Land*.

Pound's talk of sperm here is not an isolated indulgence. Six months earlier, in June 1921, in a postscript to Remy de Gourmont's *The Natural Philosophy of Love*,[34] which Pound had translated, he expatiates on the relation between creativity and sperm, and describes sperm as a shaping force not unlike Coleridge's "esemplastic power." Pound writes: "the brain itself, is, in origin and development, only a sort of great clot of genital fluid held in suspense or reserve," and "creative thought is an act like fecundation, like the male cast of the human seed." Pound asserts that the male has a privileged power to "exteriorize" forms—to create works of art: man is master of "the new upjut, the new bathing of the cerebral tissues in ... *la mousse* of the life sap." The fact that "the mind is an up-jut of sperm" has a particular bearing on the situation of a literary man in London in the 1920s, for Pound likens the phallus "charging, head-on," into "female chaos," to the frustration of "driving any new idea into the great passive vulva of London." Trying to create a revolution in poetry was a phallic act.

Pound's genital essentialism, in the context of his siring of Eliot's poem, and his self-description as source of "foaming and abundant cream," implies a scene of homosexual intercourse between Pound and Eliot. Such a scene clarifies the nature of Eliot's "Uranian muse": the phrase not only refers to Milton's muse, but to the Uranian poets, avowedly homosexual, of the late nineteenth and early twentieth centuries.[35] Rendered "hopeless and unhelped" by the spectacle of Eliot's magnificent (and now manly) *Waste Land*, Pound is "wracked by the seven jealousies," and condemns his own verse as effeminate, decadent "nacre" and "objets d'art": he confesses to Eliot, "I go into nacre and objets d'art."[36] Pound's reference to "foaming and abundant cream" strives to be merely bawdy; so does John Quinn's "feeling of stale urine exuded in the place of the cream of the jest." But dirty jokes supported more unsettling complicities. Eliot took Pound's comic verses seriously enough to suggest that they be published in italics at the beginning of *The Waste Land*—a gesture which would have revealed to all readers that the poem was a collaboration. The substance of Pound's dirty joke is that Eliot has been impregnated by Pound. Fantasies of male maternity buttress male modernism: Pound dates this letter *24 Saturnus, An 1*, signifying that 1921, the year of *Ulysses*' publication, is the Year One of Modernism, and that Joyce's epic gave birth, as it were, to a new world. In the same letter, Pound calls Eliot a "bitch," and refers, in the comic verse, to "his cervic cysts." In another 1921 letter to Eliot, Pound writes that "Yeats has given birth to a son."[37] Pound wished to believe that Joyce, Eliot, and Yeats had each given birth in 1921.

That Eliot's poem-child came from (metaphorical) homosexual intercourse with Pound is underscored by the phrase, "Vates cum fistula," in Pound's comic verse. *Vates cum fistula* means poet with reed-pipe; it also means poet (or seer) with an ulcer in his bowels. The *OED* cites: "Fostering continually this fretting Fistula within the Bowels of the Christian Commonweal." Earlier in the "obstetric" letter of December 1921, Pound wrote, "Some day I shall lose my temper, lie like a shit-arse and say 'Art shd. embellish the umbelicus.'" Paige, in his edition of the letters, omitted the phrase "shit-arse." "Shit-arse," more than jest, reinforces the sense that the male poet has given birth, and that the "umbelicus" of the male poet is in his "arse," site of "his cervic cysts." If "hysterics suffer mainly from reminiscences"—Freud's and Breuer's celebrated sentence—then *The Waste Land* suffers from Eliot's reminiscences of Jean Verdenal, a medical student with literary interests whom Eliot befriended in Paris before the war, and who died in 1915, one month before Eliot's precipitous marriage to Vivien.[38] There is a link between *The Waste Land*'s homosexual conception (Pound's sperm, Eliot's "arse") and the poem's mourning for a dead male beloved. The homosexual "nuptials" of Eliot and Pound replicate the poem's homosexual subtext, but Pound's revisions bury that subtext, for he urges Eliot to omit "The Death of Saint Narcissus," "Song for the Opherion," "Exequy," and "Dirge"—poems which are "elucidative" of Eliot's mourning for Verdenal.[39] Eliot's arguably sexual interest in Verdenal, repressed from the poem, leaves behind hysterical discontinuities.

After Eliot revised the poem, Pound made final suggestions. Paige published Pound's letter, but omitted a telling passage:

> Aristophanes probably depressing, and the native negro phoque melodies of Dixee more calculated to lift the ball-encumbered phallus of man to the proper 8.30, 9.30 or even ten thirty level now counted as the crowning and alarse too often katachrestical summit of human achievement.
>
> I enclose further tracings of an inscription discovered recently in the buildings (?) outworks of the city hall jo-house at Charleston S.C.
>
> May your erection never grow less. I had intended to speak to you seriously on the subject, but you seemed so mountany gay while here in the midst of Paris that the matter slipped my foreskin.[40]

In Paris, what evidence did Pound witness of Eliot being "mountany gay"? Given Pound's yoking of sperm and creativity, the "erection" for which Pound congratulates Eliot is both genital and literary: with Pound's help on *The Waste Land*, Eliot regained sexual potency and literary power. Eliot admitted that he "placed before ... [Pound] in Paris the manuscript of a scrawling, chaotic poem";[41] in his hesitation to claim those discontinuities as signs of power, he resembles Prufrock, unerect, indecisive, unable to come to the point. Pound treats the manuscript of *The Waste Land* as if it were an effeminate Prufrock he wishes to rouse: he "cures" the poem of its hysteria by suggesting that central representations of the feminine be expunged—thereby masculinizing the poem's core—and by urging Eliot to make his language less indecisive. Indeed, Pound's attitude toward *The Waste Land*'s neurasthenia resembled his attitude toward Eliot's sexual neurasthenia: "May your erection never grow less." In my discussion of the changes Pound suggested, I will put aside judgments of literary quality. Focusing merely on Pound's editorial genius—the fact that the passages he cut perhaps deserved to be cut—blinds us to other motives for his excisions. I would like now to suggest a different reading of Pound's Caesarean performance.

Because Pound sought to establish Eliot's primacy in literary history with *The Waste Land*, he disapproved of beginning the poem with an epigraph from Joseph Conrad, a living writer. In the "obstetric" letter, Pound wrote to Eliot: "I doubt if Conrad is weighty enough to stand the citation." I suspect that Pound objected not merely to Conrad's lack of eminence, but to the content of the epigraph: a passage from *Heart of Darkness*—"The horror! the horror!"—it records a man's fear of the dark continent. Beginning the poem with a cry of emasculated terror would not help keep Eliot erect. However, in this letter to Eliot, Pound echoes the very language of horror he disliked in the epigraph: "(It also, to your horror probably, reads aloud very well. Mouthing out his OOOOOOze.)" Pound uses words that reflect *The Waste Land*'s fear of things that gape: he mentions "the body of the poem," and describes his "Sage Homme" verses as a "bloody impertinence," which should be placed "somewhere where they would be decently hidden and swamped by the bulk of the accompanying matter." Pound's language of mouths, horror, blood, and swamps echoes Eliot's characterization of his own poems as a woman's "purulent offensive discharge."

Pound separated Eliot's verse from female discharge by critiquing Eliot's moments of identification with feminine behavior. Pound questioned Eliot's lines—"'You gave me hyacinths first a year ago'; / 'They called me the hyacinth girl'" (*F*, p. 7)—with the marginal annotation, "Marianne," which, according to Richard Ellman, refers to that woman of letters, Marianne Moore.[42] Did Pound object to these lines because Eliot, by using quotation, was adopting the style of Marianne Moore, a woman writer? Or, recognizing that "hyacinth" signified homosexuality, did Pound dislike the passage because Eliot was impersonating a hyacinth girl? Valerie Eliot, in a footnote to the facsimile, asserts that by "Marianne," Pound meant Tennyson's Mariana. Perhaps Pound disapproved of Eliot's identification with Mariana, hardly a masculine, decisive figure; indeed, she was a pining hysteric and an emblem of the Victorian poetry which, by Pound's modernist credo, signified effeteness. Pound also questions the lines—

> "My nerves are bad tonight. Yes, bad. Stay with me.
> "Speak to me. Why do you never speak? Speak.
> "What are you thinking of? What thinking? ~~Think~~ What?
> "I never know what you are thinking. Think."

—with the annotation, "photography," and disputes the line—"Are you alive, or not? Is there nothing in your head?"—with the same criticism, "photo" (*F*, pp. 11, 13). Pound faulted the lines for being photographic—cheaply realistic, insufficiently wrought by artistic muscle—and for the scene which was being photographed: the lines portray Eliot as neurasthenic, silent, unable to satisfy his wife, and portray Vivien as hysterically adamant. "Is there nothing in your head?" is a photograph of Eliot as absence, the gaping "horror" of the canceled epigraph; Pound did not want Eliot to admit affinities with Prufrock. Vivien, the camera's subject, commented that these lines were "WONDERFUL," and added a further photographic line which Eliot kept: "What you get married for if you don't want to have children." Vivien's line concerns a woman's refusal to comply with a marriage's demands, but this passage's core is not the woman's refusal to have children, but the man's sexual failure.

Another portrait of a lady that Pound blotted out was the Fresca section in "The Fire Sermon." In the typescript, Pound dismissed the whole passage with the comment—"Rhyme drags it out to diffuseness"—but only crossed out the four lines which portrayed Fresca as a poet:

> From such chaotic misch-masch potpourri
> What are we to expect but poetry?
> When restless nights distract her brain from sleep
> She may as well write poetry, as count sheep.
>
> (*F*, p. 41)

Eliot had described his own poem as "chaotic"; Pound called it a "masterpiece."[43] Pound's role as collaborator and editor is to separate Eliot's chaotic *Waste Land* from Fresca's chaotic potpourri, Eliot's masterpiece from Fresca's hysteric fits, and Eliot's Uranian Muse from Fresca's forays into homosexual and lesbian writers: "Fresca was baptised in a soapy sea / Of Symonds—Walter Pater—Vernon Lee." Pound's revisions intend to save Eliot from seeming like Symonds. By crossing out Fresca, Pound suggests that Eliot begin "The Fire Sermon" with the "I": "Musing upon the king my brother's wreck / And on the king my father's death before him." Pound only tolerated the tableau of the dead king and the wrecked brother because their dismemberment and ruin did not infect Eliot's language with symptoms of decline.

Pound particularly objected to syntactic inversion; and syntactic inversion, in turn, suggests sexual inversion. "Inversion" was one of the fin de siècle's words for "homosexual"; the word was most notoriously circulated by John Addington Symonds' and Havelock Ellis' *Sexual Inversion*. In a letter to Eliot, Pound wrote, "I should leave it as it is, and NOT invert," and in the manuscript, he commented, "inversions not warranted by any real exigence of metre" (*F*, p. 45). Syntactic inversion, a dated poetic affectation, implied for Pound the decadent world of "nacre" and "objets d'art." Pound wrote "1880" and "Why this Blot on Scutchen *between* 1922 and Lil'" beside the following lines:

> And if it rains, the closed carriage at four.
> And we shall play a game of chess:
> The ivory men make company between us
> Pressing lidless eyes and waiting for a knock upon the door.
>
> (*F*, p. 13)

These lines clashed with the modernity of the surrounding "O O O O that Shakespeherian Rag" and "HURRY UP PLEASE IT'S TIME." But Pound's annotation, "1880," also found fault with the scene of sexual inaction between the husband and wife; Pound accused Eliot of a stylistic as well as sexual listlessness. Modernism defined itself in opposition to that "1880" of literary and sexual decadence.

In keeping with his wish to remove traces of inversion from the poem, Pound quibbles with Eliot's diminutives, writing "'one' wee red mouse" (from a Rudyard Kipling poem) in the margin of Eliot's "From which one tender Cupidon peeped out" (*F*, p. 11). Similarly, Pound put a box of disparagement around the word "little" in the lines, "Carrying / Away the little light dead people" (*F*, p. 13). In the passage,

> Above the antique mantel was displayed
> In pigment, but so lively, you had thought
> A window gave upon the sylvan scene,

he objected to the "had": "had is the weakest point" (*F*, p. 11). Pound deplored the weakness of "little" in the line, "Spread out in little fiery points of will," and objected to the phrase "of will" because it was a "dogmatic deduction but wobbly as well." Pound weeded out echoes of Prufrock: writing "Pruf[rock]" and "cadence reproduction from Pr[ufrock] or Por[trait of a Lady]" in the margins, Pound objected to "Time to regain the door" and to "And if I said 'I love you' should we breathe / Hear music, go a-hunting, as before?" (*F*, p. 107). Instead of the inverted "should we breathe," he suggested the straightforward "we should breathe." To be Prufrock and to be inverted were pathologies that Pound wished to cure.

Accusing Eliot of Prufrock's indecision, Pound writes, beside the line, "Across her brain one half-formed thought may pass": "make up yr. mind you Tiresias if you know know damn well or else you don't" (*F*, p. 47). By assuming that Tiresias, though bisexual, at least knows his mind, Pound expresses that it is possible to embrace bisexuality without losing stylistic decisiveness. Tiresias, then, is the key to Eliot's cure: Pound teaches Eliot, through the example of Tiresias, that one can be inverted *and* a masterpiece. In a footnote to *The Waste Land*, Eliot declares that Tiresias is "the most important personage in the poem," the character where "the two sexes meet." Pound convinced Eliot, by addressing him as Tiresias, that this androgynous seer was the poem's center.

Pound encourages Eliot to act, whatever the sexual act in question may be. Where the "I" makes a date with the apparently homosexual Mr. Eugenides, Eliot had vacillated: Mr. Eugenides

asked me, in ~~abominable~~ French,
To luncheon at the Cannon Street Hotel,
And perhaps a weekend at the Metropole.
(*F*, p. 43)

Beside the "perhaps," Pound wrote: "Damn per'apsez."

In a 1922 volume of short stories about unmarried and implicitly homosexual men and women, George Moore used the word "perhaps" to signify a state of Tiresias-like androgyny, a pathological indecision about gender and sexual preference: "neither man nor woman, just a perhapser," sighs one of Moore's celibates.[44] Pound thought that Eliot's reliance on "perhaps" signified a similar indecisiveness: "perhaps" is the symptom of Eliot's inability to act, erotically or linguistically. Pound cures this hysteria by omitting the "perhaps," encouraging Eliot's "I" to indulge in that illicit weekend. In the margin of the line, "Perhaps his inclinations touch the stage," Pound wrote "Perhaps be damned" (*F*, p. 45). Pound seizes on that "perhaps"—the code for Eliot's ambiguous "inclinations"—as his primary hysterical symptom. Pound objects to a third "perhaps," writing "Georgian" beside the line, "Perhaps it does not come to very much" (*F*, p. 99). This Georgian line occurs in the context of the narrator's fear of sexual action: "The golden foot I may not kiss or clutch / Glowed in the shadow of the bed." This "I" is a Prufrock, afraid of desire and of direct statement; the golden foot he may not kiss or clutch is a poetic foot. Eliot's fear that "perhaps it does not come to very much" is a fear that the poem, *The Waste Land*, does not come to very much. Crossing out that doubt, Pound asserts the poem's power.

When Eliot confessed hysterical speechlessness—"I could not speak"—Pound underlined the phrase (*F*, p. 7). Did Pound dislike that confession, or did he underscore it because he recognized its importance? By emphasizing the words, Pound points out that Eliot *has* spoken, that the very act of confessing "I could not speak" means that silence is over. By articulating hysteria, Eliot conquers it, for Pound is always there to hear the hysterical utterance. I will now look at these articulations of hysteria.

The Waste Land was originally called "He Do the Police in Different Voices." The poem lost this title but remained inhabited by different voices and characters, many of them hysterical women. Eliot may have been trying to do the police—a symbol of male authority—but he ended up doing *woman* in different voices. The original title implied those states of speech which Freud described as "oracular," when the hysteric utters cryptic fragments, like the "I want to die" of the epigraph's Sibyl. Because the first line, "April is the cruellest month," repeats the Sibyl's death wish, the opening lines seem to be spoken by her. The metamorphosing speaker of the poem—now a sibyl, now Marie, now Tiresias—is herself or himself a hysteric, moving, like Charcot's Geneviève, through the stylized phases of a fit.

In *The Waste Land*, the Sibyl is the representation of Eliot's death wish, and his own vatic powers, as feminine. The poem's second sibyl is Madame Sosostris, "known to be the wisest woman in Europe"—a female Ezra Pound, whom Eliot certainly thought the wisest *man* in Europe, a soothsayer guiding Eliot toward his destiny. Like frigid Marie, who goes "south in the winter," Madame Sosostris suffers from the hysteric's chronic neuralgia: she has a "bad cold." Madame Sosostris, like Ezra Pound, reads Eliot's cards—the leaves of *The Waste Land*'s manuscript, which Pound, as late as 1969, called "the lost leaves" (*F*, p. xii). If the fragments of the poem are sibyl's leaves, then Pound is Madame Sosostris. In that seer, Eliot reconciles two contradictory representations of the hysteric: fraudulent, frigid malingerer, and oracle.

The other female hysteric in "The Burial of the Dead" is Marie, the poem's first "I" (if we do not count the epigraph): the sexless speaker of "April is the cruellest month" metamorphoses into Marie's "I":

> And when we were children, staying at the archduke's,
> My cousin's, he took me out on a sled,
> And I was frightened. He said, Marie,
> Marie, hold on tight. And down we went.
> In the mountains, there you feel free.
> I read, much of the night, and go south in the winter.

This apparently affectless reminiscence reads like a childhood trauma in *Studies on Hysteria*, a memory without meaning or emotional charge. Marie remembers nothing but holding on tight to her male cousin, going down, and feeling free. She is a reader, like Madame Sosostris, who reads the cards, or Fresca, who reads the "pathetic tale of Richardson" (*F*, p. 23); the implication of Marie's nocturnal reading is either that she is i somniac, or that she is *not* having sex "much of the night." Her sexual desires are repressed, with her childhood trauma, and as Eliot went to Lausanne, she goes south, in search of warmth and a cure.

Marie's male counterpart in "The Burial of the Dead" is the speaker who remembers the scene in the hyacinth garden—a reminiscence like Marie's, uprooted from its context, unexplained: "... I could not / Speak, and my eyes failed, I was neither / Living nor dead, and I knew nothing ..." Anna O. suffered loss of speech, as well as "a high degree of restriction of the field of vision: in a bunch of flowers which gave her much pleasure she could only see one flower at a time" (*SH*, p. 26). Eliot's vision here is restricted not to one flower, but to one head of hair—the hyacinth girl's wet hair, which provokes hysterical loss of speech and vision. Images of women's hair return in the Medusa ("Around that head the scorpion hissed!" [*F*, p. 117]) and the woman who "drew her long black hair out tight / And fiddled whisper music on those strings."

This Medusa, who represents one trauma beneath Eliot's hysteria, as well as a projection of Eliot's own vatic verbal incandescence, reappears on a "burnish'd throne" in "A Game of Chess." Eliot uses Elizabethan and neoclassical styles for misogynistic ends: this passage's satiric thrust arises from dread of the woman's supremacy. She holds court over an array of vials which "troubled, confused / And drowned the sense in odors," like the voices at the end of "Prufrock." The smell of a woman—"Is it perfume from a dress / That makes me so digress?"—drowns Eliot's "sense": his sight. The speaker's eyes failed when he saw the hyacinth girl; that blind man returns in the Cleopatra set piece as a golden Cupidon who "hid his eyes behind his wing." What he wishes not to see is the woman on the burnished throne, on the seat of power. When the men in the poem, like Tiresias—or Tom, "boiled to the eyes, blind," at Tom's place—lapse into states of hysterical absence, and lose vision, the women ascend to the throne, where they are then dethroned by Eliot's satiric neoclassical voice (*F*, p. 5).

The male "I" admits "I could not speak"; Philomel is too far gone in her hysteria for even those four words. Raped and tongueless, she converts her speech into unintelligible bird-song, the hysteric's alternative language. She relives her trauma in hysterical code that is powerless as protest: "yet there the nightingale / Filled all the desert with inviolable voice / And still she cried, and still the world pursues, / 'Jug jug' to dirty ears." Philomel metamorphoses into Vivien: "My nerves are bad tonight. Yes, bad. Stay with me. / Speak to me. Why do you never speak. Speak." This wife is supposedly the hysteric, but it is her husband—like the man in the hyacinth garden passage—who cannot speak or see, and who can only remember "Those are pearls that were his eyes." Vivien is the interrogating analyst: "Do / You know nothing? Do you see nothing? Do you remember / Nothing?" Under the pressure of her questions he breaks into a song—"O O O O that Shakespeherian Rag": this rag is "Full Fathom Five," which signifies Phlebas the drowned Phoenician, and, obliquely, the dead Verdenal. Memories of dead men induce the poem's hysteria. If Tom Eliot is "boiled to the eyes, blind," he can remain blind to his own love for the drowned man. Blindness—as hysterical symptom—signifies the fact that a memory of some erotic significance has been drowned.

Drowned Phlebas is the male version of the drowned Ophelia. When Ophelia, the Victorian's favorite image of the madwoman, intones "Good night, ladies, good night, sweet ladies, good night, good night," she performs a poetic closure that eluded Eliot. By using the voice of a madwoman to end "A Game of Chess," which contained a "photographic" portrait of his own marriage to Vivien, Eliot demonstrates how deeply he identifies with her "Shakespeherian" hysteria. This ending—"Good night, ladies"—is parallel to the ending of "The Burial of the Dead"—"You! hypocrite lecteur!—mon semblable,—mon frère!" Both endings address the reader; in one, Eliot impersonates Baudelaire, and addresses the reader as brother, and in the other, he impersonates Ophelia, and addresses the reader as sister—"sweet ladies." Ophelia—with Verdenal and Phlebas—is drowned by the poem's hysterical discourse. She drowns to the interjected, syncopated tune of "HURRY UP PLEASE IT'S TIME," a hysterical feature of Eliot's text: it is a formulaic screen, a verbal tic that punctuates and disturbs the narrative, and leads to the shutting down of all rational speech, represented by the closing of Albert's bar ("Tom's place," Tom Eliot's mind) and by the allusion to Ophelia's madness and drowning.

In the original "Fire Sermon," Eliot satirized what Fresca reads; however, like Madame Sosostris' cards, what she reads is close to the poem's heart. Eliot first intended her to read "a page of Gibbon," whose chronicle of imperial decline suggests "broken Coriolanus" and his "falling towers" (*F*, p. 23). Eliot, however, replaced her "page of Gibbon" with "the Daily Mirror": In Dickens' *Our Mutual Friend*, Sloppy, who does the police in different voices, is a "beautiful reader of a newspaper," and so Fresca's reading of newspapers is connected to the activity of the poem's original male subject (*F*, p. 125). Fresca also reads "the pathetic tale of Richardson," *Clarissa Harlowe*: Clarissa, like Philomel, was raped. Like tongueless Philomel, and speechless Eliot (in the hyacinth garden), Fresca has "much to say—/ But cannot say it—that is just my way" (*F*, p. 23). However, Eliot distances himself, through satire, from this image of the poet as a depressed woman who "scribbles verses of such gloomy tone / That cautious critics say, her style is quite her own" (*F*, p. 27). He must distance himself from her because hysteria and poetry spring from the same source:

The Scandinavians bemused her wits,
The Russians thrilled her to hysteric fits.
From such chaotic misch-masch potpourri
What are we to expect but poetry?
When restless nights distract her brain from sleep
She may as well write poetry, as count sheep.
(*F*, p. 27)

Like Marie in "The Burial of the Dead," who spent her sleepless nights reading, Fresca writes poetry much of the night.

Eliot's misogynistic portrait of Fresca, however, is a screen: on the back of the first page of the "Fresca" typescript, Eliot penciled the first draft of the opening lines of "The Fire Sermon" as we know it: "The rivers tent is broken and the last fingers of leaf / Clutch and sink into the wet bank" (*F*, p. 25). This passage depicts disappointed sexuality; "the loitering heirs of City directors" have abandoned their "nymphs." In this free-verse irruption of his own voice behind the screen of the clipped couplets of the Fresca satire, Eliot repudiates the misogynistic projection of hysteria onto women, and recognizes that the experience of being "broken"—"the river's tent is broken," "the broken fingernails of dirty hands," "a broken Coriolanus"—is the story of his own dejection. The last words on the verso of the Fresca passage are "By the waters." When completed, the line reads "By the waters of Leman I sat down and wept," a reference to himself recovering from hysteria at Lausanne (on Lake Geneva, also called Lake Leman). When Eliot abandons misogynistic satire, he returns to autobiography: the hysterical technique of the poem results from his only fitful ability to speak directly from painful experience.

In the figure of Tiresias, Eliot experiences his affinity with the female hysterics of the poem. Through that bisexual seer, Eliot acknowledges that a male body can exist in conjunction with the oracular and hysterical powers of a Madame Sosostris. Tiresias' blindness allies him with the male hysteric whose sight fails when he sees the hyacinth girl, and with "old Tom, boiled to the eyes, blind"; with his "wrinkled female breasts," he resembles the woman in "Hysteria," whose shaking breasts were an emblem of her hysteria. Through Tiresias, Eliot enters the female typist's consciousness, for Tiresias, with the typist, "awaited the expected guest." Crucially, Tiresias enables Eliot to experience vicariously the sexual advances of the man who "assaults at once," for Tiresias foresuffers all.

All of the women in the poem—Philomel, the typist, the Rhine Maidens, Tiresias—are sexually violated, and respond in hysterical code to this violation. "Twit twit twit / Jug jug jug jug jug jug" (like the "Drip drop drip drop drop drop drop" of Eliot's water-dripping song, which he considered the sign of his cure) comes from a condition like Anna O.'s "deep-going functional disorganization" of speech in "moments of extreme anxiety"; indeed, Anna O.'s feeling of "profound darkness in her head, of not being able to think, of becoming blind and deaf, of having two selves" resembles Tiresias—double and blind—and the husband in "A Game of Chess," whose wife accuses him of knowing, seeing, and speaking nothing (*SH*, p. 24). What the Rhine Maidens know is that their river has been violated, its gold stolen: "weialala leia" is the hysteric response to that violation. A Rhine Maiden gives voice to Eliot's own experience of breakdown at Margate:

> 'On Margate Sands.
> I can connect
> Nothing with nothing.
> The broken fingernails of dirty hands.

Eliot first wrote "He had / I still feel the pressure of dirty hand" (*F*, p. 53)—but as Coriolanus falls from power and becomes "broken," the "I" who feels the pressure of the dirty hand is repressed, and Eliot leaves a predicate—"The broken fingernails of dirty hands"—without a subject who experiences it. More than fingernails are broken: "broken" is the sign of Eliot's sexual failure, shattered memory, and disorganized language. At the end of "The Fire Sermon," the quotation marks which placed Eliot's linguistic hysteria in the voice of a Rhine Maiden vanish, and he becomes the "I":

> la la
>
> To Carthage then I came
>
> Burning burning burning burning
> O Lord Thou pluckest me out
> O Lord Thou pluckest
>
> burning

Repression plucks away, word by word, his language.

Losing his language, Eliot resembles Anna O., who, deprived of words, "put them together laboriously out of four or five languages and became almost unintelligible." Each of the poem's five sections traces the same trajectory of depletion: memories of enacted desire return so intensely that by each section's end, Eliot's language is fractured. In the conclusion of "The Fire Sermon," the hysteria of "Burning burning burning burning" arises from the sexual scenes that came earlier: the intercourse of typist and young man, Philomel's rape, the Rhine Maidens' violation, the trysts of the nymphs and their City Directors, and the narrator's weekend with Mr. Eugenides. In "What the Thunder Said," the hysteria of the final pastiche of tongues is a response to Eliot's return, within that section of the poem, to the moment in the hyacinth garden: "My friend, blood shaking my heart / The awful daring of a moment's surrender / Which an age of prudence can never retract." In this passage, Eliot remembers a surrender so awful no repression can thoroughly bury it. In "What the Thunder Said," desire is ultimately stronger than prudence, for desire returns when broken Coriolanus revives, and when language resurges in "Here is no water." These revivals are followed by the conclusion's extreme retreat from desire into hysteria:

> London bridge is falling down falling down falling down
>
> *Poi s'ascose nel foco che gli affina*
> *Quando fiam ceu chelidon*—O swallow swallow
> *Le Prince d'Aquitaine à la tour abolie*
> These fragments I have shored against my ruins
> Why then Ile fit you. Hieronymo's mad againe.
> Datta. Dayadhvam. Damyata.
>
> Shantih shantih shantih

The disorderly endings of "The Fire Sermon" and "What the Thunder Said" translate sexual desire into religious language. The "burning" of desire alternates with a passionate prayer, "O Lord Thou pluckest"; the sexual violation coded in "O swallow swallow," and the sexual impotence figured in "*Le Prince d'Aquitaine à la tour abolie*" (abulia?) or "London bridge is falling down," give way to the mysticism of "Shantih." Similarly, the *attitude passionnelle* of the hysteric involved enactments of alternately sexual and spiritual ecstasy. "Burning burning burning burning" is a linguistic *attitude passionnelle*, like a tableau of Charcot's Geneviève, who "would fall and tumble on the floor as if making love, then in a minute strike the crucifixion pose or be in ecstasy like a saint."[45]

As hysterical discourse, *The Waste Land* remains passive: it invites a reader to master it. Unwilling to explain itself or move past hysterical disjunction, requiring a reader-as-collaborator ("mon semblable,—mon frère!") to unravel its disguises, it is a feminine text, and implies a male reader. Eliot's abulia creates antitheses of itself in the "flushed and decided" young man carbuncular, or the sailor (in excised portions from "Death by Water") who aims his "concentrated will against the tempest and the tide" (*F*, p. 63). Despite these representations of masculine agency, the poem's heart is in its passivity toward interpretation, the moments of collage or fragmentation which place enormous faith in the reader as analyst. In this sense, Eliot's manuscript was already inscribed with the necessity for a second man, Pound, to interpret its absences. Eliot's attitude toward his own poem as merely "chaotic" and his passivity toward revision correspond to a femaleness which we find in the poem itself. Eliot could "connect nothing with nothing"; it remained for Pound to redefine disjunction, to convert female hysteria, through male collaboration, back into a discourse of male power. Indeed, Pound's revisions changed *The Waste Land* from a series of *poems* into a unity which Pound trumpeted as "the longest *poem* in the English langwidge," nineteen pages "without a break."[46] Eliot owed Pound this illusion of seamlessness, and the accompanying sense of power.

Pound's symbolic act of taking up the poem, revising it, giving it value, and Eliot's symbolic act of surrendering his poem to Pound, convert the female text into an object within a homosocial economy. Similarly, the hysterical discourse of Anna O. lost meaning as female language when it was exchanged between Breuer and Freud, when its rebellious if not revolutionary language was subsumed within a text produced by two men. Luce Irigaray observes that "women are marked phallicly by their fathers, husbands, procurers": Pound fathered, husbanded, and procured Eliot's feminine *Waste Land*, and marked it as male.[47] By giving his text to Pound, Eliot set up the paradigm for the relationship that readers and critics have established with *The Waste Land*: man to man.

Eliot's footnotes are the embodiment of the implied male reader: they are an invitation to him. They demonstrate that the poem has absences which an external body must fill. The footnotes valorize the poem's hysteria, and convert it from meaningless chaos into allusiveness. Readers armed with the notes have approached *The Waste Land* not as if it were a fragment of hysterical discourse, but an artifact already converted, by Pound's mediation, into something masculine. Conrad Aiken, on the poem's publication, wrote that it succeeds "by virtue of its incoherence, not of its plan": if a woman had written a text with the properties of *The Waste Land*, its incoherence might not have been judged successful.[48] *The Waste Land* has always been a scene of implicit collaboration between the male poet and his male reader, in which Eliot's hysterical discourse, by the act of collusive, collaborative interpretation—by the reader's analytic listening—suffers a sea change into masculinity.

Notes

I wish to thank Sandra M. Gilbert, Andrew Kappel, A. Walton Litz, and Elaine Showalter, who read earlier drafts of this essay, and offered valuable suggestions.

 Acknowledgment is given, as well, to the Collection of American Literature, Beinecke Rare Book and Manuscript Library, Yale University.

1. T. S. Eliot, quoted in Ronald Bush, *T. S. Eliot: A Study in Character and Style* (New York: Oxford Univ. Press, 1983), p. 70.

2. Quoted in Richard Ellman, "The First Waste Land," in A. Walton Litz, ed., *Eliot in His Time* (Princeton: Princeton Univ. Press, 1973), p. 51; quoted in Litz, "The Waste Land Fifty Years After," in Litz, *Eliot in His Time*, p. 4.

3. I. A. Richards, "The Poetry of T. S. Eliot," in Jay Martin, ed., *A Collection of Critical Essays on The Waste Land* (Englewood Cliffs, N.J.: Prentice-Hall, 1968).

4. D. C. Fowler, in Martin, *Critical Essays*, pp. 97, 35.

5. John Crowe Ransom, in Martin, *Critical Essays*, p. 15.

6. Julia Kristeva, "Oscillation between 'Power' and 'Denial,'" in Elaine Marks and Isabelle de Courtivron (editors), *New French Feminisms* (New York: Schocken Books, 1981), pp. 166–67.

7. Dianne Hunter, "Hysteria, Psychoanalysis, and Feminism: The Case of Anna O.," *Feminist Studies*, 9 (1983), 474.

8. My account of hysteria depends largely on Elaine Showalter, *The Female Malady: Women, Madness, and English Culture, 1830–1980* (New York: Pantheon Books, 1985).

9. Josef Breuer and Sigmund Freud, *Studies on Hysteria*, trans. James Strachey (New York: Basic Books), p. 46. Subsequent references are cited parenthetically in the text as *SH*.

10. For a discussion of the archetype of the sibyl, see Nina Auerbach, *Women and the Demon: The Life of a Victorian Myth* (Cambridge, Mass.: Harvard Univ. Press, 1982).

11. My account of the Eliots' marriage, and of their ailments, depends on Peter Ackroyd, *T. S. Eliot: A Life* (New York: Simon and Schuster, 1984). Subsequent references are cited parenthetically in the text as *L*.

12. See Showalter, *The Female Malady*, chap. 7; see also Sandra M. Gilbert, "Soldier's Heart: Literary Men, Literary Women, and the Great War," *Signs*, 8 (1983), 422–50.

13. T. S. Eliot, *The Complete Poems and Plays, 1909–1950* (New York: Harcourt, 1971), p. 25.

14. *Ibid.*, p. 19.

15. See T. S. Eliot, *The Waste Land: A Facsimile and Transcript of the Original Drafts Including the Annotations of Ezra Pound*, edited and with an introduction by Valerie Eliot (New York: Harcourt, 1971), xviii. I will not give line references for quotations from *The Waste Land*, but will give page references to the facsimile (cited as *F*) when discussing Pound's comments or omitted passages.

16. Quoted in Bush, *T. S. Eliot*, p. 56.

17. See Grover Smith, "The Waste Land in the Making," *The Waste Land* (London: Allen & Unwin, 1983), p. 67, and Harry Trosman, "T. S. Eliot and *The Waste Land*: Psychopathological Antecedents and Transformations," *Archives of General Psychiatry*, 30, No. 5 (May 1974), 709–17.

18. Conrad Aiken, "An Anatomy of Melancholy," in Allen Tate, *T. S. Eliot: The Man and His Works* (New York: Dell, 1966), p. 195.

19. See Trosman, "T. S. Eliot and *The Waste Land*," for an account of Dr. Vittoz' methods.

20. T. S. Eliot, "The *Pensèes* of Pascal," *Essays, Ancient and Modern* (London: Faber, 1936), p. 142.

21. See Bush, *T. S. Eliot*, p. 56; T. S. Eliot, "The Modern Mind," *The Use of Poetry and the Use of Criticism* (London: Faber, 1980), p. 144.

22. Quoted in James Miller, *T. S. Eliot's Personal Waste Land* (Philadelphia: Penn. State Univ. Press, 1977), p. 43.

23. Quoted in Bush, *T. S. Eliot*, p. 8.

24. Letter to Henry Ware Eliot, Sr., June 28, 1915, in the Beinecke Library, Yale University.

25. For an account of Pound's and Eliot's relationship, see Donald Gallup, *T. S. Eliot and Ezra Pound: Collaborators in Letters* (New Haven: Yale Univ. Press, 1970).

26. Eliot, *The Use of Poetry and the Use of Criticism*, p. 70.

27. Letter to Ezra Pound, Feb. 2, 1915, in the Beinecke Library, Yale University.

28. These undated letters of Vivien Eliot are in the Beinecke Library, Yale University.

29. Bush, *T. S. Eliot*, p. 55.

30. For an account of homosociality, and its relation to misogyny, see Eve Kosofsky Sedgwick, *Between Men: English Literature and Male Homosocial Desire* (New York: Columbia Univ. Press, 1985).

31. Letter to Pound, Apr. 15, 1915; letter to Pound, Sept. 23, 1917; letter to Pound, Oct. 31, 1917. All three letters are in the Beinecke Library, Yale University.

32. Letter to Pound, Oct. 16, 1920. I have excerpted these passages from a longer letter.

33. D. D. Paige, *The Letters of Ezra Pound* (New York: New Directions, 1971), p. 170. The letter is dated 24 Saturnus, An 1. Unexpurgated Paige transcription of the letter is in the Beinecke Library, Yale University.

34. Remy de Gourmont, *The Natural Philosophy of Love*, trans. and with a postscript by Ezra Pound (London: Neville Spearman, 1957). I thank A. Walton Litz for leading me to Pound's postscript.

35. See Timothy d'Arch Smith, *Love in Earnest: Some Notes on the Lives and Writings of English "Uranian" Poets from 1889–1930* (London: Routledge and Kegan Paul, 1970).

36. See letter to Eliot, Dec. 24, 1921, in Paige, *The Letters of Ezra Pound*, p. 169. In a letter to John Quinn, Pound restated, in similar words, his fear of artistic decadence: "I don't want to go soft, or get to producing merely 'objets d'art' instead of 'oeuvres.'" Quoted in B. L. Reid, *The Man from New York: John Quinn and His Friends* (New York: Oxford Univ. Press, 1968), p. 437.

37. Pound's letter to his mother, Sept. 18, 1921, in the Beinecke Library, Yale University.

38. See Miller, *T. S. Eliot's Personal Waste Land*.

39. In a letter to Pound, Eliot described the original epigraph to the poem as "somewhat elucidative." Paige, *The Letters of Ezra Pound*, p. 171.

40. Paris letter to Eliot, numbered 182 in Paige, *The Letters of Ezra Pound*, and dated approximately January 1922. Unexpurgated Paige transcription of the letter is in the Beinecke Library, Yale University.

41. Quoted in Bush, *T. S. Eliot*, p. 70.

42. Ellman, "The First Waste Land," p. 65.

43. Paige, *The Letters of Ezra Pound*, p. 173.

44. George Moore, *Celibate Lives* (London: Chatto and Windus, 1922), p. 80. I thank Elaine Showalter for pointing out to me Moore's "perhapsers."

45. See Showalter, *The Female Malady*, pp. 150–54; quotation from George Frederick Drinka, *The Birth of Neurosis: Myth, Malady, and the Victorians* (New York: Simon and Schuster, 1984), pp. 95–96.

46. Paige, The Letters of Ezra Pound, p. 169.

47. Luce Irigaray, *This Sex Which Is Not One*, trans. Catherine Porter (Ithaca, N.Y.: Cornell Univ. Press, 1985), p. 31.

48. Aiken, "An Anatomy of Melancholy," p. 202.

ERIC W. SIGG

Being Between Two Lives: *Reading* The Waste Land

> [Dandyism is] above all a burning need to acquire originality, within the apparent bounds of convention. It is a sort of cult of oneself, which can dispense even with what are commonly called illusions. It is the delight in causing astonishment, and the proud satisfaction of never oneself being astonished.
>
> Charles Baudelaire, "The Painter of Modern Life"

> Man is an analogist, and studies relations in all objects.
>
> Emerson, "Nature"

> The essential Relativity of all knowledge, thought, or consciousness cannot but show itself in language. If everything that we know is viewed as a transition from something else, every experience must have two sides; and either every name must have a double meaning, or else for every meaning there must be two names.
>
> Alexander Bain, *Logic: Deductive and Inductive*, Book 1, Chapter 1

Though it is rare to find a discussion that does not add to one's understanding of *The Waste Land*, a sense nonetheless persists that something about the poem remains disembodied, out of context, just beyond critical

From *The American T. S. Eliot: A Study of the Early Writings*, pp. 185–218. © 1989 by Cambridge University Press.

reach. However necessary, the decades of source hunting and literary sleuthing proved to be only an intermediate stage that, far from slowing down the proliferation of interpretation, probably accelerated it. Despite renewed attention to *The Waste Land* recently, asking "How do we read this poem?" remains a legitimate question. Perhaps it is the only question. Yet as if this fundamental inquiry were not difficult enough, the subsidiary problems of linking *The Waste Land* to Eliot's prose criticism and fitting it into his poetic development also remain to be explored. We perhaps rightly do not know just how to regard *The Waste Land*. It is not inconceivable that the poem that causes our confusion might deliberately have been designed to create it. The manuscript evidence suggests that Eliot himself felt differently about it as he went along, changing his procedure as the poem developed. A change of procedure is a change of emphasis, and therefore of meaning, which in turn reflects matters in Eliot's career that happened before and after *The Waste Land*. These remarks try to shed some light on the rights and responsibilities the reader may expect, and must accept, upon picking up Eliot's poem.

As is well known, Eliot's earliest poems imitated Laforgue (and other nineteenth-century French poets) and the Jacobean dramatists. In a 1939 letter, "Eliot parle de l'influence de Laforgue comme d'une 'espèce de possession par une personnalité plus puissante,' comme d'une possession démoniaque."[1] Eliot discovered Laforgue in Arthur Symons's *The Symbolist Movement in Literature*, some of whose judgments and language today seem quaint but which contains many passages reminding us how deeply the book nourished Eliot's imagination. Eliot felt indebted to Symons, and acknowledged that by leading him to Laforgue and to the other French Symbolists, Symons's book had affected his life.[2] The book's main themes—self-consciousness; the problematic nature of human identity and a corresponding interest in essence versus exteriority; the Symbolist cultivation of strangeness; the idea of universal analogy and correspondences; the need for masks; the conventionality of time; the extremes of solipsism, mysticism, and aestheticism—all appear at some stage of Eliot's work.

Laforgue, however, influenced not only Eliot's poetry, but his personality as well. Symons quotes Gustave Kahn's impression of his friend Laforgue: "D'allures? ... fort correctes, de hauts gibus, des cravates sobres, des vestons anglais, des pardessus clergymans, et de par les nécessités, un parapluie immuablement placé sous le bras."[3] Conrad Aiken, Eliot's best friend during his Harvard years, called him a "singularly attractive, tall, and rather dapper young man." After a year in Paris, Eliot returned to Harvard "perceptibly Europeanized: he made a point, for a while, a conspicuously un-

American point, of carrying a cane—was it a malacca?—a little self-conscious about it, and complaining that its 'nice conduct' was no such easy matter."[4] Aiken would later render Eliot as

> an extremely controlled, precise, disciplined person—as much so in his own life as in his poetry.... "Manners" is an obsolete word nowadays, but he had them.... Sometimes I've thought Tom might have liked to have been an actor.... His urge for the theatre was unconquerable. There was some of the actor in Tom and some of the clown, too. For all his liturgical appearance (he only lacked a turned-around collar, it sometimes seemed) he was capable of real buffoonery.

Eliot, it seems, borrowed more than Laforgue's irony. The diffidence, the manners correct almost to superciliousness, the severe, nearly liturgical costume, the cane (later transformed into his notorious umbrellas, custom-made with outsized handles, with which in the early 1920s Eliot once defended a performance of "Le Sacre du Printemps" from the audience's derision), and the clownish or ironic undertone: All suggest that Laforgue legitimized aspects of Eliot's sensibility and behavior.[5] The borrowing from Laforgue seems to have been a double one—with a serious side (the somber, if dapper, attire, the cane, the manners) tending toward the dandy and a comic side (the buffoonery Aiken mentions, as well as the bathos, ironies, vaudeville quotation, and self-mockery) tending toward the clown. Many memoirs, anecdotes, and poems indicate how Eliot's personality admitted these apparently contradictory impulses: the music hall mixed with metaphysics and intellectual, theological seriousness alternated with jokey, role-playing clownishness.

Both moods influence Eliot's inaugural poem. Written just two or three years after Eliot first read Symons and discovered Laforgue, "The Love Song of J. Alfred Prufrock" culminates a series of Laforguian experiments, a few of which appear in *Poems Written in Early Youth*, others surviving only in manuscript. Prufrock's sartorial punctilio gives his game away; he is the dandy in action:

> My morning coat, my collar mounting firmly to the chin,
> My necktie rich and modest, but asserted by a simple pin—

Though the opposites—"rich" yet "simple," "modest" but also assertive and "mounting firmly"—perfectly express Prufrock's ambivalence, they also reflect his careful, almost fussy self-presentation. However fearsome his inner demons, we should not forget he wears a "morning coat," or cutaway, a coat with tails for formal daytime occasions. Acutely sensitive to his own external appearance, Prufrock defiantly observes the latest fashions in cuffed trousers ("I shall wear the bottoms of my trousers rolled"), broods tonsorially ("Shall I part my hair behind?"), and portentously declares himself on the matter of shore wear ("I shall wear white flannel trousers, and walk upon the beach").

Prufrock's attention to detail seems so correct, so anxiously serious, that it reduces him to a clown. He wears, wearily, a mask. The eternal Footman, despite (or because of) Prufrock's overwrought demeanor, responds with a "snicker." (Even in metaphysical circles, it would seem, good help is hard to find.) And Prufrock calls himself

> Deferential, glad to be of use,
> Politic, cautious, and meticulous;
> Full of high sentence, but a bit obtuse;
> At times, indeed, almost ridiculous—
> Almost, at times, the Fool.

The sad clown, Pierrot, mingles the serious and the comic, the liturgical with the buffoonish. These elements, and even the bald spot in the middle of his hair (both clowns and monks are bald)—suggest that Prufrock's "Fool" descends from Laforgue's "Hamlet" and *L'Imitation de Notre Dame de la lune*.[6]

From nineteenth-century France Eliot also inherited the legacy of the dandy. The dandy relied as much on the sartorial, social, and personal surface as did the clown, but with different motives and dramatic intentions. Instead of comic excess, the dandy emphasized severity, angularity, sobriety, and an almost fierce suppression of instinct. Pierrot's vacant, vulnerable passivity signaled his availability as a victim. By contrast, the dandy devotes himself to aggressive, total control and enselfment almost to superfluity, sharpening his wit and demeanor should he need them to parry a riposte or avenge a slight. By making life a matter of control and by measuring conduct against stylistic norms,[7] the dandy counts upon his mastery of custom and personality to subdue any social matrix and dominate it dramatically. Instead of cultivating his character—the "central self"—and expecting it to conform to abstract, moral criteria, the dandy polishes his manners—the "social self"—evaluating them according to criteria no less elevated and severe, yet concretely gestural. Against morals he pits mores and manners, which he takes quite seriously indeed.

Even in this respect, then, Eliot's attention extends in opposite directions: toward a private self sad, disillusioned, and victimized—a

Pierrot—and toward a public self rigorous and polished—a dandy. That Prufrock contains both these qualities is what makes him so convincing a character, as well as one so imbued with pathos. We remark his unshakable conviction about his own shortcomings, while noting his summary dismissal of whoever bores him. Prufrock's complexity explains something about that of his creator and, given these predilections, about Eliot's exile. In America, the dandy cuts an almost revolutionary figure, his disdain of popular acceptance emphasizing those aspects of the gentlemanly ideal that have been most thoroughly discredited socially, culturally, and, perhaps especially, sexually. American culture, as has been remarked, treats dandies and aesthetes even less kindly than do most other countries.[8]

Eliot's interest in dandies descends primarily from Baudelaire, who in moralizing the dandy's role modernized it as well, making it a vehicle with which to rebel against democratic, materialistic mediocrity. As Ellen Moers describes the progression, after Dickens's dandyism of failure and Barbey d'Aurevilly's mode of dissatisfaction, Baudelaire offered a dandyism of despair, detached, irresponsible, self-absorbed, and idle, but also morally critical of contemporary life. Defying respectable society, Baudelaire's dandy reasserted Original Sin, observing and accepting evil in a modern form.[9] Dandy gravity thus exerted a stronger influence upon the young Eliot than did the clownish Pierrot (though that role still held a greater appeal than is commonly assumed).[10] We do not ordinarily think of Eliot as a renegade, but only because the refinement upon which he reneged has so largely disappeared and because his apostasy necessarily remained of a refined, if not always subtle, kind.

"Baudelaire," although a later essay, confirms this view of Eliot's relation to his own pose and his own verse. Either Baudelaire must reject the contemporary world in favor of heaven and hell because he cannot adjust to the actual world, or because he perceives heaven and hell he must reject the world: Both ways of explaining Baudelaire's dualistic, negative metaphysic, Eliot concludes, are tenable.[11] Somewhat trivialized, this reversible formula applies to Prufrock; considerably enlarged, it describes *The Waste Land*. So does Eliot's comment upon how personality relates to artistic form. By their superficial coherence, excellence of form, and perfection of phrasing, Baudelaire's poems might give an appearance of presenting a definite, final state of mind. To Eliot, however, they seemed to have "the *external* but not the *internal* form of classic art. One might even hazard the conjecture that the care for perfection of form, among some of the romantic poets of the nineteenth century, was an effort to support, or to conceal from view, an *inner* disorder."[12] If we substitute "self" (especially the "social self") and "dandies" for "form" and "romantic poets," the substituted formulation makes a concise theory of the dandy, and of the Puritan. His comment, moreover, seems to acknowledge that Eliot's position vis-à-vis his early poetry resembled that of "some of the romantic poets of the nineteenth century." As had many nineteenth-century French Symbolist and "decadent" writers, Eliot created compensatory literary worlds because of a deep dissatisfaction with reality.[13] *The Waste Land* exemplifies this effort, and we overlook its author's critical, negative stance toward contemporary life at the risk of misunderstanding one of the poem's important motives.

"Baudelaire" further suggests that Eliot understood the strategies that the self—and the poet—may use to divert attention from a vulnerable, fragile, or socially unacceptable inner identity and fix it instead upon the external surface. *The Waste Land* itself arguably employs such a strategy. Alternatively, the dandy's intensively developed social self converts what society regards as subsidiary or peripheral into matters of primary importance. What many people view as concessions to social reality—dress, manners, small talk, quotidian politesses of diverse kinds—become for the dandy a kind of weapon.[14] The dandy's expert hypercivility exploits a smooth social surface, his offensive politeness discomfiting those who fail to keep pace. So that they may obscure inner facts, the dandy's external features proliferate. His superficial conformity may become so pronounced that it codifies itself in structured, formalized rebellion; it becomes "impersonal" through exaggerating personality.

This formula contributes to Eliot's emphasis on craft and technique, by which various rhetorical skills shift attention from the poet to his verse. Eliot's doctrine of impersonality thus in one sense implies its opposite upon deciphering his code. He called the bad poet unconscious where he ought to be conscious, and conscious where he ought to be unconscious. These two "errors," as Eliot termed them, tended to make the bad poet "personal," when in fact poetry did not cause a release of emotion or the expression of personality, but permitted instead an escape from them.[15] This famous formulation cancels conventional connections between poetry and sincerity and affirms Eliot's dandiacal poetic motives. Poetry did not explore and reveal the personality and emotions. Instead, it offered a respite from these burdensome aspects of the self. Dandyism, then, supported Eliot's anti-Romanticism, a classical tendency at once serious and stylized almost to mannerism or parody.

The dandy aimed to be himself not by relaxing or unbuttoning, but by tightening and controlling. Conceiving of the self as a gentleman, the dandy subjected it to the perfection of its accessories, resistance to vulgarity, and abomination of instinct, passion, and enthusiasm.[16] Thus to the dandy, certain kinds of freedoms and pleasures remained alien indulgences. In its rigorous dominion over the visible self, recoil from whatever was emotional, instinctual, or animal, and disgust with vulgarity, the dandy's posture did not preclude moralism. Both the dandy and the Puritan were elitist (the one socially, the other spiritually) and jointly condemned what they perceived as "animal." A dandyism capable both of criticizing conventional morals by flouting them and of expressing moral suffering as a way, of escaping it may partly explain Eliot's affinities to the French tradition. The English dandy, descended from Brummell, tended to be useless, sensual, and merely foppish. Brummell, in his biographer's words, had every quality to make him "agreeable, amusing and ornamental, but not one that tended, in the most remote degree, to make him useful."[17] In the Victorian era, then, one chose to be either entirely useful or utterly useless, with a no man's land in between. In France, however, Baudelaire launched an alternative, serious dandyism, symbolically clothed—before it became fashionable—in black, the mourning color, admirably suiting (so to speak) a declining age: "Nous célébrons tous quelque enterrement."[18] Laforgue's liturgical costume fit into this line of melancholy, diffident resistance to "ce stupide dix-neuvième siècle," which like Eliot's both proclaimed a badge of class disaffection and masked inner turmoil.[19]

Beyond these personal affinities, Eliot's critics have largely overlooked how Eliot's attraction to nineteenth-century France reached beyond purely literary influence and how that literary choice matched his other early model, the Elizabethans and Jacobeans. Eliot's choice of sources remains neither arbitrary nor fungible and reflects distinct historical preferences. Jacobean and nineteenth-century French literature resembled one another historically and socially. Seventeenth-century English society was unsettled; its aristocracy was inexperienced; its religious establishment was divided; its court and monarchs were suspect economically, morally, and sexually. These schisms caused individual tensions as well, but in social terms the stress of doubleness arose as two social ideologies developed into distinct, competing cultures within a single society, which led finally to war.[20]

The similarities between Jacobean England and nineteenth-century France, though far from being identities, nonetheless seem significant. The primary resemblance consists in the notion of two antagonistic cultures occupying a society undergoing a prolonged shift from one *Weltanschauung* to another. Whereas the social and ideological friction heated up to a civil war and a regicide in seventeenth-century England, nineteenth-century France began at that point. A century after 1789, after assorted monarchies, empires, communes, and republics, there still existed in France, especially among artists and intellectuals, alienation from some of the same forces—that in England had been on the ascendancy before 1641.[21]

Eliot's allegiances tethered him to the more traditional, "orthodox" ideology, seemingly doomed to decline along with the social class whose property it was. His literary choices represent his untheoretical but sure grasp of different historical periods undergoing a similar struggle. Eliot's sensitivity to this struggle owed much to what had happened in his own country, and to his own class, after the American Civil War. America, like Jacobean England and post-revolutionary France, underwent a civil war, the assassination of its head of state, and the conversion of its economy from regional, agricultural bases to national, urban, industrial ones. The class loyal to traditional ideology found itself displaced by economically motivated, democratic, less well educated "new men," a displacement producing emotional and ideological responses for which the literature of seventeenth-century England and nineteenth-century France provided rhetorical analogues and historical models. Ideological change and social displacement, and the notion that such developments elicit similar emotional and literary responses, provide the assumption from which to reason that Eliot's social experience affected his choice of literary models.

Such responses and experience reveal a sensibility with peculiar appetites and therefore satisfied by distinct rhetorical preferences. Something of this appears in Eliot's discussion of Andrew Marvell's wit—the "structural decoration of a serious idea," which Eliot found in Gautier, as well as in the "*dandysme*" of Lafargue and Baudelaire.[22] In "The Metaphysical Poets," setting forth a theory that glances forward to *The Waste Land*, Eliot linked the two periods explicitly. Because modern civilization contains "great variety and complexity," Eliot proposed that its poets must therefore be "difficult." They must become more indirect, allusive, and comprehensive, forcing and if necessary dislocating language into their meaning. This produces something resembling the metaphysical poets' conceit and also close to Eliot's nineteenth-century French models. Corbière and Laforgue, Eliot concluded, more closely resembled the school of Donne than did any modern English poet.[23] The Jacobeans and French Symbolists supported Eliot's rhetorical predilection for effects of doubleness, plurisignation, irony, ambiguity, and semantic disarrangement. Moreover, these models strengthened Eliot's preference for Gothic effect, proved that connotation could be cultivated until it surpassed denotation, showed how poetic craft could divert attention from the author's emotions to the verbal surface, and complemented Eliot's use of suggestion and techniques of strangeness. In *The Waste Land* and elsewhere, Eliot also drew upon the fund of historical incident and iconography the Jacobean and especially the Symbolist eras offered.[24]

Eliot ransacked the Jacobeans and Symbolists for rhetorical correlatives to his mental environment. Extremes within the same society appear to engender extremes within individual consciousness: They dissociate the sensibility. In an atmosphere overheated by social friction or violence, poets may prefer vagueness, ambiguity, suggestion, obscurity, allusion, and ellipsis instead of valuing precision, clarity, coherent narrative and syntax, and fixed, paraphrasable content. When formerly shared values must compete against newer ones, what was once absolute becomes merely relative; a temple of thought gives way to the marketplace of ideas. The emotional and intellectual complexity this competition calls forth in turn elicits verbal ambiguity and complexity. Politics, ideology, and the movement of social classes affect consciousness, which in turn influences verbal technique. This equation links nineteenth-century France and seventeenth-century England to Eliot as a post-Civil War American.

"From Poe to Valéry" suggests how social unease seems to hasten the progression from unconscious to self-conscious language, leading ultimately to *la poésie pure*. Eliot's use of ambiguity, however, extended deeper than the purely verbal or superficial borrowing. For reasons having to do with his cultural inheritance, self-division, and emotional dualism, Eliot apparently had to master the techniques of obscurity in order to write at all. Those contrivances therefore cannot be divorced from the matter they set forth. A sense that existence is obscure or unknowable engenders a search for literary devices connoting doubleness or conflict—ambiguity, paradox, irony, or tension—with which to represent that ambivalent sense of things. The presence of such elements in Eliot's early verse, as well as in his early life, suggest that this verbal ambiguity flows from a more deeply ambiguous sense of experience.

Ambiguity of experience, however, suggests experience unformed, whereas ambiguity of language signifies that language has maximally realized its formal properties. This paradox recalls the crux dividing the moral (or serious) from the rhetorical (or dramatic) perspective. Ambiguity of response toward experience may demonstrate a failure of moral, evaluative, and conceptual apparatus to account for a reality that outdistances or contradicts it. As intellectual and social structures crumble, so the structures of consciousness—and art—disperse. Yet ambiguity of language—using a single word to convey multiple meanings or connotations or attaching several meanings to one word—signifies the *success* of a verbal address toward the same world. In an ambiguous world, verbal ambiguity may thus become the most complete mimesis. Eliot's mastery of these techniques accounts for some of the singular attractions of the early verse—the images, music, and especially Eliot's voice and rhythms, which are among the most personal and distinct of all poetry in English.

The Waste Land, however, enlarges verbal and semantic disestablishmentarianism to encompass poetic form as a whole. Instead of complicating words and phrases by double reference, it multiplies the referentiality of each phrase, sentence, or paragraph by making it potentially significant to any other. The fragment, the poem's generic staple, and the lack of explicit authorial connective tissue dislodge expectations about a poem's form. On one level, the fragments mimetically render a disconnected reality and criticize its confusion. Portraying a culture and its *Weltanschauung* breaking apart, *The Waste Land* posits a moral center and a remembered order, but insists that the center is no longer shared and that the order persists only in memory. Our frustrations with the poem's discontinuous form, as it were, imitate Eliot's with the disorderly world. Semantic, verbal, and formal disconnection, upsetting expectations about poetic discourse, also dispatches preconceived ideas about order applied to the world. There may have been in 1922, and now certainly are, readers who do not expect much in the way of order in either the poem or the world. Just as surely, however, Eliot was not one of them. *The Waste Land* loses much of its moment if we forget the poetic and social predispositions to order that it deliberately violates and depicts being violated.

This is far from the entire picture, of course. The poem's fragmentary quality raises the question why its separate scenes appear in sequence, in the same poem. "Whispers of Immortality," for instance, though stating the relation between Donne and Webster expressly, leaves the connection between those two poets and Grishkin unstated and implicit. Origen, Sweeney, and similarly disparate characters appear side by side, yet their relation—though felt to be more than merely spatial—is nowhere made explicit. If the poem means to sustain attention, such characters must bear some relation, either of resemblance or of contrast, beyond simply appearing in the same poem. Spatial relation precedes, but also presupposes, intellectual relation.[25] In *The Waste Land*, voices, fragments, multiple genres, and narrative discontinuity reproduce Eliot's sense of a world withholding the aesthetic and moral order he expected it to supply.

Yet the poem's emotional consistency provokes another sort of scrutiny; though stylistically discrete, to have any larger significance its rhetorical units must establish reference beyond themselves. As Eliot had written in his dissertation, "meaning involves relations; at least (we need) the relation of identity through which a universality of function is recognized through a diversity of situation."[26] In Bradleyan terms, the discovery of relations objectifies feeling into thought. In this sentence, Eliot probably refers to the necessity that a word mean the same thing in different semantic circumstances. If it does not, and means something new every time it is used, the word can hardly be said to have a meaning, or indeed, any meaning. Yet words *can*, within limits, acquire meanings in different situations, a property poetic language so clearly exploits. There exist "relations" other than identity; a word also establishes relations with other words through syntax, connotation, metaphor, etymology, and dozens of other ways. The process by which individual words or the rhetorical units of a long poem become meaningful involves their linkage by author and reader to other termini: no meanings but in relations.

Eliot did not write *The Waste Land* to produce a meaningless poem or well-crafted, arty chaos. Arguing how the poem upsets predispositions to poetic order tells only half the story and explains why focusing only on its experimental form, without more, can so easily overstate the case. Its fragmentary, sudden shifts of scene, character, tone, time, and language deliberately forestall the habitual suspension of disbelief and thereby create a state of readiness. It is the first of many acts of aggression the reader will encounter. Yet if we listen for the "under-pattern" Eliot heard in the Jacobeans, *The Waste Land* reveals a web of subcutaneous nerve cells whose synapses fire periodically as we proceed through the poem. Underlying relation counterbalances the poem's epidermal confusion. The diverse methods by which *The Waste Land* builds up this tissue of relatedness, and just what sorts of relations it contains, I shall explore and illustrate in the following pages.

Separate scenes with similar reference, for instance, imply one sort of relation. In "The Burial of the Dead," a speaker says he could not speak; his eyes failed; he knew nothing; he was neither living nor dead. At least on a first reading—and how quickly one loses touch with that experience—a reader cannot yet know that later on, a woman (the hyacinth girl, whose wet hair, now dry, spreads out in fiery points?) asks a man (the same man?) a series of questions to which, out of the usual sequence, he seems already to have responded. Answer first, and ask questions later. In "A Game of Chess," she commands him to speak to her and asks him why he never does. She asks him if he knows, sees, and remembers nothing. And she asks him if he is alive or dead. When similar words or incidents appear in distant scenes, their intentional similarity enables us to recognize a "universality of function" in diverse situations. Answer and question bring two otherwise unlike scenes into relation, forcing the reader to identify what that relation is.[27]

One of the poem's premonitory nerve centers, the visit to Madame Sosostris, predicts several future scenes and illustrates another kind of relation. Here diverse parts begin to relate, not only as a plot, but through thematic and verbal associations the Tarot scene anticipates and later events will recall. Her visitor treats Sosostris skeptically, even patronizingly, noting how she throws a "wicked" pack of cards. Although not uncomplimentary, the American slang sense of "wicked" (meaning excellent, capable, keen)[28] also helps declare the speaker's independence from what he observes. The jaunty, journalistic "Madame Sosostris, famous clairvoyante" and the ironic "known to be the wisest woman in Europe" disclose his facile doubts about her acumen. And by snidely mimicking her slightly flawed English—"Tell her I bring the horoscope myself"—the speaker betrays his own vanity. Neither he—nor the reader—can as yet suspect that each card she interprets taps a spring of meaning that will seep throughout the poem. We shall follow some of these as they surface in later scenes, tying the poem together each time they emerge.

"Belladonna" glances forward to "A Game of Chess." "Bella" denotes "beautiful" but also borrows something from "warlike," as in bellicose. The folk etymology "beautiful lady" appears to have been influenced by the cosmetic use of *Atropa belladonna* to dilate the eye. The plant's opposite properties preserve the ambiguity: Its cosmetic use recalls the sense of "beautiful" in "bella," while its lethal chemistry (it is the deadly nightshade, source of the poisonous crystalline alkaloid, atropine) echoes its' "warlike" connotation. "Belladonna" sums up the woman's twofold nature as "A Game of Chess" begins. The opening scene details her boudoir (replete with marble, jewels, colored glass, copper, gold, and colored stone: "the Lady of the Rocks") and her toilette (surrounded by luxurious furnishings, mirrors, and perfumes). Beauty presently changes to belligerence, and as the scene unfolds she metamorphoses into the lady of situations.

In another prolepsis, Sosostris mentions "your card, the drowned Phoenician Sailor" and "the one-eyed merchant," whose associations attach to Eugenides and to Phlebas, reinforced by the clairvoyante's comments on "the wheel" and other cards: "Fear death by water. I see crowds of people, walking round in a ring." The poem will develop each of these references, though at this stage they appear to be only an unreliable clairvoyante's random observations, not to be taken particularly seriously.

The subsequent encounter with Eugenides contains several curiosities of reference and association. One recalls Eliot's father, who before T. S. Eliot's birth spent seven years working at a St. Louis wholesale grocery concern in various capacities. As shipping and receiving clerk, he prepared commercial documents and oversaw the flow of goods. His memoir recorded his dockside visits and knowledge of the boats' names, one of which was *The Sultana*, which it is possible to link both to Eugenides' Turkish origin and to the dried fruit he carries.[29]

Another recalls Bertrand Russell's description of Eliot's graduate school colleague, with whom he once arrived to ask Russell a question. "Eliot is very well-dressed and polished with manners of the finest Etonian type. The other, an unshaven Greek appropriately named Demos, who earns the money for his fees by being a waiter in a restaurant. The two were obviously friends and had on neither side the slightest consciousness of social difference." Also "unshaven," Eugenides speaks "demotic" French.[30]

Finally, employed in Lloyds Bank and perhaps by way of his father's experience, Eliot introduced the commercial shorthand "c.i.f. London" into his poem. Oddly, Eliot's original note incorrectly defined the phrase.[31] "C.i.f." followed by a destination abbreviates "cost, insurance, and freight," terms of a once-common shipping contract for the sale and transport of goods. The quoted price includes not only the goods, but also insurance and freight to the stated destination. Thus the seller performs his contract upon delivering goods to the shipper and tendering documents to the buyer. Even though the goods have not yet arrived at their ultimate destination, title passes to the buyer, who assumes all risks after the goods have been placed on board. "The seller completes his contract when he delivers the merchandise called for to the shipper, pays the freight thereon to the point of destination, and forwards to the buyer bill of lading, invoice, insurance policy, and receipt showing payment of freight."[32]

Though Eugenides, the Smyrna merchant, is cognizable as a modern Phlebas—one of the ancient trading tribe, the Phoenicians—other evidence joins the two. Eugenides quotes a price for a shipment of "currants"; another sort of "current" browses upon Phlebas' skeleton. The link involves more than a simple homonymous pun. Both these Aegeans, Phlebas and Eugenides, pursue waterborne commerce. Himself a sailor, Phlebas turned the wheel and looked to windward, keeping his eye, like the "one-eyed merchant," on "the profit and the loss." So had Eugenides to calculate when quoting a commodity "c.i.f."; although adaptable to other forms of shipping, in practice this contract was used primarily to allocate the risks of long distance, oceanic conveyance, risks Phlebas' demise makes evident.

"Current," moreover, derives etymologically from the same root as "currency," and the two words share a number of overlapping associations. We speak today, for example, of "cash flow" and of an "income stream." As in Eliot's time, goods enter the "stream of commerce," borrowers and corporations "float" loans and bond issues, and in banking the total value of uncollected checks or drafts in transit adds up to the "float." "Water," then as now, means stock issued at below par value or for discounted, nonmonetary, or nonexistent consideration, thus reducing the value of previously issued shares because it diffuses ownership but does not correspondingly increase capital. And for an investor or venture to be "under water" refers to heavy debt or imminent bankruptcy and failure. Eliot's work in the City would have acquainted him with these and similar terms and with the financial facts to which they figuratively alluded. (In the 1870s, two friends induced Henry Ware Eliot, Sr., to invest in a business manufacturing pyroligneous acid for the St. Louis lead industry. After four years' struggle against fire, floods, and an "intemperate" partner, the two friends at short notice abandoned Eliot and the business, which then failed. H. W. Eliot's memoir implies that Rev. Eliot bailed him out.)[33] Phlebas thus turns both his ship's wheel and the wheel of fortune. Even business parlance contains an "undertone" making it a kind of poetry and contributing to the imagery Eliot used to express moral anxiety about commercial culture and his participation in it.

We also speak of "liquid" assets and of liquidity, the relative ease or difficulty of converting assets into "currency," or cash. The related sense, "liquidation," occurs when a bankrupt corporation settles accounts with debtors and creditors and goes out of business. These overlapping associations between water and commerce, currents and currency, highlight another quality of Eliot's verbal practice throughout *The Waste Land*, his use of Gothic language to supply a subliminal menace of death. A "current" is a distinct flow, stronger, swifter, or of a different temperature, within a larger body of water. Just as liquidating a person leaves a corpse, so liquidating a business terminates a corporation: Another meaning of "liquidate" is to murder. This double sense makes it possible to associate a corpse and a business corporation. Incorporation creates an economic body enjoying legal rights like those of a person—the ability to buy, sell, contract, borrow, litigate—but also distinct from and superior to those of individuals. The law, that is, endows a corporation not only with limited liability—limiting a shareholder's liability to corporate creditors in bankruptcy to his ownership interest—but with eternal life.

The concluding scene of "The Burial of the Dead" first draws attention to this submerged ambiguity. After visiting Madame Sosostris, the speaker reappears in the London financial district, where a river of commuters crosses London Bridge and travels down King William Street toward the precinct where the great financial institutions are located: the Bank of England and the Royal Exchange, hard by the Stock Exchange, not far from the Cannon Street Hotel, Upper Thames Street, Moorgate, and other locations the poem names. They reverse the journey after the workday, "at the violet hour," echoing Sosostris's prophetic warning of "the Wheel," and "crowds of people, walking round in a ring." Recognizing one of the commuters, the speaker hails him:

'Stetson!
'You who were with me in the ships at Mylae!
'That corpse you planted last year in your garden,
'Has it begun to sprout? Will it bloom this year?
'Or has the sudden frost disturbed its bed?

The "corpse" has several associations.[34] Its overt, if metaphoric, sense concerns a bulb (compare the other plant called belladonna, *Amaryllis belladonna*, the hyacinth girl, and "Lil" in Part II) or the "roots" and "tubers" of the poem's opening lines. The "corpse," however, has been "planted." That garden-variety horticultural verb also has an exotic, "Gothic" meaning. As the facsimile edition shows, the original manuscript of *The Waste Land* contained an opening section full of colloquial American speech (e.g., "boiled to the eyes, blind" and "fly cop," meaning, respectively, "drunk" and a "detective"). One of many elements that the revisions nearly effaced was the poetry of slang, but traces of it survive nevertheless. In contemporary American slang the word "plant" was a synonym for burying a corpse or a cache of money.[35] The black-humored locution might accuse Stetson of murder or peculation. More likely the excited apostrophe reflects the speaker's surprise, or dismay, that Stetson (whose presence at Mylae—the first major naval victory of Imperial Rome—suggests that he, too, was once a sailor before succumbing to the horse latitudes of finance and commerce) has declined into a commuter, tending a suburban garden. There he has interred his past, and perhaps also his hope for the future. Having buried himself in his work, his living leaves him one of those whom death has "undone."

The speaker's question, "Or has the sudden frost disturbed its bed?" reprises many of these associations. The horticultural sense of a garden or flower bed extends themes present in "corpse," "planted," "sprout," and "bloom." But the "bed" also shares the mortal, murderous associations of "corpse" and "planted" and the notion that death has undone so many. "Bed," that is, may connote a "final resting place" or being "laid to rest," a cemetery as well as a garden plot. Phlebas' corpse occupies its final resting place in yet a third sense of the word "bed," that of a river- or seabed, a sense relevant to the currents, rivers, and bodies of water throughout *The Waste Land*. A fourth meaning involves the sexual or marital bed, here rendered as "disturbed," as a kind of death.

These associations do not exhaust "Death By Water," another of the poem's nerve centers, extending fibrous relations in many directions. The homonymous "current" and "currants" underscore the Gothic tone: Eugenides' currants were eaten; the current now eats Phlebas. It "picked his bones in whispers," that is, removed bit by bit, as meat from bones, eating sparingly or mincingly, without enthusiasm, as in picking at one's food. The irony is hardly subtle; Eugenides, a seller and consumer of food (he asks the speaker to luncheon), is the unconscious opposite of Phlebas, once engaged in the same business but now himself consumed by the current—and the currency—upon which he formerly floated. Buried at sea, his corpse rises and falls, like the commuters flowing up the hill and down King William Street. Phlebas' fate merges the "crowds of people, walking round in a ring" with "death by water," leaving him to perish, "entering the whirlpool."

These associations point to a theme that further illuminates the poem's mood. In due time we shall explore the theme of aggression in *The Waste Land*. Now it is appropriate to point out how Eliot's disillusion with business, commerce, and money joins with it to frame the theme of spiritual deadness. Eliot's family history supplies one source of this ambivalence. Notwithstanding his father's and grandfather's financial success, Eliot inherited their sense of an irreconcilable antinomy between God and mammon. "The whole district smells of fish," Sir John Betjeman once observed of the area around St. Magnus the Martyr. Its dozens of empty churches must constantly have reminded Eliot how financial prosperity had displaced Christian devotion.

In 1921, reporting a proposal to sell for demolition nineteen City of London churches, Eliot's renewed attack upon the pachydermatous "True Church" scarcely concealed his loyalties. Few visitors, he supposed, paid much attention to those empty sanctuaries,

> but they give to the business quarter of London a beauty which its hideous banks and commercial houses have not quite defaced.... the least precious redeems some vulgar street.... As the prosperity of London has increased, the City Churches have fallen into desuetude.... The loss of these towers, to meet the eye down a grimy lane, and of these empty naves, to receive the solitary visitor at noon from the dust and tumult of Lombard Street, will be irreparable and unforgotten.[36]

Aesthetic transport occasioned by religious architecture was not new to American aestheticists; Adams had written in the same vein. And as we have observed other American aesthetes do, Eliot's condemnation expresses moral disgust in an aestheticist vocabulary: The banks are "hideous" and "deface" their surroundings, and the streets and lanes are "vulgar" and "grimy." But the churches have a "beauty" that is "precious" and "redeems" their prosperous surroundings, the final verb connoting the two transformations of the precinct, conversion of securities and negotiable instruments into cash as well as delivery from sin and its penalties. His attitude discloses an inherited recoil from mammon merged with an acquired cultural ideal of beauty, refinement, and repose, the latter appearing as the "inexplicable splendour of Ionian white and gold." Though it is possible to exaggerate the extent to which Eliot held commerce to account for spiritual deadness, his thinking at this stage nonetheless warns against acquisitive, commercial motives in the most dire terms.

Aside from reiterating that warning, "Death By Water" illustrates another device Eliot uses to unify the poem's disparate episodes. We have so far discussed several such devices: puns; predictions; verbal echoes and repetition; semantic and thematic association; and anchoring separate episodes geographically. Besides these more or less internal mechanisms, Eliot incorporates extraneous sources to tie his poem together. For example, *The Waste Land* quotes or echoes lines 388–408 of act I, scene ii, of *The Tempest*. As I have observed, several crucial nerve centers of *The Waste Land* influence later or resolve earlier portions, as if by remote control. Some parts of the poem—"Death By Water," for one, or the Tarot scene—are simply more important than others, at least in terms of interpreting the whole. Eliot's references to *The Tempest*, however, take the unusual step of locating a governing nerve center *outside* his own poem, in the work of another author.

Eliot's notes make the point several times, most clearly by stating that "the one-eyed merchant, seller of currants, melts into the Phoenician Sailor, and the latter is not wholly distinct from Ferdinand Prince of Naples." Though if not wholly distinct, that is to say, not wholly identical either. In act III, scene iii, for example, Ariel spoke of the "never-surfeited sea," which now leisurely nibbles Phlebas' corpse. In some suggestive lines concerning "Death By Water" and "What the Thunder Said," Alonso cried out for his conscience:

O, it is monstrous, monstrous!
Methought the billows spoke and told me of it;
The winds did sing it to me; and the thunder,
That deep and dreadful organ pipe, pronounced
The name of Prosper; it did bass my trespass.
Therefore my son i' th' ooze is bedded; and
I'll seek him deeper than e'er plummet sounded
And with him there lie mudded.

Of course, the difference between Phlebas and Ferdinand is that Alonso misapprehends the state of things. Ferdinand is lost, but not dead; unlike Phlebas, who is both, he does not rest at the bottom of the seabed. When Ferdinand sits on the bank "Weeping again the King my father's wrack," he is mistaken, unlike the speaker in *The Waste Land*, and in due time will learn the facts.

Many other similarities between Eliot's poem and Shakespeare's play exist—water metaphors, the conflict between legitimacy and usurpation, and the theme of metamorphosis, for only a few examples; here simply note how widely Eliot has distributed them. Pluck any reference to *The Tempest*, and like a thread in a blanket, others woven elsewhere into the poem's four corners will twitch in response. This example seems to illustrate the theory in "Tradition and the Individual Talent." Allusion, that is, fits into the existing system of reference and meaning, which supports the contemporary work of art but is also altered by it. As the contemporary work of art forms a terminus of relations tying it to previous works of art, new relations thereby established shift preexisting ones. This Bradleyan premise underpins the method by which allusive literary networks grid *The Waste Land*, building up its own meanings through afferent and efferent pathways of extraneous literary relation to and from Shakespeare as well as Jacobean tragedy, Dante, Baudelaire, and other nineteenth-century French writers. *The Waste Land*, indeed, casts its referential net wide enough to include the Bible, the Upanishads, St. Augustine, and the Buddha, as well as *From Ritual to Romance* and *The Golden Bough*. By alluding to "Dans le Restaurant" and "Burbank with a Baedeker: Bleistein with a Cigar," Eliot even incorporates his own earlier writing, altering the meaning of earlier poems even as he uses them to create meaning in his latest one.[37]

It is neither possible nor necessary to pursue all these extraneous sources. What details this analysis provides can only illustrate Eliot's rich procedure. The innumerable details and the relations they arrange may nevertheless tend to distract attention from the "substance of the poem." That substance, though not always easy to pin down, sends another kind of pattern cunning through *The Waste Land* like a current. The theme of aggression emerges in scenes establishing the poem's principal emotional coordinates. It is particularly important because it suggests, by negative implication, the poem's primary positive values.

Emotional aggression pervades the initial scenes of "A Game of Chess." In her luxurious boudoir, a woman endeavors through jewels, perfumes, and other high-style artifice to provoke her taciturn lover. She evidently fails, but because her tricks arise from a genuine need for contact, she takes his reluctance personally. Frightened and frustrated, she becomes angry and then abusive, interrogating him with questions recalling what was said to the hyacinth girl. That moment captured a blinding perception of the force of love. Now, however, the woman fairly screams, while the man keeps silent (at least to her; the reader, significantly, is permitted access to his thoughts). Threatened by being "drowned"—intimations of Phlebas' fate—in her perfume and overwhelmed by her rage, the man is protected by his silence, or so he imagines. In truth, it precipitates the storm of abuse that rains down upon him. The woman, tortured by an agony of love remembered but now attenuated or gone irretrievably bad, wants him to lead, to give her something, to make some sign. Her questions simply state how desperately she wants something—anything—to happen. But nothing does. The marital game of chess produces a stalemate: out of wedlock, deadlock. Despite her threat to embarrass him into intimacy by going out in public *en deshabille*, he is the one who exits the perilous straits of a rocky marriage, fleeing domestic danger into the safety of a public house.

There he overhears a tale of another marriage and observes a different kind of aggression. The woman at her vanity received too little attention; Lil suffers because she receives too much—more, apparently, than she wants or than her health can take. Albert, however, presents little immediate peril compared with the narrator's recollected conversation, in which she had the knives out for Lil. She calls Lil dowdy, telling her to replace her decaying teeth with a store-bought set (anticipating the "carious teeth" in "What the Thunder Said"). She hints at Lil's dishonesty (spending teeth money to purchase pills for an abortion) and calls her selfish, foolish, and immature ("You *are* a proper fool.... What you get married for if you don't want children?"). She also pointedly threatens Albert's philandering if Lil does not stop looking "so antique." Miraculously, Lil took most of this sitting down, even inviting her inquisitor to dinner—with Albert—the next Sunday. As the group breaks up at closing time, slightly drunk and slurring their words—"Goonight"—it evidently forgives and forgets such aggression in short order. Despite the brass tacks of birth, marriage, life, and death raised as items of gossip, pub culture dismisses such verbal violence as harmless, refusing to let grudges hold up the eating and drinking for long.

What ensues after the typist arrives home at teatime occupies a position farther along the poem's developing spectrum of desire and aggression. This scene elaborates a minor theme introduced when Eugenides inquired after his companion's luncheon and weekend plans. His sexual query altered the center of gravity of his "business proposition," abruptly shifting the emphasis from the former to the latter word. The young man carbuncular, a "small house agent's clerk," also moves in the business world, if in a petty way. He has grandiose plans and an attitude to match: all the assurance—and, the comparison implies, all the moral acuity—of a war millionaire, if without the enabling fortune. His assurance and "bold" stare, his ego swollen to maximum tumescence, his avidity to overwhelm someone weaker than he suggest his own ultimate fragility. He is all aggression: "flushed and decided," he "assaults" and is "exploring," yet he "gropes," as if blinded, when he leaves. The typist makes no "defence" to his onslaught. Ironically balanced opposites render their interaction: His caresses are "unreproved, if undesired," and his vanity makes a "welcome of indifference." Hardly participating, she treats the episode routinely, as much a part of her daily round as a hurried breakfast, crushing commute, or a half-heard tune on the gramophone.

In "A Game of Chess," a frightened, angry woman had emotionally bullied a taciturn man, probably himself frightened into silence and emotional withdrawal. In "The Fire Sermon," by contrast, the bully is a young man, still adorned in adolescent acne ("carbuncular" also ironically denoting a semiprecious gem), yet vain and aggressively sexual. Though something short of rape, his technique seems mainly to consist of an utter lack of interest in his partner. Consumed by his desire, unassuaged by easy, private conquest in the typist's bedsit, the house agent's clerk, seeking novelty or danger, attempts sex in a "narrow canoe" floating down the Thames.

The venture fails. "Undid" denotes the unfastening of her clothing, recalling the catalogue of her "drying combinations," "stockings, slippers, camisoles, and stays." A related sense connotes her ruin by seduction, while a third echoes, "I had not thought death had undone so many," connoting cosmic, spiritual ruin, leaving the body alive but the soul dead. Referring to the canoe, the original manuscript's inclusion of "perilous" in place of "narrow" bolsters an intuited link between this scene and the typist's combinations "perilously" spread, as well as underscoring the theme of spiritual peril.[38] She then says, "My feet are at Moorgate, and my heart under my feet." Moorgate lies near King William Street, Saint Mary Woolnoth, and the bell's funereal peal. There the speaker met Stetson, who had planted a "corpse" in the ground where the typist's heart now lies. (The Elizabethan idiom "under ... feet" denotes subjection, ruin, conquest, with a subliminal connotation of burial, as in 1 Corinthians 15: 24–7, quoted in the Anglican service "At the Burial of the Dead": "Then cometh the end, when he shall have delivered up the kingdom to God, even the Father; when he shall have put down all rule and all authority and power. For he must reign, till he hath put all enemies under his feet. The last enemy that shall be destroyed is death. For he hath put all things under his feet.")

This time, however, the canoeing incident also undoes the "young man carbuncular." The inversion, noun before adjective, implies that he is heraldically "rampant," a word deriving from "climbing" and "claw." "Rampant" suggests luxuriant growth, like the vegetation they drift past at the great botanical garden at Kew. More insidiously, it suggests how the young man and his desires—socially climbing and sexually clawing—spread unchecked, barbarically out of control. Does the "event" simply repeat the assault on the divan? Evidently not, given what follows in each case. She earlier seemed to have taken no offense, nor does she now. Yet here, he "wept." If he attempted sex in the canoe and failed, the house agent's clerk (inane enough to conceive the plan, and then unable to bring it off) might well have "wept" from his bruised vanity, or even a pang of guilt that he had "gone too far." He might as well promise a melodramatic "new start."

Expiatory promises after sexual humiliation—thus a "non-event"—also make her response plausible. "I made no comment. What should I resent?" If nothing happened in the canoe except some disrobing, a demoralized woman, victimized on other occasions, might conclude that on this one at least she had not been ill treated. Despite the vague action of these scenes, we do know that this latest disaster occurs on the river-bed, and that the next section, "Death By Water," presents another sailor's corpse, resting on the seabed, who like the loveless lovers "was once handsome and tall as you."

The man and woman in the canoe seem to have been brought face to face with their respective predicaments. Sexual failure has occasioned his spiritual crisis; subsequent sexual access will most likely relieve it. Hers, however, seems a crisis of dispiritedness; she lacks even the resources to "resent," to "connect," or to "expect." Thus matters stand at the end of "The Fire Sermon," after a series of scenes in which an aggressor victimizes a passive recipient. As if to point out the paradox of this earthly pattern, the same one essentially repeats itself when a divine aggressor "pluckest out" the passive subject. For once, however, the passive character is the beneficiary, instead of the victim, of an active power. Divinity exercising its power on our behalf: Modern people experience that kind of power only rarely, the poem seems to say, perhaps, like the typist, having lost the knowledge that they may hope for grace, or something like it, to be extended. (Under the circumstances, synergism is presumably out of the question.) The moment, however, does not last. "Death By Water" illustrates the cruel fact of human impotence. The predictable accident to which first the spirit (crowds of people, walking round in a ring) and then the body (devoured by the current of time) succumb, mortality undoes us all.

Where, then, does "What the Thunder Said" arrive, if passivity before earthly aggression reflects spiritual weakness, but passivity before divine power makes grace possible? Both themes inform this fifth section, especially insofar as its chapel perilous might offer a forum for resolving the paradox between spiritual passivity and mundane aggression. Indeed, at several moments something does seem about to happen. The initial verse paragraphs allude to the primal Christian act of aggression and passivity, the Crucifixion, out of which the victim perfects divine fortitude. Christ's corporeal death and resurrection into everlasting life make this salvation concrete and available, broadcasting the redemptive Holy Spirit to all willing to receive it. The story makes the fundamental Christian distinction that Christ, once corporeally alive but mortal, through resurrection enjoys everlasting spiritual life. Yet the poem states, "He who was living is now dead." And instead of acknowledging that Christ's example makes resurrection and everlasting life available to all who accept the Holy Spirit, the poem concludes, "We who were living are now dying." Christian believers would have phrased it the opposite way; before Christ, they were physically alive, but spiritually dead. After Christ's great example, their faith ensures that they wax spiritually even as they wane physically.

"What the Thunder Said" alternatively offers the Grail legend as an initiation into spiritual power and a way to penetrate divine mystery. Yet the section seems rather to state the difficulty to be surmounted, and the chances of surmounting it, than to succeed in actually overcoming that obstacle. Weston's theory requires some violent contest in the chapel perilous to effect the initiation. Spiritual adventure must complete itself in physical contest; an enemy must threaten the quester's life.[39] Despite many signs of the before and after of struggle, however, what happens falls short of the spirit- and body-concentrating event of focused, physical conflict. "Dry bones can harm no one." Yet without physical jeopardy, no spiritual victory may result. So while the section exhibits a degree of progression, the absence of anything by which to account for the change deprives it of the force it is surely meant to possess. Instead of a resolution, "What the Thunder Said" seems to bring about only an ending. Michael Levenson justly perceives that of the themes mentioned in the introductory note to "What the Thunder Said," Eliot attends only to "*incipient* phenomena ('journey,' 'approach,' 'decay') the stages that precede realization. He employs ... 'three themes' in this section of the poem, but none of the three achieves dramatic resolution; they remain, indeed, poised in 'continuous parallel.' The result is a particular dramatic inconclusiveness. Parallels multiply, but they do not meet."[40]

To be sure, in fine-tuning the climactic cosmic theater, Eliot cranks up some splendid poetic machinery:

Then a damp gust
Bringing rain

Ganga was sunken, and the limp leaves
Waited for rain, while the black clouds
Gathered far distant, over Himavant.
The jungle crouched, humped in silence.
Then spoke the thunder.

These lines, the fulcrum of the poem's energy and a moment of maximum compression—literally the calm before the storm—develop a pattern of vowels and consonants to express the nervous tension they contain. The *u* vowel predominates: "sunken," "jungle," "crouched," "clouds," "humped," and "thunder." Like the bed of the river Ganga, the *u* lies open to the sky, ready to receive water and meaning, yet with upright sides to collect and retain them. By contrast, the *m* and *n* consonants, often adjacent to the *u* vowel, also pervade the passage: "damp," "Bringing rain," "sunken," "limp," "Himavant," "jungle," "humped," "silence," "Then," and "thunder." The *m* and especially the *n*, "humped" like the sacred mountain "Himavant," add weight to a word's volume. Closed to the sky and positioned like a dome or arch, they resemble structures that protect, support, and shelter. The *u* collects and conserves, like a cup; its opposite, the *n*—a *u* inverted—protects and shelters, like a cap.

Both responses are appropriate to the coming storm. The onomatopoeic "DA," resembling a clap of thunder, and "shantih," the soft susurrus of a life-giving rain-shower: these marvelous devices give pleasure with every reading. If ever one wished to suspend disbelief, this is the moment. Once translated from exotic Sanskrit to plain English, however, the very ordinariness of "give, sympathize, control" suggests how little has happened, despite the superb *deus ex natura*. The components of a Gangetic peace that passeth all understanding—detached from the Westonian and Frazerian apparatus and the poetic business—turn out to be familiar Unitarian imperatives, the Sunday school virtues. They pretty much require the Unitarian procedure, as well: not the drama, blood, and thunder of sudden conversion, but years of conscious self-direction.[40a] The poem's grand finale, pretending to be something that makes the soul cohere, turns out to be merely the assertion that it does—or that it could.[41]

At the time, Eliot wrote that "in art there should be interpenetration and metamorphosis."[42] *The Waste Land* contains quantities of the former, but a certain absence of the latter quality raises questions. It is not that these ethical prescriptions are irrelevant, or wrong, or even that they do not fit in this poem. They do: giving to and sympathizing with others, and controlling oneself, prescribe fitting responses to the various incidents of aggression the poem contains. And the modern world contains innumerable people who could profit from them. (One hastens to point out that not many—like Eugenides, the young man carbuncular, or Lil's beery persecutor—will be the sort to read *The Waste Land*, much less heed its precepts.) The difficulty is rather that given the exotic machinery framing these imperatives, a measure of incongruity accompanies their appearance, not so bad as bathos but something of a letdown nevertheless. It is as if the author could not bring himself to set forth such familiar propositions without extraordinary labor. Given their similarity to his ancestral formulas, perhaps for Eliot to profess them required something like this toil and trouble.

The antinomies in the "give, sympathize, control" paragraphs—by far the poem's most obscure—reflect Eliot's personal difficulty, and, I think, an American difficulty. "Surrender" and "prudence," "given" and "retract," "daring" and "obedient," the prison of the isolated self and the calm, carefree responsiveness of intimacy: these ambivalences reflect a self unformed, afraid of the step that will force the identity's precarious possibilities to closure, yet desperate to take it. Americans tend to resist the notion that anything other than a knowing, voluntary choice may bind them individually. This idea, inherited from Protestantism and rationalism and reinforced by Romanticism, seems established in American common wisdom, on one hand, and in law and public policy, on the other. It was the motive behind Unitarianism, as we have seen, refusing to admit either the imputed guilt of Adam's sin or the sudden gift of God's grace, leaving the matter of salvation or damnation to the individual's own resources.

In a modern, secular context, the idea tends to dissolve the claims upon us of the past, of our ancestors, of our birth, of our bodies, of even our own seemingly irrevocable commitments. Shading off into antinomianism, criminality, laissez faire, or an anarchic unwillingness to plan, it challenges the right and reach of law, legislation, and decisions taken by society. Many Americans routinely take pleasure in dismissing facts they did not influence or decisions in which they took no part as unjust impositions, satanic conspiracies, or simply matters of grand irrelevance. American identity itself, in this context, becomes a subject of conscious, individual choice to come, and to stay. What is voluntarily chosen, however, may be relinquished, as Eliot's life suggests. Voluntarily choosing to be involuntarily bound, he chose, or thought he chose, to live in a society where one's life was more a fact and less a choice. But the very possibility of making that choice implies that the un-self-conscious fact of living no longer survived to be recovered. Painfully mixing erotic death by burial or drowning with an excruciating labor of rebirth, *The Waste Land* may be read as a poem about the costs of choosing identity, of consciously altering something originally formed unconsciously. It struggles with the question of choice in general, asking how much may be left to the conscious mind, how strong are the claims of ancestral, parental, and national bonds, how much of the life and self one has must be given up to get the life and self one wants.

The poem's final lines further undercut the likelihood that coherence for the soul—or of the world outside—can pretend to be anything more than temporary. The conclusion quotes, inter alia, "*Le Prince d'Aquitaine à la tour abolie.*" *Abolie*—literally, "ruined" or "downed"—seems close to the heart of the matter. In 1921, at work on the poem, Eliot diagnosed his own problem with nerves as an "aboulie and emotional derangement which has been a lifelong affliction."[43] A single vowel separates the physical ruin of "*abolie*" from the emotional ruin of "aboulie," a loss of the ability to exercise willpower and make decisions. The quotation, in which is buried Eliot's self-diagnosis, does not place much confidence in the regenerative power of the ideal so symmetrically proposed a few lines earlier.

"These fragments I have shored against my ruins" seems to confirm the difficulty of spiritual change. No metamorphosis—no miracles—without faith. The very familiarity of this line makes it easy to overlook its implied paradox: Ordinarily ruins result in fragments, instead of fragments protecting against ruin. "Fragments," on one hand, refer to the poem's discrete parts, and perhaps to its allusive cultural diversity. On the other, it suggests that "give, sympathize, control" are fragments of a larger—presumably Christian and orthodox—system, an ethic without the glue of faith, Incarnation, and dogma that will incorporate them into a complete, spiritually reconstituting system. Even though they fall short of that completion, these ethical imperatives nonetheless refer and aspire to it. Indeed, inasmuch as they *do* argue against disillusion, they perform that positive function, despite remaining necessarily negative because, as yet, incomplete. They do not simply call a solution impossible. If anything, they—indeed the entire poem—point toward the solution's ultimate necessity. That a solution is postponed does not subtract from the necessity of persisting to seek one.

Perhaps it is the better part of poetic candor to suggest an ideal and acknowledge its practical insufficiency, rather than to propose that no ideal is possible. The poem's ultimate indeterminacy, that is, hardly seems a particularly grave flaw. Indeed, remembering its indeterminacy helps blunt the interpretive implements that constrain the poem as they force it into one of various schematic cubbyholes. Though *The Waste Land*, and especially the notes, seemingly welcome that kind of hermeneutic shoehorning, the more of these interpretative schema the poem can bear, the more one tends to mistrust any one of them, whether Christian, Hindu, anthropological, mythological, or otherwise. One can make an ambiguity precise by insisting upon one of its terms and dismissing the others. But Eliot wrote ambiguously because he wished to say many things, not because he wished to say only one.

Even the "single-protagonist theory," though welcome because of its procedural focus, does not quite hang together. The poem, to be sure, contains enough consistency of incident, tone, and voice to encourage the notion that a single narrator sees, experiences, speaks, and acts. It is one sort of "relation" to which the poem may plausibly give rise. But a good deal of *The Waste Land* contradicts the protagonist's existence; Levenson's example of Eugenides and the narrator in "The Fire Sermon" is only one embarrassment of this theory. No fictional being could encompass all the poem's variation and still remain sufficiently unified to cohere into something cognizable as a protagonist.[44]

The process of collating the poem's diversity contributes something necessary and interesting to understanding *The Waste Land*. To establish relations among the poem's various parts requires a critical vantage point that commands these diverse elements. To state the proposition in reverse, reader's must immerse themselves in the poem's particulars *a priori* so as to discover and create relations between them *a posteriori*. By attaining greater knowledge about the poem's incidents and characters, the reader rises to a prospect from which to view them in more detail and greater breadth. Thus the poem's transcendent, synthetic method: glimpse the ideal by establishing relations. (To paraphrase Emerson's "Circles," discovering relations is a new influx of divinity into the mind. "Hence the thrill that attends it.") Although essentially passive and intellectual, this procedure and the related ethic of give, sympathize, and control make it possible for the poem to incorporate the reader into its activity. Whether one calls it the author or some dramatized, foreshortened, or inflected version of him, the poem's controlling consciousness shares with the reader the task of infusing relations into an inert, lifeless text. He invites the reader to adopt his own, supervening perspective, all-knowing, all-seeing, and all-relating, *the perspective of the maker*.

The Waste Land, then, superficially disjointed, remains fundamentally capable of revealing relations part to part, and part to whole. Yet unless we apply the term to something so odd and partial as to fall into a category sui generis, the poem withholds a protagonist. Among other problems, the vital element of Christian accession or consistency with the Grail legend is missing. The Hindu excursion to the Ganges, moreover, turns out to have ventured not far from the Unitarian River Charles. Ultimately the theatrical and poetical rendering, the ambitious procedure of superficial fragmentation concealing relational unity, and the ubiquitous sense of an independent moral, emotional, and intellectual center carry the poem; not the action or substantive incident, much of whose core remains indefinite. This indefiniteness, I reiterate, is not necessarily a flaw. The chief use of a poem's meaning, Eliot argued, may be only to divert the reader's mind while the poem proceeds to do its work. Some poets, however, "become impatient of this 'meaning' which seems superfluous, and perceive possibilities of intensity through its elimination."[45]

The poem illustrates how the aesthetic difficulty—unifying the poetic fragments—and the psychological and spiritual crux—unifying the self and the soul—compose a single problem. It is nevertheless not unreasonable to conclude that although art can render and organize the fragments, art without faith cannot alone fuse the fragments into the peace which passeth understanding. An extra-artistic, extra-aesthetic thing, faith is what *The Waste Land* points and aspires to, but cannot itself create. As Eliot concluded after his religious conversion:

> Nothing in this world or the next is a substitute for anything else; and if you find that you must do without something, such as religious faith or philosophic belief, then you must just do without it. I can persuade myself, I find, that some of the things that I can hope to get are better worth having than some of the things I cannot get; or I may hope to alter myself so as to want different things; but I cannot persuade myself that it is the same desires that are satisfied, or that I have in effect the same thing under a different name.[46]

Is it unreasonable to suppose that Eliot could not have written these two sentences until he had completed *The Waste Land* and exhausted its particular possibilities? Only two years before, literary tradition had thrived in a prose garden beneath the filtered, aesthetic shade of *The Sacred Wood*; there the trees flourished, and the gods lived. In *The Waste Land* of contemporary poetry, however, something afflicts the power of art; the gods have fled and the trees have withered, leaving a barren emotional landscape not unlike what Eliot would later call the "well-lighted desert of atheism."[47] In Eliot's career, *The Waste Land* establishes the limit of art, and hence a boundary of his aestheticism. The poem seems to show that even though they may function in similar ways (as I have argued elsewhere), philosophy, art, and religion are not simply different names for the same thing. Though *The Waste Land* may illustrate the effect and desideratum of faith, it cannot by itself supply the cause or the fact of faith. It catches Eliot at the middle point of his long transit from cynic to visionary: In "Preludes," "the worlds revolve like ancient women gathering fuel in vacant lots," while "Burnt Norton" begins "at the still point of the turning world." *The Waste Land*, however, only sets forth what must be done, acknowledges that it should be done, and shows how it might be done. But it does not do it. Yet.

The dandy—at least the *dandysme moral* of Baudelaire and Laforgue—gave a literary embodiment to Eliot's earliest skepticism, which progressed into disillusion before metamorphosing into religious vision. The dandy and the visionary form a curious collection of similarities and differences. Both, for instance, aspire to superiority, mastery, and power, the difference being the realm over which they seek to obtain dominion. The dandy moves in a social arena, applying his wit's sharp blade to trim any rough edges it encounters. The visionary moves at the level of metaphysics, the spirit, and the supernatural, grasping layers of truth and reality beyond everyday consciousness. Whereas the dandy emphasizes personality, impersonality—if not objectivity—distinguishes the visionary.

If *The Waste Land* finds Eliot at midpoint in his journey from skeptical dandyism to religious vision, formally speaking the poem occupies the middle ground between Eliot's early use of personae and dramatic monologue and his late recourse to a first-person, lyric poetic voice. Departing from a technique that typified Eliot's early poetry, *The Waste Land* contains no central, named persona—no Prufrock, no Gerontion—even though at times named characters, such as Tiresias, appear to speak. It merges aspects of both: containing a multitude of voices and characters, yet retaining the recognizable presence of its author. *The Waste Land* portrays Eliot's singular interests and emotions, yet filters them through diverse characters, incidents, and allusions quite distinguishable from him. Presenting dramatized personae as well as Eliot's identifiable lyric voice, *The Waste Land* probably remains something sui generis, profitably (though incompletely) analyzed from either point of view, because containing both of them. What needs to be said—perhaps all that can be said—is that the voice in *The Waste Land* belongs to the poem's author, from whom the voice is partly distinct but with whom it is also partly identical. We may not want it both ways, but that is the way we have it. Ambiguities concerning the author's distance from and presence in his poem constitute perhaps the most difficult "relation" that *The Waste Land* requires the reader, with all possible delicacy, to adjust.

The Waste Land mediates the polarities of Eliot's poetic journey in yet another sense. Tiresias, that is, remains the poem's "most important personage" not simply because he "unites all the rest" or because he joins sexual opposites, male and female. Cynicism and vision also meet in Tiresias.

His disillusion arises from seeing too much. Although physically blinded, even "at the violet hour," Tiresias "can see." He need not even look; having "perceived the scene" and having been condemned to await the expected guest, he has not only "foretold" but has "fore-suffered" all enacted there, before it even happened. "What Tiresias *sees*"—Eliot's emphasis—"is the substance of the poem." Yet he sees only a more inclusive version of the waste land than the typist and clerk; it cannot yet be called "vision." Despite his vantage point, no more than a typist, a house agent's clerk, and their predictable carryings-on fill his view; only repetition, sameness, and lack of progression reward his superior acuity. Thus his point of view only feeds his cynicism; he has the means to see, but not yet the power of vision.

For Eliot, vision did not simply reach above and beyond; it also extended below and beneath. In literary terms, this inclusiveness involved contacting that "inexhaustible and terrible nebula of emotion which surrounds all our exact and practical passions and mingles with them" or using words having a "network of tentacular roots reaching down to the deepest terrors and desires." It also involves qualities Eliot found in Elizabethan dramatists: a pattern, or "undertone, of the personal emotion, the personal drama and struggle," and a dimension distinct from the literal actions and characters, "a kind of doubleness in the action, as if it took place on two planes at once."[48] Likewise, it involves a wide-ranging emotional inclusiveness, uniting extremes of upper and lower, inner and outer, width and depth. Comparing the characters of Shakespeare and Jonson, Eliot suggested that Falstaff represented the satisfaction of feelings not only more numerous, but more complicated. Calling Falstaff the offspring of feelings deeper and less apprehensible, although not necessarily more intense or strong, than Jonson's, Eliot concluded that Shakespeare's creation did not differ because of the distinction between feeling and thought, or because of Shakespeare's superior perception or insight. Eliot accounted for the difference by pointing to Shakespeare's "susceptibility to a greater range of emotion, and emotion deeper and more obscure."[49]

An upper and lower, a visible surface and an undertone or underpattern, a superficial fragmentation concealing a network of relations uniting disparate parts, and an emotional breadth: These aspects of *The Waste Land* construct an incipient visionary architecture. This must be why the notes exist. Eliot added them so readers would not miss the framework that held the poem's detailed façade in place. (Of course, besides telling readers how to treat the poem, these analogues, allusions, and attributions that link it to external sources must also have reassured the author of its objectivity, that it was not wholly personal. They act as a kind of control to Eliot's poetic experiment.)

Reading *The Waste Land* requires scrutiny of this double structure. Beneath the poem's detailed, shifting surfaces, the reader must discover the relational filigree the fragments conceal. Eliot addressed one of the crucial problems this architecture poses, the task of deciding whether a voice, self, or center ties it together. Speaking of Pound's "peculiarity of expressing oneself through historical masks," Eliot implied how a reader might distill—or "collate"—the author's presence in *The Waste Land*. Pound, Eliot wrote, imposed upon himself the restless condition of changing his mask continually, which in turn required readers to shift their ground. Eliot called Pound more himself and more at ease behind one of his masks than when speaking in his own person. "He must hide to reveal himself. But if we collate all these disguises we find not a mere collection of green-room properties, but Mr. Pound."[50] Masks and poetic surfaces, that is, both conceal and reveal the poet and the meaning beneath and behind.

Two years before *The Waste Land*, Eliot thus suggests a way of placing, or replacing, the poet in his poem. Many years later, writing of St. John Perse's *Anabasis*, Eliot set forth the other, more impersonal demand upon the reader, perhaps recollecting his own long poem:

> Any obscurity of the poem, on first readings, is due to the suppression of "links in the chain," of explanatory and connecting matter, and not to incoherence, or to the love of cryptogram. The justification of such abbreviation of method is that the sequence of images coincides and concentrates into one intense impression of barbaric civilization. The reader has to allow the images to fall into his memory successively without questioning the reasonableness of each at the moment; so that, at the end, a total effect is produced.
>
> Such selection of a sequence of images and ideas has nothing chaotic about it. There is a logic of the imagination as well as a logic of concepts.[51]

Such a method may tax a reader's intellectual and aesthetic faith, but it emphasizes two points about the author and his reader. First, the images and their sequence do succumb to conscious—even "logical"—control; they are neither random, arbitrary, nor the indulgent gamesmanship of difficulty for its own sake. Second, a reader must maintain an ambivalent, two-pronged attitude toward such writing, combining passive receptivity (allowing images to fall into memory "without questioning" their reasonableness) and active analysis (constantly collating the disguises and synthesizing the relations). Any obscurity, that is, should progressively dissipate after the "first readings."

Rereadings, by coincidence and concentration of the images, should create an impression described by the word to which Eliot increasingly attached the highest poetic value as he progressed toward vision: The impression should be "intense."

The Waste Land ultimately arrives at a relationship to the reader that posits a controlling consciousness aware of all the poem's parts, yet also *aware, like the reader, that its parts know nothing of one another*. The reader must assume the point of view, or adopt the assumptions, of the poet vis-à-vis his creation, becoming necessarily more aware than the characters within it. Like such characters, the poem's parts have no awareness of other parts. The poet, however, has placed those parts in relation, which relation gives the parts a meaning intelligible to—and in a sense co-created by—a reader, even though the relations a reader draws between the parts will not invariably match those of the poet. Hence, though on one level it allows the poet to withhold his personality, suppressing the "links in the chain" means that on the interpretative, functional level the reader and poet converge almost to identity. Unlike the people in the poem, the author and reader can apprehend all the fragments and discern their relation to one another. And knowing that we may imitate the poet's superior, more inclusive consciousness makes us resemble not only the poet in relation to his poem, but also Eliot's poetic heroes in relation to their surroundings. Such co-creative reading demands a vision that can incorporate above and below, surface and depth, disorder and "relations." Eliot defined the poet's essential advantage as not that of having "a beautiful world with which to deal: it is to be able to see beneath both beauty and ugliness; to see the boredom, and the horror, and the glory."[52]

We may thus approximate the inclusive consciousness of the poet and visionary, able to join the opposites of beauty and ugliness, sublimity and practicality. The dandy poet Baudelaire spread before Eliot the possibility of extracting high beauty—"intensity"—from the meanest, most "sordid" surroundings. And not only was this beauty composed out of metropolitan imagery, but it was to be presented in a double aspect: both literally—"as it is"—and as something else, as part of an inclusive poetic vision. Baudelaire, Eliot wrote, did not create for others a mode of expression simply by using sordid, metropolitan imagery or images of common life. Instead, by presenting such imagery as it was, while causing it at the same time to represent something more than itself, Baudelaire elevated it to the "*first intensity*."[53] Throughout his early poetry, Eliot had endeavored to capture what had formerly been considered "the impossible, the sterile, the intractably unpoetic." When writing *The Waste Land*, he thought in visionary terms, with an inclusive poetic unity. The five-line stanza beginning "I am the Resurrection and the Life," almost formulaically gathered the opposites of spirit and flesh, mortal and eternal life, fixity and flux, man and woman, suffering and aggression. All these themes appear in *The Waste Land*, yet what is remarkable about this visionary fragment from the facsimile is that Eliot could not fit it into the poem with which it was in many ways so consistent.

It might have pointed in the direction he wished to move but could not yet do so in his poetry. Eliot's progress toward vision transpired only in stages, pursuant to models set forth by the dandies, skeptics, and cynics. Baudelaire, for instance, left Eliot

> a precedent for the poetical possibilities ... of the more sordid aspects of the modern metropolis, of the possibility of fusion between the sordidly realistic and the phantasmagoric, the possibility of the juxtaposition of the matter-of-fact and the fantastic. From him, as from Laforgue, I learned that the sort of material that I had, the sort of experience that an adolescent had had, in an industrial city in America, could be the material for poetry.[54]

Needless to say, this "precedent" influenced a major poem that intended to represent the sort of experience an adult had in a financial city in England. Eliot carefully phrased this lesson in terms of balanced doubleness—the "fusion" and "juxtaposition" of opposites, the "realistic" and "matter-of-fact" versus the "phantasmagoric" and "fantastic." The quotation also outlines how Eliot approached and defended himself against the sordid, urban reality by seeing it as material for art.

The city—evil, ugly, fascinating—captured Eliot's early awareness. He ransacked St. Louis, Boston, Paris, and London, retrieving images of a decaying, implicitly corrupt civilization. This search, however, set in motion a process that transfigured Eliot's poetry a second time, requiring a new literary model with a different sort of visionary precedent. As the Jacobeans and nineteenth-century French poets had satisfied Eliot's early poetic needs, so Dante ultimately guided his developing awareness of visionary poetry:

> The great poet should not only perceive and distinguish more clearly than other men, the colours or sounds within the range of ordinary vision or hearing; he should perceive vibrations beyond the range of ordinary men, and be able to make men see and hear more at each end than they could ever see without his help.... The Divine Comedy expresses everything in the way of emotion, between depravity's despair and the beatific vision, that man is capable of experiencing.[55]

What had once been ambiguities, precisely distinguished subtleties, and hardheaded ironies in Eliot's vocabulary have now become something new, and mystical. Now the poet not only sees more clearly what ordinary people see. He sees beyond ordinary things: He sees "vibrations." No word could more suitably distinguish Eliot at the close of his poetic career from his earliest attitude. Had Eliot encountered this notion of the poet's task in his late twenties, it is almost pleasant to imagine the firestorm of disdain such an indefinite, indefinable word as "vibrations" would have touched off. Yet three decades later, he could seriously and un-self-consciously propose it as an indicium of the poet's uniqueness. It was not the only one, of course, for simply seeing better, and seeing more, do not alone make a poet. The poet must return to earth, into society, using the language of his fellow human beings. Though his visionary self remains isolated, the poet must retain his social personality, expressing what he sees in a social—even democratic—medium. Without language, or an audience, the visionary act remains, from the poet's point of view, incomplete. The seer must also be a sayer. Dante constantly reminded Eliot of the poet's

> obligation to explore, to find words for the inarticulate, to capture those feelings which people can hardly even feel, because they have no words for them; and at the same time, a reminder that the explorer beyond the frontiers of ordinary consciousness will only be able to return and report to his fellow-citizens, if he has all the time a firm grasp upon the realities with which they are already acquainted.[56]

Each step along Eliot's journey from cynicism to vision involved a poetic hero, whose very flaws implied a heroic estimate of the poet's role, of his special abilities, and of his ethic. Eliot's introduction to *Adventures of Huckleberry Finn* sums up the values of these poetic heroes. Published in 1950, well after his major poems and criticism, this essay reflects an interesting engagement with a fellow Missourian. The essay is late in two senses; it is among Eliot's last major literary essays, and because Eliot's parents kept Twain's novel from him as a child, he apparently did not read it until middle age. Eliot's comparison of Tom and Huck nevertheless illuminates values that informed his poetry from its very beginning. It seems a particularly sweet irony that Eliot found the moral, ethical, and perceptual qualities of his visionary poetic hero distilled in a quintessentially American figure, Huck Finn.

Unlike Tom, whom Eliot calls "wholly a social being" with "imagination," Huck "has, instead, vision. He sees the real world; and he does not judge it—he allows it to judge itself.... Huck Finn is alone.... The fact that he has a father only emphasizes his loneliness; and he views his father with a terrifying detachment.... He is the impassive observer." Penetrating vision; nonjudgmental observation of a world that will convict itself; aloneness and loneliness; and a terrifying detachment: All these qualities set the stage for Eliot's central statement about Huck, which states Eliot's conclusions about his own poetry. "Huck is passive and impassive, apparently always the victim of events; and yet, in his acceptance of his world and of what it does to him and others, he is more powerful than his world, because he is more *aware* than any other person in it."[57]

The key figures in Eliot's early poetry—the speaker in "Preludes," Prufrock, Gerontion, Tiresias—all share this quality; all are somehow more "aware" than any other person they come into contact with. It would furthermore appear by analogy that the same analysis fixes Eliot vis-à-vis his poetic creations; the author is likewise more completely "aware" than his characters, even when they reflect aspects of his own moods, interests, and problems. Perhaps most crucially, passivity and victimization, instead of the products of powerlessness, become the means to power inasmuch as they permit a superior awareness, a more capacious, inclusive consciousness. The observer's detached passivity may subtract from his ability to act, but it adds to his ability to see, and thus to know. Hence even if knowledge is not necessarily power in the world, his superior awareness gives the poetic hero the power to prevail over it. Cynicism, by merely seeing through things, at first sees only disillusion. But having pierced the negative, the ugly, the compromised, seeing through may ultimately lead to insight, to understanding, to vision. The cynic feels he sees too much, too clearly; the visionary wants to see all he possibly can, as intensely as he can.

These values characterize not only Eliot's principal characters, and not only Eliot in relation to his own poems. They also describe Eliot's ideal reader. Given its unusual form, of no poem is this more true than *The Waste Land*. The poem's demands—collating the masks; establishing the relations part to part and part to whole; staying receptive to stylistic shifts and verbal nuance; and remaining detached throughout that process, lest the adoption of a final point of view obscure some relation or bar it from penetrating the consciousness—require the suspension of judgment and preservation of detachment, the *impersonality* and *surrender*, that become critical values not only in reading poetry, but in relation to life.

The Waste Land, then, and our relationship to it, reproduce consciousness, which boils down to the juxtapositions and fusions we arrange between things that have no relation other than that which we give them. Eliot's—and our, once we read and understand the poem—command of reality remains so much more complete than that of its scenes and characters that we and Eliot exist both privileged and burdened by the knowledge. This superior, if painful, consciousness—which includes as an axiom the awareness of how unconsciously most people behave—explains one of Eliot's characteristic emotions: arrogance mitigated by frustration, distance combined with sympathy, and acute regret that this knowledge, such as it is, compensates for the loss of innocence so meagerly. His characters—from "Preludes" forward—inhabit a more limited, less complete, and less conscious universe than Eliot, who appears at various moments to regard their omissions as both unforgivable and tragic.

Nowhere, however, does the method bear greater import than in *The Waste Land*, where a feeling of the dispiriting unreality of things coexists with a kind of voyeurism: observing people who are unaware of any scrutiny heightens the sense of real life while emphasizing the observer's detachment and inability to intervene. *The Waste Land*, then, lies beyond, but also within. It is finally a damaged or partial consciousness that has rendered the world and the self such deadly, boring, and futile places to be. By being an artifact and an allegory of self-consciousness (at equally a personal, aesthetic, historical, and social level), *The Waste Land* epitomizes its author's uniqueness, and his dilemma. Eliot's self-consciousness condemns the self to paralysis, but also may present it with irrevocable, privileged vision. Its ambiguities invite ambivalence, yet also characterize our modern consciousness and our historical time. They preserve Eliot as the characteristic poet of our age, with its curious spiritual demoralization amid material and erotic plenty, its tendency toward credulous emotion and overwrought intellect, and the loneliness of individuals stranded among its crowds. Eliot wrote with a deep doubt of progress insofar as the complexity of human endeavors outruns our capacity to comprehend and perhaps even to exist with them. Are we fated—or doomed—to discover if our self-consciousness can survive our creations? Eliot once wrote hypothetically that advanced, extreme self-consciousness, whether of language—as in the poetry of Valéry—or of indefinitely elaborated scientific, political, and social machinery, might produce a strain against the human nerves, and mind would rebel, producing an "irresistible revulsion of humanity and a readiness to accept the most primitive hardships rather than carry any longer the burden of modern civilization."[58] Has such a point been reached; does it approach; or has it already been surpassed?

Notes

1. See T. S. Eliot's Introduction to Ezra Pound, *Selected Poems* (London, Faber & Gwyer, 1928), p. viii, and E. J. H. Greene, "Jules Laforgue et T. S. Eliot," *Revue de Littérature Comparée*, July–September 1948, p. 365, quoting Eliot's October 18, 1939, letter.

2. T. S. Eliot, "[A Review of] *Baudelaire and the Symbolists: Five Essays*. By Peter Quennell," *Criterion*, January 1930, p. 357.

3. Arthur Symons, *The Symbolist Movement in Literature* (New York, Dutton, 1958), p. 56.

4. Conrad Aiken, "King Bolo and Others," in *T. S. Eliot: A Symposium*, ed. Richard March and Tambimuttu (Freeport, N.Y., Books for Libraries Press, 1968), pp. 20–1.

5. Conrad Aiken, "T. S. Eliot," *Life*, January 15, 1965, p. 92. Harford Powel, in "Notes on the Life of T. S. Eliot, 1888–1910," Master of Arts Thesis, Brown Univ., 1954, p. 42, confirms that Eliot "was something of a dandy in dress" at Harvard. According to a classmate, however, when Eliot attended Smith Academy, "he was always in need of a haircut" and was "rather careless about his clothes and linen" (p. 72). Eliot recorded his attempts to restrain his neighbors with his umbrella at a performance by Sokalova in "A Commentary," *Criterion*, October 1924, p. 5.

6. "*L'Imitation de Notre Dame de la Lune* includes forty-one poems, of which twenty-three deal with Pierrot and his ideas" (Martin Green, *Children of the Sun: A Narrative of "Decadence" in England after 1918* [New York, Basic Books, 19761, pp. 32–3). See also Warren Ramsey, *Jules Laforgue and the Ironic Inheritance* (New York, Oxford Univ. Press, 1953), pp. 140–6, and Robert F. Storey, *Pierrot: A Critical History of a Mask* (Princeton, N.J., Princeton Univ. Press, 1978).

7. Hugh Kenner, *A Homemade World: The American Modernist Writers* (New York, Morrow, 1975), p. 114.

8. Green, *Children of the Sun*, p. 94. Dandyism, aestheticism, and Symbolism nonetheless affected Pound, Faulkner, and Stevens considerably. See Kenner, *A Homemade World*, on Hemingway, esp. p. 152, and on Faulkner, pp. 195–8; and Daniel Fuchs, *The Comic Spirit of Wallace Stevens* (Durham, N.C., Duke Univ. Press, 1963), pp. 3–30.

9. Ellen Moers, *The Dandy: Brummell to Beerbohm* (Lincoln, Univ. of Nebraska Press, 1960), p. 283. Something about dandyism prefers the aftermath of a war. Parisian, distinctly Anglophile French dandyism began the year after Waterloo with Brummell's flight in disgrace to Calais. Perhaps the most widespread English dandyism (in a culture with an extraordinarily long tradition of it) transpired during the 1920s and 1930s as Green's *Children of the Sun* explores so imaginatively and thoroughly. That era observed a milder manifestation in America, presumably because the United States suffered less during World War I but also because of its deep-seated cultural reservations—understating the matter considerably—about dandy phenomena. Nonetheless, Eustace Tilley (complete with pince-nez, high collar, and top hat), the most famous symbol of American literary dandyism, appeared in 1925, when the *New Yorker* commenced publication. As Stanford M. Lyman and Marvin B. Scott discuss in *The Drama of Social Reality* (New York, Oxford Univ. Press, 1975), pp. 141–6, America created its own, less derivative dandyism after the Civil War, when ex-Confederate soldiers and, their sons spread dandyism through the American West as dispossessed but well-dressed *banditti*. The South still supplies America's best literary dandies, such as Tom Wolfe: "I used to solve writer's blocks by going out and getting clothes made, you could use up a lot of time that way" (Peter York, "Tom, Tom, the Farmer's Son," *Style Wars* [London, Sidgwick & Jackson, 1983], p. 225). Social strains—which included, in America at least, an unpopular war—in the late 1960s and early 1970s produced yet another phase of Anglo-American

dandyism. Its most dazzling and talented figure was David Bowie, whose life and personae pursue many patterns described here almost note for note.

10. "Mrs. Scratton had me to tea again, and ... she told me of a summer twilight in the Roman theater at Verona when, sitting between Pound and young Eliot, she had been startled and had said to Eliot, 'Why, you're rouged!' at which he had drawn from his pocket a woman's compact and shown it smiling. I felt the musing lady understood this to have been neither androgyny nor histrionics but something more exceptional and strange" (Robert Fitzgerald, "The Third Kind of Knowledge," *Atlantic*, June 1980, p. 80). Then there is the incident of the pale green face powder; see John Pearson, *Facades: Edith, Osbert, and Sacheverell Sitwell* (London, Macmillan, 1978), p. 239, and Pearson's references to Virginia Woolf's diary, p. 240. Whatever was going on at Verona, Eliot's writing otherwise cocks an eye at the tradition of the dandy, of Pierrot, of aesthetes, "decadents," and Symbolists, in whose lives a degree of sexual experimentalism or ambivalence frequently surfaces. Farther down the road, conversion to Christianity, particularly the more Catholic varieties (Eliot, by becoming an "anglo-catholic," winks at this tradition even as he places himself within it) seems to go with the territory.

11. "Baudelaire," *S.E.*, p. 423.

12. Ibid, pp. 423–4; emphasis added.

13. Jean Pierrot, *The Decadent Imagination, 1880–1900*, trans. Derek Coltman (Chicago, Univ. of Chicago Press, 1981), p. 45.

14. Examine the defiant sneer and indolent posture in Whistler's portrait of Count Robert de Montesquiou, whose vestigial cane has so withered that it has surrendered any value as either weapon or support. Montesquiou relied on his personality instead. Whistler directs the viewer's attention to the formal surface not only of his aristocratic subject, but of his portrait, which achieves the formally impossible—painting a man wearing a black suit on a black background. See also Philippe Jullian's *Prince of Aesthetes: Count Robert de Montesquiou, 1855–1921* (New York, Viking Press, 1967).

15. "Tradition and the Individual Talent," *S.E.*, p. 21. A passage from "Virgil and the Christian World," *O.P.P.*, pp. 122–3, reflects Eliot's awareness of the way rhetorical craft may transfer attention from the poet to his verse and shows Eliot reacting to the reaction to *The Waste Land*. A poet, Eliot explained, may think his poem expresses only his private experience, with the poetry providing a "means of talking about himself without giving himself away." Readers, however, may regard the same poem as expressing their own secret feelings and a generation's despair or exultation. Eliot's announcement of his classicism, royalism, and Anglo-Catholicism, for instance, doubtless surprised or angered many readers who had interpreted *The Waste Land* as an instrument with which to reject the past by asserting its irrelevance to the new world of the present day. Though their outrage proves it was not, their misreading should have been obvious well before Eliot's retrograde avowal. Such readers had reversed the terms of the poem's evaluation, which indicts the present by dramatizing its disregard of the past.

16. Moers, *The Dandy*, p. 18.

17. Ibid., p. 254, quoting Captain William Jesse's 1844 biography.

18. Ibid., p. 272.

19. See ibid., pp. 122–4, and Roger Shattuck, "How Poetry Got Its Teeth: Paris, 1857 and After," *Western Review*, Winter 1959, p. 179.

20. See Lawrence Stone, *The Crisis of the Aristocracy, 1558–1641* (New York, Oxford Univ. Press, 1965), p. 502, on how "Court" and "Country" came to mean political, psychological, and moral opposites.

21. See Theodore Zeldin, ed., *Conflicts in French Society: Anticlericalism, Education, and Morals in the Nineteenth Century* (London, Allen & Unwin, 1970). Consider also Edward Lucie-Smith, *Symbolist Art* (New York, Praeger, 1972), p. 54, linking snobbery, dandyism, and decadence to a series of refusals to participate in some event or acknowledge an individual and generalizing about the negative Symbolist emotional climate. Symbolism, Lucie-Smith writes, was a way of saying no to contemporary moralism, rationalism, and the "crass materialism" of the 1880s; of protesting the oppressive doctrines of naturalism; and of reacting to the defeat of France in the Franco-Prussian War and to the ensuing civil strife of the Commune.

22. "Andrew Marvell," *S.E.*, p. 296.

23. "The Metaphysical Poets," *S.E.*, pp. 289–90. In "Andrew Marvell," pp. 292–3, Eliot again links Donne with Baudelaire and Laforgue, apparently calling Donne as much a dandy as either French poet. Donne, like Baudelaire or Laforgue, invented an "attitude," which Eliot defines as a system of morals or of feeling. Eliot wrote that Donne's "curious personal point of view," appearing at one time, could appear at another time as the "precise concentration of a kind of feeling diffused in the air about him. Donne and his shroud, the shroud and his motive for wearing it, are inseparable, but they are not the same thing."

24. See Philippe Jullian's *Dreamers of Decadence: Symbolist Painters of the 1890's* (New York, Praeger, 1971), and *The Symbolists* (New York, Dutton, 1977); Lucie-Smith's *Symbolist Art*; Robert L. Delevoy's *Symbolists and Symbolism* (New York, Skira Rizzoli, 1978); James L. Kugel, *The Techniques of Strangeness in Symbolist Poetry* (New Haven, Conn., Yale Univ. Press, 1971); and Pierrot, *The Decadent Imagination*. Less helpful is Henry Peyre, *What Is Symbolism?* trans. Emmett Parker (University, Univ. of Alabama Press, 1980). See also a rare treatment of how Symbolist art influenced Americans, Charles C. Eldredge, *American Imagination and Symbolist Painting* (New York, New York Univ. Grey Art Gallery and Study Center, 1979); and Bram Dijkstra, *Idols of Perversity: Fantasies of Feminine Evil in Fin-de-Siècle Culture* (New York, Oxford Univ. Press, 1986), arguing that the modernist painters' formal experiments obscured their fidelity to the previous generation's imagery. Eliot's formally innovative poetry likewise incorporates much Symbolist iconography virtually unchanged.

25. Joseph Frank's "Spatial Form in Modern Literature," *The Widening Gyre: Crisis and Mastery in Modern Literature* (Bloomington, Indiana Univ. Press, 1968), remains an important discussion of these ideas, although his comments on Eliot sometimes falter. A better discussion is "Dialectical Form," Chapter 3 of Anne C. Bolgan's *What the Thunder Really Said: A Retrospective Essay on the Making of "The Waste Land"* (Montreal, McGill-Queen's Univ. Press, 1973). Significantly, her chapter analogizes modern literature with the cinema—a twentieth-century permutation on the ancient relation between poetry and the visual arts. Johannes Fabricius, in *The Unconscious and Mr. Eliot* (Copenhagen, Nyt Nordisk Forlag Arnold Busck, 1967), pp. 30–46, also discusses montage, *The Waste Land*, and the "third thing." *The Diary of Virginia Woolf*, ed. Anne Olivier Bell (London, Hogarth Press, 1978), vol. 2, pp. 67–8, records: "I taxed him with willfully concealing his transitions. [Eliot) said that explanation is unnecessary. If you put it in, you dilute the facts. You should feel these without explanation." Charles Feidelson's *Symbolism and American Literature* (Chicago, Univ. of Chicago Press, 1953), pp. 49–76, also bears on these issues. Eliot's writing illustrates Feidelson's conclusion that "mid-nineteenth-century America was a proving ground for the issues to which the method of modern literature is an answer" (pp. 75–6). Feidelson's remarks are crucial to understanding that however far Eliot extended his search to European sources, the origins of his dualistic, divided sensibility

remained in the American tradition. See especially "Toward Melville: Some Versions of Emerson."

26. *K.E.P.*, p. 100.

27. Compare the echoes between lines 19–30 and 331–58, for instance, or between lines 99–103 and 203–6.

28. Harold Wentworth and Stuart Berg Flexner, *The Dictionary of American Slang*, 2d ed. (New York, Crowell, 1975), p. 579.

29. *N.S.F.B.*, p. 19.

30. See Bertrand Russell's March 27, 1914, letter to Ottoline Morrell, quoted in *Ottoline: The Early Memoirs of Lady Ottoline Morrell*, ed. Robert Gathorne-Hardy (London, Faber & Faber, 1963), p. 257; but see further information of Raphael Demos, who took his degree in 1916, later becoming a professor at Harvard, in *The Autobiography of Bertrand Russell, 1872–1914* (London, Allen & Unwin, 1967), p. 212.

31. *The Waste Land: A Facsimile and Transcript*, ed. Valerie Eliot (New York, Harcourt Brace Jovanovich, 1971), p. 147.

32. *Seaver v. Lindsay Light Co.* (1922) 135 N.E. 329, 330; see also *C. Groom, Ltd. v. Barber* (1914) 1 K.B. 316, 323–4; *Tregelles v. Sewell* (1862) 158 E.R. 600, 604; and *Smith Co. v. Moscahlades* (1920) 183 N.Y.S. 500, 503.

33. Eliot began in the Foreign and Colonial Department of Lloyds Bank, prosaically tabulating balance sheets of foreign banks to show their relative annual performance but seeking to learn "something about the science of money." He was later promoted to settling the bank's prewar German claims and debts, more sophisticated work involving international law and the peace treaties. He ultimately represented the bank in provincial industrial centers, edited a daily sheet of commercial and financial extracts from the foreign press, and wrote a monthly article on foreign currency exchange for *Lloyds Bank Economic Review*. Eliot recalled spending his time at the bank dealing with "sight drafts, acceptances, bills of lading, and such mysteries, and eventually writing articles on the movement of foreign exchanges for the bank magazine" (*On Poetry* [An Address ... on the Occasion of the Twenty-fifth Anniversary of Concord Academy] [Concord Academy, Mass., 1947], p. 7). See also *The Waste Land: A Facsimile and Transcript*, pp. xi–xii, xviii, xx, and xxviii; Donald Gallup, *T. S. Eliot: A Bibliography* (London, Faber & Faber, 1969), p. 363; and Michael Holroyd, *Lytton Strachey: A Critical Biography* (New York, Holt, Rinehart & Winston, 1968), vol. 2, p. 365.

For the story of Henry Ware Eliot's business problems, see his "Brief Autobiography" (William Greenleaf Eliot Papers, Washington Univ. Libraries, Saint Louis, Mo., n.d.), p. 57 and appended autograph of Henry W. Eliot, Sr., on the last unnumbered page of "The Reminiscences of a Simpleton."

34. Two related senses of "corpse" might be mentioned: the literary corpus, the body of an author's work; and the corpus of a trust, the principal or trust *res*, from which the beneficiary receives the income. Having inherited only the beneficial interest in his father's estate in 1919, Eliot felt the effects of this division of a financial corpus into legal and equitable title. His siblings received their share outright, but because Eliot's father disapproved of his residence in England, the principal of Eliot's legacy reverted to his family upon his death, leaving his wife, should he have predeceased her, without the income. This was another reason Eliot cited for staying at the bank, bound to the wheel of commerce (*The Waste Land: A Facsimile and Transcript*, pp. xxvii–xxviii).

35. Wentworth and Flexner, *The Dictionary of American Slang*, p. 395: Plant: "To bury, as a corpse; to bury or cache an object, goods, or money. Since 1860." On Eliot's "Gothic"

language in *The Waste Land*, see Michael H. Levenson, *A Genealogy of Modernism: A Study of English Literary Doctrine, 1908–1922* (Cambridge Univ. Press, 1986), p. 174.

36. T. S. Eliot, "London Letter," *Dial*, May 1921, pp. 690–1; reprinted by permission of Mrs. Valerie Eliot and Faber & Faber Ltd. By 1928, Eliot was even lamenting the loss of "good," "grave," and "agreeable" bank buildings in this quarter and their replacement by "grander," "expensive and smart" ones. See "City, City," in "A Commentary," *Criterion*, December 1928, pp. 189–90. Betjeman's observation occurs in John Betjeman, *The City of London Churches* (London, Pitkin Pictorials, 1969), p. 22.

37. "Death By Water" not only renders the final paragraph of "Dans le Restaurant," it also makes some submerged allusions to "Burbank with a Baedeker: Bleistein with a Cigar." A fragment not included in *The Waste Land*, "Dirge" embeds the deceased Bleistein in a Gothic parody of Ariel's song from *The Tempest*. See *The Waste Land: A Facsimile and Transcript*, p. 121. "Burbank," after some "defunctive music undersea," placed Bleistein—like Phlebas—in the "protozoic slime." "Dirge" deposits him "full fathom five." "Those are pearls that were his eyes" in *The Tempest* and *The Waste Land*; in "Burbank," combining Eugenides' single eye and ironically comparing the live Bleistein to the pearls in the dead Phlebas' eyes, Bleistein singly stares with a "lustreless protrusive eye."

38. *The Waste Land: A Facsimile and Transcript*, pp. 50–1.

39. See Chapter 13, "The Perilous Chapel," in Jessie L. Weston, *From Ritual to Romance* (New York, Anchor, 1957), pp. 175–88.

40. Levenson, *A Genealogy of Modernism*, p. 200.

40a. Compare Rev. William G. Eliot, *Discourses on the Doctrines of Christianity* (Boston, American Unitarian Assoc., 1881), pp. 128–9: "We do not believe in an instantaneous and miraculous change, by virtue of which he who is at one moment totally depraved can become in the next one of God's saints.... We have greater confidence in the change which comes through the quietness of thought. It may promise less at first, but will accomplish more in the end. It may be accompanied with less of the rapture of religious triumph, but it is more likely to bring us to that peace which passeth all understanding."

41. Eliot wrote that Bradley's Absolute responded only to an imaginary demand of thought and satisfied only an imaginary demand of feeling. Though it pretended to make finite centres cohere, in the end it turned out to be merely the assertion that they do. "This assertion," Eliot concluded, "is only true so far as we here and now find it to be so" ("Leibniz' Monads and Bradley's Finite Centres," *K.E.P.*, p. 202).

42. T. S. Eliot, "London Letter," *Dial*, September 1921, p. 453.

43. See T. S. Eliot's November 6, 1921, letter to Richard Aldington from Lausanne, Switzerland, where Eliot was undergoing psychological treatment from Dr. Roger Vittoz, quoted in *The Waste Land: A Facsimile and Transcript*, p. xxii.

44. On the "single-protagonist theory," see Robert Langbaum, "New Modes of Characterization in *The Waste Land*," in *Eliot in His Time: Essays on the Occasion of the Fiftieth Anniversary of "The Waste Land,"* ed. A. Walton Litz (Princeton, N.J., Princeton Univ. Press, 1973); Stanley Sultan, *Ulysses, "The Waste Land," and Modernism: A Jubilee Study* (Port Washington, N.Y., Kennikat Press, 1977); and Calvin Bedient, *He Do the Police in Different Voices: "The Waste Land" and Its Protagonist* (Chicago, Univ. of Chicago Press, 1986). But see Levenson, *A Genealogy of Modernism*, pp. 186–93.

45. "Conclusion," *U.P.U.C.*, p. 151.

46. "Matthew Arnold," *U.P.U.C.*, pp. 113–14; reprinted by permission of Faber & Faber Ltd.

47. *N.T.D.C.*, p. 72.

48. "Nebula": "Andrew Marvell," *S.E.*, p. 300; "tentacular roots": "Ben Jonson," *S.E.*, p. 155; "undertone": "John Ford," *S.E.*, p. 203; "doubleness": "John Marston," *S.E.*, p. 229.

49. "Ben Jonson," *S.E.*, p. 158.

50. T. S. Eliot, "The Method of Mr. Pound," *Athenaeum*, October 24, 1919, p. 1065.

51. T. S. Eliot, Preface to St. John Perse, *Anabasis* (New York, Harcourt Brace, 1949), p. 10; reprinted by permission of Faber & Faber Ltd. Compare *K.E.P.*, p. 75, disagreeing that a great poet's ideas were arbitrary. By contrast, in "really great imaginative work," logical necessity bound up the connections, and any apparent irrelevance stemmed from the poet's use of terms with "more or other than their normal meaning, and to those who do not thoroughly penetrate their significance the relation between the aesthetic expansion and the objects expressed is not visible."

52. *U.P.U.C.*, p. 106.

53. "Baudelaire," *S.E.*, p. 426.

54. "What Dante Means To Me," *T.C.C.*, p. 126; reprinted by permission of Faber & Faber Ltd. Symons's *The Symbolist Movement in Literature*, p. 59, further suggests what the French tradition gave Eliot's earliest work. Even through his disdain for the world, Symons wrote, Laforgue retained a heightened consciousness of daily life, seeing "*l'Inconscient* in every gesture," but unable to see it without these gestures. Compare T. S. Eliot, "Eeldrop and Appleplex," *Little Review*, May 1917, p. 8, describing Eeldrop—Eliot's persona in the story—as "a sceptic, with a taste for mysticism."

55. "What Dante Means to Me," *T.C.C.*, p. 134; reprinted by permission of Faber & Faber Ltd.

56. Ibid.; reprinted by permission of Faber & Faber Ltd.

57. T. S. Eliot, Introduction to Samuel L. Clemens, *The Adventures of Huckleberry Finn* (London, Cresset Press, 1950), pp. viii–x; reprinted by permission of Faber & Faber Ltd.

58. "From Poe to Valéry," *T.C.C.*, p. 42.

JO ELLEN GREEN KAISER

Disciplining The Waste Land, *or How to Lead Critics into Temptation*

> I must admit that I am, on one conspicuous occasion, not guiltless of having led critics into temptation.
>
> —T. S. Eliot, "The Frontiers of Criticism"

In what is still the best-known review of *The Waste Land*, Edmund Wilson in 1922 assured readers of *The Dial* that they would find T. S. Eliot's long poem "intelligible at first reading." Yet, in the course of arguing for the poem's intelligibility, Wilson used Eliot's own as yet unpublished notes to *The Waste Land* to explain the poem's "complicated correspondences." Wilson may have been the first to use the notes to negotiate his way through the poem, but he certainly has not been the last critic to have been "led into temptation." As Eliot acknowledged in "The Frontiers of Criticism," his 1956 essay from which my epigraph and title are taken, his notes "have had almost greater popularity than the poem itself," such that "now they can never be unstuck" (110).

Eliot's own explanation in "The Frontiers of Criticism" of his notes' genesis and influence must be taken with a large grain of salt, but it is worth reviewing nonetheless:

> The notes to *The Waste Land*! I had at first intended only to put down all the references for my quotations, with a view to spiking

---

From *Twentieth Century Literature* vol. 44, no. 1 (Spring 1998), pp. 82–99.

> the guns of critics of my earlier poems who had accused me of plagiarism. Then, when it came time to print *The Waste Land* as a little book—for the poem on its first appearance in *The Dial* and in *The Criterion* had no notes whatever—it was discovered that the poem was inconveniently short, so I set to work to expand the notes, in order to provide a few more pages of printed matter, with the result that they became the remarkable exposition of bogus scholarship that is still on view to-day. (109)

Eliot's contention that the notes were added only because his poem "was inconveniently short" has been disproved. We now know that Eliot had the notes in mind before he began serious negotiations with his eventual publisher, Liveright, and that he had finished composing them several months before the poem first appeared in *The Dial*.[1] Eliot's description of the notes as a "remarkable exposition of bogus scholarship," however, should be taken more seriously. As Peter Middleton stated so concisely almost a decade ago, "academic interpretation of *The Waste Land* has gone straight along the paths laid out by those footnotes" because "*The Waste Land* is a ready-made academic poem with interpretations already included" (175, 176). The notes not only introduce a specifically academic discourse to the poem, but, at least until recently, they have also had the effect of encouraging professional literary critics to unify the poem's fragments along interpretive lines the notes themselves suggest.

What interests me, however, is how, when, and why the notes *stopped* being so effective at convincing critics that the poem is unified.[2] Unlike Middleton, who tends to view academic discourse as an unchanging instance of an ever more stable institution, I will argue that readings of the notes—and of the poem—have changed precisely because the notes represent a particular conflict in professional literary critical discourse in the 1920s. Beginning with Wilson's review, I argue that the notes have been successful in producing ordered readings of *The Waste Land* because they deflect the cultural crisis represented in the poem onto the act of reading, suggesting that the disorder seemingly so evident in the poem is in fact the fault of the reader. The notes particularly emphasize the readerly role of the professional literary critic, parodying the two theories of reading then dominant in the professional literary field, philology and impressionism. At the same time, however, the notes hold out the possibility that professional literary critics may be able to resolve the conflicts within their own discursive field and in so doing achieve the unified sensibility necessary for reconstructing the order apparently absent in the poem. In effect, the notes suggest that professional literary critics can use their expertise to resolve the crisis of modernity represented by the poem. This presumption of cultural power has swayed most professional readers of the poem until recently. Once poststructuralist theorists, however, began demonstrating that the expertise of the professional critic is a product of the very cultural crisis it is designed to overcome, the notes have ceased to have their unifying effect.

Unlike other early reviewers of magazine versions of Eliot's poem who had to make sense of *The Waste Land* on its own terms, Edmund Wilson had access to the poem's as yet unpublished notes.[3] Before reading the notes, Wilson believed *The Waste Land* to be "nothing more or less than a most distressingly moving account of Eliot's own agonized state of mind" (*Letter on Literature and Politics* 94). Wilson found the structurally fragmented poem representative of the "chaotic, irregular, fragmentary" experiences that Eliot, in his recent essay on "The Metaphysical Poets," had used to define the "disassociated" modern mind (247). After reading the notes in October and November, however, Wilson restructured his reading of the poem. By the time he published "The Poetry of Drouth" in December, he could write that "we feel that [Eliot] is speaking not only for a personal distress, but for the starvation of a whole civilization" (616).

As "the cry of a man on the verge of insanity," the poem Wilson first read enacted the very failure of modernity it critiqued. Following Zygmunt Bauman's account, I define *modernity* as the political and socioeconomic episteme that became dominant during the seventeenth century and may be characterized by its desire for order.[4] This desire for order, however, continuously deconstructs itself, as the very imperative to "set my lands in order" assumes as its foundational ground the presence of chaos. Eliot's poem, by expressing this central dilemma, marks a significant moment of crisis in the history of modernity. Faced with the impossible task of formulating a totalizing order, the poem's speakers, like the modern inhabitants of the everyday world they represent, fragment their world into increasingly smaller segments in an attempt to achieve a local order (e.g., "If there were water / And no rock / If there were rock / and also water"). Yet the more the world—and the poem—is catalogued, divided, fragmented, the more insistent becomes the pervasive sense of disorder. Read in this way, the poem suggests the postmodern possibility that the individual's relation to the world, and to him or herself, is fundamentally ambiguous and obscure. In this postmodern, poststructuralist reading, Eliot's poem is indeed what Wilson had early termed a "cry *de profundis*, "a profound demonstration of the deconstruction not only of individual identity but also of the fundamental categories through which the individual in modernity has heretofore understood the world.

At first glance, Wilson's revised account of the poem as a representation of "our whole world of strained nerves and shattered institutions" seems only to underscore this poststructuralist reading. Yet Wilson does not believe that the representation of disorder necessitates a reconsideration of the quest for order. In his review of *The Waste Land*, Wilson asserts that the poem's apparent lack of "structural unity" is belied by "the force of intense emotion" that "provide[s] a key" to the poem's organization. In arguing for the ultimate order of Eliot's poem, Wilson is drawing on Eliot's own discussions of the craft of poetry in "Tradition and the Individual Talent" (1919) and "The Metaphysical Poets" (1921). According to Eliot, the best poets do not express their "personal emotions," but rather "transmute the passions" into an impersonal emotion, "forming new wholes" out of ordinary feelings and experiences ("Tradition" 8; "Metaphysical" 247). Those who succeed in marrying thought and feeling in this way are said by Eliot to possess a "unified sensibility." That possessing such a unified sensibility would lead to the creation of better poetry was a point already made by Ezra Pound and the imagists, who argued that presenting "an intellectual and emotional complex in an instant of time" was the ultimate aim of art (Pound 4). Wilson evokes this imagist aesthetic when he explains that Eliot's lines might "be wrung from flint ... broken and sometimes infinitely tiny," but that they are nonetheless "authentic crystals." Like crystals, the bewilderingly multifaceted nature of the poem's lines are proof for Wilson of the strength of the underlying sensibility that orders the poem.

The notes to *The Waste Land* reinforced Wilson's emerging belief that modernist literature had an order, if only the critic would look for it. Although Wilson does not acknowledge in his review that he had access to the notes, he paraphrases and sometimes quotes many of them directly to piece together a unified reading of Eliot's poem.[5] Most importantly, where Wilson previously believed that *The Waste Land* was simply a reflection of a disordered mind, he now paraphrases Eliot's headnote to define what he later calls the "key" to the poem: "Mr. Eliot asserts that he derived [the] title, as well as the plan of the poem 'and much of the incidental symbolism,' from a book by Miss Jessie L. Weston called *From Ritual to Romance*" (611). Wilson proceeds to describe Weston's version of the grail quest, in which a knightly questor must find the grail to renew a sterile land ruled by an impotent king, then draws on the notes to trace images of this "waste land" through the poem. The grail quest becomes the "key" to the poem, Wilson asserts, because this "concrete image of a spiritual drouth" enables Eliot to hear "in his own parched cry the voices of all the thirsty men of the past" and so transmute his personal despair into an expression of the sensibility of his "civilization." Thus, although Wilson claims at the end of his review that the poem's unified sensibility implies the connections made in the notes, he uses the notes at the start of his review to make the case for the existence of the poem's unified sensibility.

Wilson's reading, in hindsight, became paradigmatic for several generations of critics who have found ample evidence for the poem's unity in the notes. The genealogy of such readings can be traced from Wilson through Cleanth Brooks to Calvin Bedient, who in 1986 argued that the many voices of the poem are united by a nameless protagonist who disguises his faith with an ironic expression of disorder. All of these critics have used Eliot's notes to make their argument, even when such a use conflicted with their own theoretical methodology. Cleanth Brooks, for example, known for his description of poems as autonomous, organic wholes, admits in his essay on *The Waste Land* that he finds himself unable to resist using Eliot's notes to construct what he acknowledges to be a "scaffolding" of understanding around the poem. Although he realizes that he may "rely too much on Eliot's note[s]" (154), he finds it impossible to understand the poem without them.

How can we understand the power the notes have had to suggest that *The Waste Land* is, in the end, an orderly poem? The simplest answer is that the notes invite such a reading. It is the notes that insist that the poem has a "plan"; it is the notes that assert that the plan is based on the grail legend; it is the notes that suggest that the poem has one questor, Tiresias, in whom all the other characters "meet." As Hugh Kenner pointed out long ago, without the notes few readers would come to the same conclusions. For example, the only specific reference to the grail legend is in section V (the "empty chapel" of line 389), and the impotent Fisher King himself appears only in section III (where he is associated with Ferdinand of Shakespeare's *The Tempest*) and at the end of section V. Compared to the pervasive emphasis on the city as a locus of corruption, or even to the recurrent trope of Ariel's song, the grail quest appears at most a minor theme when considered without reference to the notes.

That the notes provide the means for unifying the poem does not, however, explain why they have had the power to do so. Many poets have annotated their texts—one thinks readily, to give just a few examples, of Spenser's "Shepheard's Calendar," Pope's "Dunciad Variorum," Byron's "Childe Harold," and more recently of James Merrill's "Yanina"—yet few such annotations have governed critical textual response in the way Eliot's notes have governed *The Waste Land*. Unlike Middleton, who suggests that all "footnotes are an institutional extension of the filing system for useful retrieval and recording of the institution's decisions" (175) and thus dictate how the text they annotate should be read, I believe that the discourses in which paratexts like the notes to *The Waste Land* participate must be understood within their own specific—and conflicted—historical contexts. Eliot's notes have served institutional purposes, but not because they simply "record institution's decisions." Indeed, if the notes did stand in for "the academy," then poststructuralist literary critics who have questioned the notes (including myself) would have to be understood as writing from a standpoint somehow outside of that same academy, a position I find untenable. Readings of the notes have changed, not because poststructuralists have somehow managed to free themselves from institutional constraints but because the notes represent a particular conflict in the professional literary critical discourse of the 1920s which no longer governs professional literary critical discourse today.

Today, professional literary criticism is practically synonymous with academic criticism, the few exceptions proving the rule. In the 20s, however, the term "professional literary critic" could include both academic critics and men of letters like Edmund Wilson, who had little use for universities or organizations like the MLA but who still made his living from his expertise in literary criticism. Throughout the first half of this century, both academic and nonacademic literary critics alike were grappling with the crisis of modernity while simultaneously attempting to establish literary study as a professional field.[6] In doing so, they faced a peculiarly difficult problem. Modern culture was in crisis precisely because the rational, ordered universe it both produced and depended on had begun to unravel under the signature of such influential authors as Nietzsche, Freud, and Einstein. Yet, the literary critic's claim to professional status in the 20s was based on that critic's ability to provide a systematic method for ordering the literary text.[7] If the crisis of modernity had put the very possibility of ordering any text into question, what could distinguish the literary critic as a professional? Professional literary critics thus needed to find a way to resolve, or at least evade, the crisis of modernity in order to establish their own credentials.

Eliot's notes, by representing his poem as a unified and orderly whole, already performed the very maneuver professional literary critics sought to enact by shifting the central issues of the poem from questions of modernity to questions of interpretation. For although the poem radically questions the possibility of order, and thus the foundations of modernity, the notes assume that order not only can be achieved but already exists. While at least one speaker of the poem knows only "a heap of broken images," the author of the notes knows that the poem has a "purpose" and a "plan." The notes thus fundamentally change the reader's orientation to the poem. Like Wilson, readers who at first reading of the poem are confronted with a deconstruction of the very idea of order (a cry *de profundis*) find in the notes that the problem is not metaphysical after all but hermeneutic. The reader is asked to shift focus from considering the very possibility that order, as a concept, has failed, to considering how this poem is—or can be—ordered. In effect, when faced with the poem's "difficulties," the reader is told to become a better reader rather than to investigate the foundational source for his or her readerly discomfort.

The note to Tiresias provides a capsule example of this discursive shift. Tiresias, Eliot tells us in this famous note, "although a mere spectator and not indeed a 'character,' is yet the most important personage in the poem, uniting all the rest." We can see how this sentence redirects the reader from questions of order to questions of reading. Perhaps the most troubling aspect of the poem is its multiplicity of voices, a cacophony that refuses to follow any singular narrative line. Some of that trouble is reflected in this sentence, as the author searches for a descriptive term for the voice Tiresias names. Is he a spectator, a character, or a personage? If a spectator, what is the spectacle? If a character, in what play? These questions of narrative order are raised, however, only to be deflected by the central claim that, whatever Tiresias may be called, he unites all the rest. The question we are led to ask is no longer whether the characters in the poem are organized in any meaningful way, but how they are organized. How does Tiresias unite all the "personages" of the poem? More to the point, how did we miss his unifying role? Are there perhaps other unifying features we missed? The hermeneutic circle thus begun, the project of modernity is allowed to continue.

The note to the Tarot deck provides an even clearer example, not only of how this shift from a crisis of order to a crisis of reading occurs in the notes but also of why pursuing this interpretive move was so attractive to previous generations of professional literary critics. The Tarot cards enter the poem through the figure of Madame Sosostris, a fortune-teller whose name links her to the transvestite character in Aldous Huxley's *Chrome Yellow*. By the usual literary conventions, Sosostris appears to be an unreliable, even comic, speaker in the poem; a clairvoyant whose vision is clouded by her "bad cold," she stands as another lost figure in the "unreal city." Her attempt to tell the future, an endeavor that assumes that the future is fixed and thus knowable, parodies the modern quest to find predictable order. In this quest, Sosostris fails. She cannot see far enough into the future to protect the horoscope she brings to "Mrs. Equitone," nor can she even see the meaning of all of her cards. She can "not find" the Hanged Man, and she advises her client to "Fear death by water," even though the waste land is plagued by drought, and the speaker of the poem's climactic fifth section waits for rain. Sosostris's advice is not necessarily bad; Phlebas the Phoenician does experience a possibly unhappy "death by water" in section IV. That, however, is precisely the point. Sosostris is wrong not in warning her client to fear water, but in masking the complicated, ambivalent role water plays in the waste land. What her comic advice underscores is the impossibility of formulating a coherent plan of action predicated on an ordered world.

Rather than focusing on the larger questions Sosostris's horoscope raises, however, this note, like the note on Tiresias, deflects our attention by suggesting that an ordered reading of the cards is, indeed, possible. Where a reader uneducated by the notes might ask whether formulating any "horoscope" is feasible in an uncertain world, the reader who follows the notes is instructed to overcome the comic disorder of Sosostris's predictions in order to find the "real" order they conceal. The note to the Tarot card implies that telling the future is possible, and advises us that Sosostris's horoscope accurately foreshadows the order of the poem, if only we know how to read it. We are told to look for the one-eyed merchant, the Phoenician Sailor and "Death by Water" later in the poem, where they appear, respectively, in part III as "Mr. Eugenides," and in part IV as "Phlebas the Phoenician" whose "Death by Water" is recounted. Despite Sosostris's own inability to find him, "The Hanged Man" is associated with the "Hanged God of Frazer," and thus with both the risen Christ the disciples see on their way to Emmaus (in part V) and with the grail quest (via the spiritual death of the King and his land's rebirth anticipated in that myth). The effect of the note is to demonstrate a method of reading that distinguishes between significant and insignificant references on the assumption that the seemingly heterogeneous images of the poem are unified by a few important themes.[8] This "elucidative method," as Eliot calls it in his headnote, orders the poem.

Not only does this method suggest a means of unifying the poem, it does so by using a language peculiar to early twentieth-century professional literary criticism. As I stated above, I do not mean that notes are or have become a distinctly academic form. Rather, the Tarot note in particular, and the notes to *The Waste Land* in general, encode a conflict then raging in professional literary criticism between philology and impressionism. Impressionism was based on Pater's claim that art can only be experienced subjectively, and on Arnold's belief in literature as the prime conveyor of a culture's spiritual values. In practice, impressionistic critics would offer their personal responses to works of art, believing that their refined sensibilities as members of an Arnoldian remnant would reveal the spiritual truths of the work before them. As literary studies became increasingly professionalized and localized in universities, however, impressionism was gradually supplanted by philology and its related forms of scholarship.[9] Originally based in linguistics, philology was developed in German universities as a scientific method using literary texts to study the history of language. Gradually, however, literary scholars, following the French critic Hippolyte Taine, became more interested in the historical background of the text than in the language in which the text was written. American philology essentially combined German philological methods with Taine's historical interest to develop a scientific study of literary sources.

Eliot's note on the Tarot deck is premised on the reader's ability to reconcile the author's personal impressions with the more "objective" citation style he uses, to reconcile, that is, the impressionistic and philological methods. Like many of the scholarly academic notes with which we are still familiar today, the Tarot note instructs the reader to examine other sources—namely, Frazer's *The Golden Bough* and the *New Testament*—in order to comprehend the full meaning of individual Tarot cards. At the same time, however, Eliot admits that he "is not familiar with the exact constitution of the Tarot pack," that he has "departed from the pack to suit [his] own convenience," and that some of his referential associations are made "arbitrarily," such as his claim that "The Man with Three Staves" is the "Fisher King." Two very different constructions of textual understanding are at play here, one based on the philologist's scientific use of annotation and citation to record evidence for textual arguments, the other based on the impressionist's intuition of the author's motives and desires to enhance the reader's pleasure in reading. Neither method, on its own, is apparently sufficient to "elucidate" the poem.

In fact, as represented in the notes, both philological and impressionistic inquiry can come to seem rather comical. Ever since the poem was published in book form, many commentators have noticed that the notes have a distinctly parodic quality.[10] In 1923, for example, one of Eliot's antagonists at Cambridge, the Renaissance scholar F. L. Lucas, attacked the notes in his review of the poem as being "as muddled as they are incomplete":

> What is the use of explaining 'laquearia' by quoting two lines of Latin containing the word, which will convey nothing to those who do not know that language, and nothing new to those who do? What is the use of giving a quotation from Ovid which begins in the middle of a sentence, without reference? And when one person hails another on London Bridge as having been with him 'at Mylae,' how is the non-classical reader to guess that this is the name of a Punic sea-fight in which a Phoenician sailor, presumably, the speaker, had taken part? (117)

Lucas quite rightly perceives that many of the notes (especially those beginning "Cf." [compare with] or "V" [see]) have the form of philological citations, but then do not deliver the appropriate scholarly information. References that would be obvious to most educated readers of Eliot's day, like the parodied lines from Marvell, are noted, while quite obscure references to Joyce, Lyly, and Kipling, among others, are omitted.[11] References to a given author and work are noted in one place, yet not in another; for example, references to Shakespeare's *Tempest* are noted for lines 192 and 257, but not for lines 48 and 125. Sources for passages in foreign or classical languages are given in those languages, which is hardly helpful for the person who does not have enough learning to recognize the passage in the first place. Obscure references to classical or historical situations are not noted, yet Eliot will take pains to describe the origins of a common ballad or the species of singing bird he has in mind. Finally, Eliot at times seems to mislead the reader deliberately, as in line 360, where he sends the reader off to investigate a "delusion" by one member of an Antarctic expedition "that there was *one more member* than could actually be counted," rather than noting the more relevant New Testament passages describing the journey to Emmaus. In short, these notes certainly do not fulfill the philological imperative of giving readers "all the references for my quotations."

At the same time, the notes hardly satisfy the expectations for impressionism that they also raise. A paradigmatic example of an impressionistic note comes at line 68, where the speaker, instead of citing the apocryphal tale in which Christ's crucifixion is said to have occurred on "the final stroke of nine," informs us that this sound was "a phenomenon which I have often noticed." Other references to the speaker's experience rather than to a textual source occur in the notes to lines 199, 210, 221, 264, and 360 (the hermit-thrush note arguably includes aspects of both philological and impressionistic discourse). In each of these cases, any source the author might mention is given not as a reference but as an impression of his experience, and thus an indication of its aesthetic value. The problem with these notes, and the source of their parodic quality, is that they ultimately refuse to give us access to the author. The impressionistic critic longs for biography—such as Coleridge's account of taking opium before writing "Kubla Khan"—yet the potentially biographical nature of these notes is itself too fragmented to be of much use. Tellingly, while Eliot's biographers have found a rich vein of material in the drafts to *The Waste Land*, they have, for the most part, left the notes to the poem alone.

The comic failure of either the philological or the impressionistic notes to have content commensurate with their theoretical objectives reflects Eliot's growing distaste for either method, a distaste he shared with many of his contemporaries.[12] His most direct criticism of philology and impressionism occurs in an important but unanthologized review essay titled "Reflections on Contemporary Poetry," which he wrote for *The Egoist* in 1917. In the second part of that essay, he complains that an otherwise well-written study of the Scottish writer John Davidson suffers from the author's inability to find an alternative to the two dominant modes of contemporary literary criticism: "In avoiding the sort of thesis subject which demands merely detective manipulation of small facts," Eliot writes, "[the author] Mr. Fineman tends to the only alternative in University criticism—aerial generalization" ("Reflections II" 133). Eliot here is not arguing that critics should never be concerned with facts, or that critics should never generalize. Rather, what concerns Eliot is that philologists are only concerned with "thought," and impressionists are only concerned with "feeling." In short, Eliot felt that most of the contemporary criticism he was reading reflected precisely the disassociated sensibility that he already had observed in contemporary poetry.

Indeed, an argument could be made that Eliot's goal throughout his career as an essayist was to correct the disassociated sensibility he continued to see in literary criticism. In the Clark Lectures of 1926, for example, Eliot explains that the Cambridge don and the "artisan critic" (i.e., men of letters like Eliot himself) are really not as different as they might appear. "The speculative critic," he writes,

> refines and intellectualizes our enjoyment, heightens, not destroys, the keeness of our immediate and irreflective apprehension; establishes standards which create a demand for the highest form of art, and so affects production. And the artisan critic, whose aim is production and novelty, production of the *best* possible, and novelty because we can only capture the enduring by perpetual movement and adaptation, must also adopt disinterestedness in the pursuit of such kind of truth as exists in his material. (45)

The don starts from thought, but must anticipate and increase feeling; the artisan starts from feeling, but must adopt the disinterested thought of the scholar. In each case, thought and feeling must be unified if great work and great criticism are to be produced. As late as 1956, Eliot was reiterating these same concerns, in perhaps his clearest formulation:

> If in literary criticism, we place all the emphasis upon *understanding*, we are in danger of slipping from understanding to

> mere explanation. We are in danger of pursuing criticism as if it were a science, which it never can be. If, on the other hand, we over-emphasize *enjoyment*, we will tend to fall into the subjective and impressionistic, and our enjoyment will profit us no more than mere amusement and pastime. ("Frontiers" 117)

Over and over again in his essays, Eliot argues that critics must neither privilege a scientific, scholarly understanding of literature nor the impressionistic, subjective enjoyment of literature, but must somehow reassociate thought and feeling to form a unified critical sensibility.

This function of criticism is all the more important in an age of disassociated sensibility. Although he liked to think of himself as a poet first, then a critic, Eliot suggests in these essays that criticism is better equipped than poetry to reassociate the modern sensibility. For Eliot, poetry can only be great when it transcends individual emotion and expresses "the mind of a whole people," the common tradition that unifies the great works of the past with the culture of the present. In an age of disassociated sensibility, however, that common tradition is precisely what is lost, as society fragments into particulars, rather than joining into wholes. It is in such an age, Eliot writes in *The Use of Poetry and the Use of Criticism*, when criticism is most needed: "The important moment for the development of criticism seems to be the time when poetry ceases to be the expression of the mind of a whole people" (12). In effect, criticism must supplement poetry by reconstructing the unified sensibility the poet both needs and lacks. In the mind of "The Perfect Critic," Eliot writes in 1920, critical perceptions will "form themselves as a structure; and criticism is the statement in language of this structure; it is a development of sensibility" (58). Here, it is criticism, rather than poetry itself, which leads to the development of sensibility. That thought is echoed in the quote from the Clark lectures above. Significantly, it is the speculative critic who makes great art possible; it is he who "establishes standards which create a demand for the highest form of art, and so affects production." The artisan is able to produce "the best possible" only once the speculative critic has done this cultural work.

Faced with the crisis of modernity, Eliot in the early 20s looked to criticism, rather than to poetry, to reunite the disassociated sensibility of his age. In this light, the function of the notes to *The Waste Land* and the source of their rhetorical effectiveness for professional literary critics become much clearer. *The Waste Land* is a poem that demonstrates that the poetry of modernity has ceased to be "the expression of the mind of a whole people." The notes reveal the same disarray in the critical field by parodying the oppositional strategies of philology and impressionism. Yet, the notes also suggest that these critical methods can be joined. To fully "elucidate" his poem, Eliot insists, the reader of the notes must be receptive to both the philological and the impressionistic annotations he offers; we must be able both to perceive that a line alludes to Sappho and that the allusion "may not appear as exact as Sappho's lines," since the poet "had in mind" a slightly different scene (see note to line 221). The notes hold out the possibility that if critics would only become better readers, learning how to find formal unity in the poem's apparent chaos, the poem's wishful ending might in fact be realized as the fragments coalesce into a "peace which passeth understanding."

The notes thus not only appeal to the language of professional literary criticism but also represent the discourse of professional literary criticism as the best and perhaps the only solution to the crisis of modernity. What the notes do not do, however, is describe exactly how professional literary critics might achieve a unity of thought and feeling, philology and impressionism. Instead, the implication of the notes is that professional literary critics will be able to realize this unified sensibility through the proper exercise of their expertise. It is by suggesting this faith in professional literary critical expertise that the notes reassert the possibility of an ordered world in a poem that everywhere denies that order.

The note to line 309 provides a good example of the way in which the notes call on the expert reader to establish an order lacking in the poem. This note refers to the end of section III, where the song of the three Thames daughters dissolves into fragments from Augustine's *Confessions* and Buddha's *Fire Sermon*. It reads, "From St. Augustine's *Confessions* again. The collocation of these two representatives of eastern and western asceticism, as the culmination of this part of the poem, is no accident." As with the headnote on Jessie Weston, this note encourages us to believe that the poem has a definite order: Not only are the references to Augustine and Buddha "no accident," but also the note suggests they are "the culmination" of a greater plan. Yet we are not told what the plan is, or how the metonymic "collocation" of east and west may be understood symbolically as a metaphor for "this part of the poem." Instead, what the note to line 309 offers is a new kind of faith, a faith in the reader's ability to recreate a common tradition out of his or her expert knowledge of the past.

Early in his career, Eliot had believed the roles of poet and critic to be so closely related that he insisted, in essays like "Professionalism, Or ...," that the poet was a professional literary critic, and should be treated as such. By 1956 however, Eliot was arguing that his criticism was only "a by-product of my private poetry workshop," and not at all the same as that produced by the professional critic. Eliot could disassociate his poetic work from his critical work in these later essays because he no longer needed or wanted to invest criticism with the charge of reunifying the disassociated sensibility of his age. Eliot had begun to resolve the crisis of modernity for himself as early as 1926, when he gradually began to place his hope for order in the Anglican Church.[13] Once converted, Eliot continued to believe that critics should attempt to overcome an increasingly disassociated sensibility by encouraging both "understanding" and "enjoyment." However, he had come to the conclusion that only religious faith—in particular, his brand of Christianity—could restore a common culture and an ordered tradition.

Professional literary critics in the 50s, however, still based their claim to professional status on their ability to provide a systematic method for ordering the literary text, and thus still had a stake in the faith in criticism the notes offered. Indeed, the New Criticism, for which Eliot held himself partly responsible, emphasized the critic's role in ferreting out the underlying unity of the literary work. In 1956, Eliot saw the result of having led such critics into temptation, and was not pleased with what he saw. In the 20s, he confessed, he had been more worried about the impressionists than the philologists ("Frontiers" 117). My guess is that the notes, while introducing both impressionism and philology, were meant to tip the balance a bit towards the philologists. By the 50s, however, academic scholars had largely replaced the traditional men of letters, and Eliot thought these new academics read the notes with altogether too much understanding and not enough enjoyment. "My notes," he writes, "stimulated the wrong kind of interest among the seekers of sources.... I regret having sent so many enquirers off on a wild goose chase after Tarot cards and the Holy Grail" ("Frontiers" 110). In "The Frontiers of Criticism," Eliot hoped to unstick the notes from the poem in order to once again balance out thought and feeling, understanding and enjoyment.

Eliot could not get rid of the notes, however, as he himself acknowledged. It has only been with the rise of poststructuralist theory that professional literary critics have been able to describe once again the sense of disorder *The Waste Land* evoked for many of the earliest readers of the poem. We no longer need to look to the notes to order the poem for us, because the basis of literary professionalism itself has undergone a significant change. Understanding what Sam Weber has called "the limits of professionalism," we no longer feel compelled to "discover" the underlying unity of any literary work. The notes to *The Waste Land* remain important, however, precisely because they reveal the stake professional literary critics have had in continuing the project of modernity. Seeking to validate their expertise, professional literary critics responded to the suggestion, expressed in the notes, that the project of modernity and the project of professional literary criticism were one and the same. Providing a sense of order for the profession and for the poem became synonymous goals. Ironically, however, this made the notes a necessary supplement, underscoring the lack of order in a poem they were designed to correct, the conflicted nature of a literary professionalism they were designed to support. The notes, now, can never be unstuck. Rather, they should be read as a reiteration of the very crisis of modernity that the poem represents, a reiteration that illuminates how embedded professional literary discourse has been in the cultural situations it has sought to transcend.

Notes

1. Stanley Sultan has put together a convincing chronology of the notes in his *Eliot, Joyce and Company* (see particularly the chapter "Ulysses and *The Waste Land*"). Sultan concludes that the notes were complete before any publication, but "were withheld from a prior periodical publication to protect the value of the book" (143).

2. Since Middleton published his essay in 1986, Eliot's poem increasingly has been read as a postmodern work expressing a negative hermeneutics. The first critical reading of *The Waste Land* as a postmodern text was Ruth Nevo's in 1985, although Gregory Jay and Andrew Ross had already signaled that direction, and Harriet Davidson developed it more fully in her *T. S. Eliot and Hermeneutics* of the same year. Such poststructuralist readings have become mainstream: Among the best is Michael North's, who reads the poem as reflecting, rather than resolving, the fragmentation it records.

3. Ronald Bush gives a complete account of Wilson's engagement with Eliot's text in "T. S. Eliot and Modernism at the Present Time: A Provocation." I am indebted to his suggestion there that the history of Wilson's reading of the poem and its notes provide a clue to our own reception of the poem.

4. See Bauman's *Postmodern Ethics*, especially p. 8. For an excellent overview of the ever-shifting definitions of the concept of modernism, see Astradur Eysteinsson's book by that title.

5. For example, Wilson's list of the "voices of all the thirsty men of the past" is based on references made in the notes to passages from Ecclesiastes, the journey to Emmaus, the Buddha's *Fire Sermon*, Dante's *Inferno*, Webster's dirge, and so forth. Wilson's view that Tiresias is "in the centre of the poem" undoubtedly owes a debt to Eliot's note fingering Tiresias as "the most important personage in the poem," while his claim that the nightingale in the mantel's painted panel belongs in Milton's paradise is so far-fetched that he can only have gotten it from Eliot's cryptic note to Milton's "sylvan scene."

6. A large literature has been written in the last decade on the role of professionalization in shaping literary studies, starting with Graff's *Professing Literature: An Institutional History*. The collection of essays Graff edited with Micnael Warner, *The Origins of Literary Studies in America*, is especially useful for analyzing the rhetoric of early disciplinary battles. For a more general overview of the development of the American university, see Veysey's *The Emergence of the American University*. Similarly, for a general overview of the history of professionalization in the United States, see Bledstein's *The Culture of Professionalism*. Finally, Bourdieu, while focusing on the French academy, gives a good theoretical account of academic professionalism in particular in *Homo Academicus*.

7. See Graff, chs. 8 and 9. Golding also makes this point in the context of his discussion of New Critical readings of *The Waste Land*.

8. For an example of a reader who became engrossed in the method the Tarot deck offers, see Creekmore's "The Tarot Fortune in *The Waste Land*."

9. Wilson's attack on the MLA in 1968 provides an excellent example of the response of an impressionist/man of letters to philologists/academics. The date of his pamphlet is a good reminder of just how long this particular conflict lasted.

10. Among those who have noted the parodic quality of the notes, most, beginning with F. O. Matthiessen, have proceeded to demonstrate that what at first appeared irrelevant is actually relevant by pointing toward some important theme in the poem. That is, just as some readers have argued that the poem's fragmentary voices can be united in a thematic whole, these critics have argued that the notes' parodic voices ultimately point to precisely those unifying themes. The latest critic to deal with the notes in depth has been Stanley Sultan, who disagrees with Matthiessen on several points. Yet even Sultan concludes that the "irrelevant material" that "certain notes contain" is "a playful device enabling Eliot to slip in statements that do real work in his poem" (173). In arguing that the notes are "functional play," Sultan assumes that the poem is unified and that the notes serve to illuminate its mythic themes. I am arguing that the poem is governed by a negative hermeneutic, and that the poem's unity is not revealed by the notes but is constituted by the notes.

11. Sultan has argued convincingly that in line 74, the "Dog" is based on Stephen's fox-dog in ch. 3 of *Ulysses* (138–39); Eliot gets his "jug jug jug" from Lyly's *Euphues*, as H.D. pointed out in her *By Avon River*. "O Tis the ravished nightingale / Jug jug jug terue she cryes...." In a footnote to his essay on Kipling in *On Poetry and Poets*, Eliot himself gives evidence that in line 380 we can hear overtones of both Kipling's *In the Same Boat*, "Suppose you were a violin string—vibrating—and someone put his finger on you," and his *The Finest Story in the World*, where he describes a "banjo string drawn tight."

12. In America, Eliot had learned from his mentor Irving Babbitt that the study of literature should be based neither on our impressionistic likes and dislikes nor on a scientific attempt to treat art as a natural object, but on our inner principle of restraint, which enables us to discern the authentic tradition from the "melange" of texts that have been produced (*New Laokoon* vii). Similarly, in Britain, men of letters like John Middleton Murry advocated a new, "truly aesthetic philosophy" that would guide critics to refine their powers of "discrimination" in an attempt to uncover the "organic" nature of art (*Aspects* 13). While Eliot rejected both Babbitt's and Murry's solutions (in "The Humanism of Irving Babbitt" and "The Function of Criticism," respectively), he was intent on finding an alternative to the two dominant modes of literary criticism.

A good source on Eliot's relationship to professional literary criticism is McDonald's *Learning to Be Modern*. Although I disagree with her view that Eliot uses *The Waste Land* as an education in relativism, I think she gives a good account of Eliot's complex response to Babbitt.

13. Peter Ackroyd does an excellent job of detailing the connection between Eliot's desire for order and his conversion to Anglicanism. See pages 160–61.

Works Cited

Ackroyd, Peter. *T. S. Eliot: A Life*. New York: Simon, 1984.

Babbitt, Irving. *The New Laokoon*. New York: Houghton, 1910.

Bauman, Zygmunt. *Postmodern Ethics*. Oxford: Blackwell, 1993.

Bedient, Calvin. *He Do the Police in Different Voices:* The Waste Land *and Its Protagonist.* Chicago: U of Chicago P, 1986.

Bledstein, Burton. *The Culture of Professionalism.* New York: Norton, 1978.

Bourdieu, Pierre. *Homo Academicus.* Trans. Peter Collier. Stanford: Stanford UP, 1988.

Brooks, Cleanth. *Modern Poetry and the Tradition.* Chapel Hill: U of North Carolina P, 1939.

Bush, Ronald. "T. S. Eliot and Modernism at the Present Time." *T. S. Eliot: The Modernist in History.* Ed. Ronald Bush. Cambridge: Cambridge UP, 1991.

Creekmore, Betsy. "The Tarot Fortune in *The Waste Land.*" *ELH* 49 (Winter 1982): 908–28.

Davidson, Harriet. *T. S. Eliot and Hermeneutics.* Baton Rouge: Louisiana State UP, 1985.

Eliot, T. S. "The Frontiers of Criticism." *On Poetry and Poets.* London: Faber, 1957. 103–21.

———. "The Metaphysical Poets." *Selected Essays.* New ed. New York: Harcourt, 1950. 241–51.

———. "The Perfect Critic." *Selected Prose of T. S. Eliot.* Ed. Frank Kermode. New York: Harcourt, 1975. 50–59.

———. "Professionalism, Or ..." *The Egoist* 5, 4 (Apr. 1918): 61.

———. "Reflections on Contemporary Poetry." *The Egoist* 4, 9 (Oct. 1917) 133–34.

———. "Tradition and the Individual Talent." *Selected Essays.* 3–12.

———. *The Use of Poetry and the Use of Criticism.* Cambridge: Harvard UP, 1933.

———. *The Varieties of Metaphysical Poetry.* Ed. R. Schuchard. New York: Harcourt, 1993.

———. *The Waste Land: A Facsimile and Transcript.* Ed. Valerie Eliot. New York: Harcourt, 1971.

Eysteinsson, Astradur. *The Concept of Modernism.* Ithaca: Cornell UP, 1990.

Golding, Alan. *From Outlaw to Classic: Canons in American Poetry.* Madison: U of Wisconsin P, 1995.

Graff, Gerald. *Professing Literature: An Institutional History.* Chicago: U of Chicago P, 1987.

Jay, Gregory. *T. S. Eliot and the Poetics of Literary History.* Baton Rouge: Louisiana State UP, 1983.

Kenner, Hugh. *The Invisible Poet.* New York: Ivan Obolensky, 1959.

Lucas, F. L. Review of *The Waste Land. New Statesman* 22 (3 Nov. 1923): 116–18.

Matthiessen, F. O. *The Achievement of T. S. Eliot,* 3rd ed. New York: Oxford UP, 1959.

McDonald, Gail. *Learning to Be Modern: Pound, Eliot and the American University.* Oxford: Oxford UP, 1993.

Middleton, Peter. "The Academic Development of *The Waste Land.*" *Demarcating the Disciplines.* Ed. with an introd. by Sam Weber. Minneapolis: U of Minnesota P, 1986. 153–80.

Murry, John Middleton. *Aspects of Literature.* New York: Knopf, 1920.

Nevo, Ruth. "*The Waste Land*: Ur-Text of Deconstruction." *T. S. Eliot: Modern Critical Views.* Ed. Harold Bloom. New York: Chelsea, 1985. 95–103.

North, Michael. *The Political Aesthetic of Yeats, Eliot, and Pound.* Cambridge: Cambridge UP, 1991.

Pound, Ezra. *Literary Essays of Ezra Pound.* New York: New Directions, 1935.

Ross, Andrew. "*The Waste Land* and the Fantasy of Interpretation." *Representations* 8 (Fall 1984): 134–58.

Sultan, Stanley. *Eliot, Joyce, and Company.* New York: Oxford UP, 1987.

Veysey, Laurence. *The Emergence of the American University.* Chicago: U of Chicago P, 1965.

Warner, Michael, and Gerald Graff. *The Origins of Literary Studies in America: A Documentary Anthology*. New York: Routledge, 1989.
Weber, Sam. "The Limits of Professionalism." *Institution and Interpretation*. Minneapolis: U of Minnesota P, 1987.
Wilson, Edmund. *Fruits of the MLA*. New York: The New York Review, 1968.
———. *Letter on Literature and Politics*. New York: Farrar, 1977.
———. "The Poetry of Drouth." *Dial* (Dec. 1922): 611–16.
———. "The Rag-bag of the Soul." *The Literary Review* (Nov. 25, 1922): 237–38.

Chronology

1888	Born Thomas Stearns Eliot on September 26 in St. Louis, Missouri to Henry Ware Eliot and Charlotte Eliot.
1898–1905	Attends Smith Academy in St. Louis. Puts out his own magazine, *Fireside*. Publishes poems in the *Smith Academy Record*.
1906	Enters Harvard University.
1908	Discovers Arthur Symons's *The Symbolist Movement in Literature*, where he reads the poetry of Jules Laforgue.
1909	Earns bachelor's degree.
1910–1911	Studies in France and Germany. Completes "The Love Song of J. Alfred Prufrock."
1911–1914	Studies as a graduate student at Harvard, working on the philosophy of Francis Herbert Bradley.
1915	World War I breaks out. Publishes "Prufrock" in *Poetry*. Marries Vivienne Haigh-Wood.
1916	Completes dissertation but never returns to Harvard for his degree.
1917	Begins work for Lloyd's Bank. *Prufrock and Other Observations* is published by the Egoist Press.
1920	Publishes *Poems* and *The Sacred Wood*.
1922	Wins the *Dial* Award for *The Waste Land*. Commences editorship of *The Criterion*.

1925	Publishes "The Hollow Men" in the *Dial.* Leaves Lloyd's Bank to become a director at Faber and Gwyer. Publishes *Poems 1909–1925.*
1927	Joins the Church of England and becomes a naturalized British citizen.
1930	"Ash Wednesday" is published by Faber and Faber. "Marina" published by Blackamore Press.
1932	Gives Charles Eliot Norton Lectures at Harvard. Publishes *Selected Essays 1917–1932.*
1933	Publishes *The Use of Poetry and the Use of Criticism.*
1934	Publishes *After the Strange Gods and The Rock.*
1935	Writes *Murder in the Cathedral.* Publishes *Poems,* 1909–1935.
1939	Writes *The Family Reunion.* Last issue of *The Criterion* appears.
1943	Publishes *Four Quartets.*
1945	Ezra Pound is arrested for pro-Fascist broadcasts in Rome. Eliot asks for public support from poets to stand by Pound.
1947	Vivienne Eliot dies in a nursing home.
1948	Receives the Nobel Prize for literature.
1952	*The Complete Poems and Plays 1909–1950* is published.
1953	*The Confidential Clerk* opens at the Edinburgh Festival.
1957	Marries Valerie Fletcher, his secretary. Publishes *On Poetry and Poets.*
1965	Eliot dies on January 4, at home in London.
1971	The original manuscript of *The Waste Land*, rediscovered in 1968, is published by Faber and Faber.

Contributors

HAROLD BLOOM is Sterling Professor of the Humanities at Yale University. He is the author of 30 books, including *Shelley's Mythmaking* (1959), *The Visionary Company* (1961), *Blake's Apocalypse* (1963), *Yeats* (1970), *A Map of Misreading* (1975), *Kabbalah and Criticism* (1975), *Agon: Toward a Theory of Revisionism* (1982), *The American Religion* (1992), *The Western Canon* (1994), and *Omens of Millennium: The Gnosis of Angels, Dreams, and Resurrection* (1996). *The Anxiety of Influence* (1973) sets forth Professor Bloom's provocative theory of the literary relationships between the great writers and their predecessors. His most recent books include *Shakespeare: The Invention of the Human* (1998), a 1998 National Book Award finalist, *How to Read and Why* (2000), *Genius: A Mosaic of One Hundred Exemplary Creative Minds* (2002), *Hamlet: Poem Unlimited* (2003), *Where Shall Wisdom Be Found?* (2004), and *Jesus and Yahweh: The Names Divine* (2005). In 1999, Professor Bloom received the prestigious American Academy of Arts and Letters Gold Medal for Criticism. He has also received the International Prize of Catalonia, the Alfonso Reyes Prize of Mexico, and the Hans Christian Andersen Bicentennial Prize of Denmark.

HUGH KENNER taught English at Johns Hopkins University and the University of Georgia. His many books include *The Pound Era*, *The Stoic Comedians*, *The Counterfeiters*, and *A Homemade World*.

ELEANOR COOK is professor of English at the University of Toronto. She is the author of *Poetry, Word-Play, and Word-War in Wallace Stevens*, and *Against Coercion: Games Poets Play*.

JAMES E. MILLER, JR. is Helen A. Regenstein Professor Emeritus of English at the University of Chicago. His books include *T. S. Eliot's Personal Waste Land*, *The American Quest for the Supreme Fiction: Whitman's Legacy in the Personal Epic*, and *Leaves of Grass: America's Lyric-Epic of Self and Democracy*.

GREGORY S. JAY is professor of English at the University of Wisconsin, Milwaukee. He is the author of *American Literature and the Culture Wars* and *T. S. Eliot and the Poetics of Literary History*.

CLEO MCNELLY KEARNS is the author of *T. S. Eliot and Indic Traditions*. She is associate professor of humanities at the New Jersey Institute of Technology.

LOUIS MENAND teaches at Harvard University. A regular contributor to the *New Yorker*, he is the author of *The Metaphysical Club*, which won a Pulitzer Prize in 2002.

JAMES LONGENBACH is Joseph Henry Gilmore Professor of English at the University of Rochester. His scholarly books include *The Resistance to Poetry* and *Modern Poetry after Modernism*. He is also the author of two collections of poetry: *Threshold* and *Fleet River*.

WAYNE KOESTENBAUM teaches at the City University of New York. He is the author of *Andy Warhol*, and *Cleavage: Essays on Sex, Stars, and Aesthetics*, and several collections of poetry.

ERIC W. SIGG is the author of *T. S. Eliot: A Study of the Early Critical Writings* and *California Public Gardens: A Visitor's Guide*.

JO ELLEN GREEN KAISER is a freelance publishing consultant and a Senior Editor at *Tikkun*. She has taught at the University of Kentucky and written numerous articles.

Bibliography

Ackroyd, Peter. *T. S. Eliot: A Life*. New York: Simon and Schuster, 1984.

Bedient, Calvin. *He Do the Police in Different Voices:* The Waste Land *and Its Protagonists*. Chicago: University of Chicago Press, 1987.

Behr, Caroline. *T. S. Eliot: A Chronology of His Life and Works*. New York: St. Martin's Press, 1983.

Bishop, Jonathan. "A Handful of Words: The Credibility of Language in *The Waste Land.*" *Texas Studies in Literature and Language* 27 (Summer 1985): 154–177.

Blasing, Mutlu Konuk. "*The Waste Land*: Gloss and Glossary." *Essays in Literature* 9 (1982): 97–105.

Braybrook, Neville, ed. *T. S. Eliot: A Symposium for His Seventieth Birthday*. New York: Farrar, Straus & Cudahy, 1958.

Bush, Ronald. *T. S. Eliot: A Study in Character and Style*. New York: Oxford University Press, 1983.

Childs, Donald. "Stetson in *The Waste Land.*" *Essays in Criticism* 38 (April 1988): 131–48.

Cook, Eleanor. "T. S. Eliot and the Carthaginian Peace." *ELH* 46 (1979): 341–355.

Cooper, John Xiros. *T. S. Eliot and the Politics of Voice: The Argument of* The Waste Land. Ann Arbor: UMI Research Press, 1987.

Cox, C. B., and Arnold P. Hinchcliffe, eds. *T. S. Eliot: The Waste Land*. Nashville: Aurora, 1970.

Douglas, Paul. "Reading the Wreckage: De-Encrypting Eliot's Aesthetics of Empire." *Twentieth Century Literature* 43 (Spring 1997): 1–26.

Drew, Elizabeth. *T. S. Eliot: The Design of His Poetry*. New York: Scribner's, 1949.

Erwin, Mark. "Wittgenstein and *The Waste Land*." *Philosophy and Literature* 21 (October 1997): 279–91.

Froula, Christine. "Eliot's Grail Quest: Or, the Lover, the Police, and *The Waste Land*." *Yale Review* 78 (Winter 1989): 235–253.

———. "Corpse, Monument, *Hypocrite Lecteur*: Text and Transference in the Reception of *The Waste Land*," *Text: An Interdisciplinary Annual of Textual Studies* 9 (1996): 304–314.

Gardner, Helen. *The Art of T. S. Eliot*. New York: E. P. Dutton, 1959.

Gilbert, Sandra. "'Rats Alley': The Great War, Modernism, and the (Anti)Pastoral Elegy." *New Literary History* 30 (Winter 1999): 179–201.

Gish, Nancy K. *Time in the Poetry of T. S. Eliot*. London: Macmillan, 1981.

Gordon, Lyndall. *Eliot's Early Years*. New York: Oxford University Press, 1977.

Grant, Michael. *T. S. Eliot: The Critical Heritage*. London: Routledge, 1982.

Harmon, William. "T. S. Eliot's Raids on the Inarticulate." *PMLA* 91 (1976): 450–459.

Houghton, R. L. "*The Waste Land* Revisited." *Cambridge Quarterly* 18 (1989): 34–62.

Jay, Gregory S. *T. S. Eliot and the Poetics of History*. Baton Rouge, LA: Louisiana State University Press, 1983.

Kearns, Cleo McNelly. *T. S. Eliot and Indic Traditions*. New York: Cambridge University Press, 1987.

Kenner, Hugh. *The Invisible Poet*. New York: Harcourt, Brace & World, 1959.

———, ed. *T. S. Eliot: A Collection of Critical Essays*. Englewood Cliffs, NJ: Prentice-Hall, 1962.

Kermode, Frank. *T. S. Eliot: An Appetite for Poetry*. Cambridge, MA: Harvard University Press, 1989

Knoll, Robert E., ed. *Storm over The Waste Land*. Chicago: Scott, Foresman, & Co., 1964.

Koestenbaum, Wayne. "*The Waste Land*: T. S. Eliot's and Ezra Pound's Collaboration on Hysteria." *Twentieth Century Literature* 34 (Summer 1988): 113–139.

Leavis, F. R. *New Bearings in English Poetry*. Ann Arbor: University of Michigan Press, 1960.

Levenson, Michael. "Does *The Waste Land* Have a Politics?" *Modernism/Modernity* 3 (1999): 1–13.

Lewis, Paul. "Life by Water: Characterization and Salvation in *The Waste Land*." *Mosaic* 11 (1978): 81–90.

Litz, A. Walton, ed. *Eliot in His Time*. Princeton, NJ: Princeton University Press, 1973.

Longenbach, James. "Hart Crane and T. S. Eliot: Poets in the Sacred Grove." *Denver Quarterly* 23 (Summer 1988): 82–103.

———. *Modernist Poetics of History*. Princeton, NJ: Princeton University Press, 1987.

March, Richard, and Timbimuttu, eds. *T. S. Eliot: A Symposium*. Chicago: Regnery, 1949.

Margolis, John D. *T. S. Eliot's Intellectual Development*. Chicago: University of Chicago Press, 1972.

Martin, Jay, ed. *A Collection of Critical Essays on "The Waste Land."* Englewood Cliffs, NJ: Prentice-Hall, 1968.

Matthiessen, F. O. *The Achievement of T. S. Eliot*. New York: Oxford University Press, 1958.

McGrath, F. C. "The Plan of *The Waste Land*." *Modern British Literature* 1 (Fall 1976): 22–34.

McGee, Daniel. "Dada Da Da: Sounding the Jew in Modernism." *English Literary History* 68 (Summer 2001): 501–527.

McRae, Shannon. "Glowed into Words: Vivien Eliot, Philomela, and the Poet's Tortured Corpse." *Twentieth Century Literature* 49 (Summer 2003): 193–218.

Menand, Louis. "T. S. Eliot After His Time." *Raritan* 8 (Fall 1988): 88–102.

Miller, J. Hillis. *Poets of Reality*. New York: Atheneum, 1969.

Miller, James. *T. S. Eliot's Personal Waste Land*. University Park, PA: Penn State University Press, 1977.

Moody, A. D. *The Waste Land in Different Voices*. London: Edward Arnold, 1974.

Pearce, Dan. "Repetition Compulsion and 'Undoing': T. S. Eliot's 'Anxiety of Influence.'" *Mosaic* 21 (Fall 1988): 45–54.

Rainey, Lawrence, ed. *The Annotated "Waste Land" with Eliot's Contemporary Prose*. New Haven: Yale University Press, 2005.

Rajan, Balachandra. *The Overwhelming Question*. Toronto: University of Toronto Press, 1976.

Riquelme, John Paul. "Withered Stumps of Time: Allusion, Reading, and Writing in 'The Waste Land.'" *Denver Quarterly* 15 (1981): 90–110.

Schneider, Elizabeth. *T. S. Eliot: The Pattern in the Carpet*. Berkeley: University of California Press, 1975.

Scott, Peter Dale. "Pound in *The Waste Land*, Eliot in *The Cantos*." *Paideuma* 19 (Winter 1990): 99–114.

Sicker, Philip. "The Belladonna: Eliot's Female Archetype in *The Waste Land*." *Twentieth Century Literature* 30 (Winter 1984): 420–431.

Sigg, Eric W. *The American T. S. Eliot*. New York: Cambridge University Press, 1989.

Smith, Grover. *T. S. Eliot's Poetry and Plays: A Study in Sources and Meaning*. Chicago: University of Chicago Press, 1956.

Southam, B. C. *A Guide to the Selected Poems of T. S. Eliot*. New York: Harcourt Brace Jovanovich, 1969.

Spanos, William V. "Repetition in *The Waste Land*: A Phenomenological Destruction." *Boundary 2* 7 (1979): 225–285.

Surette, Leon. "*The Waste Land* and Jessie Weston: A Reassessment." *Twentieth Century Literature* 34 (Summer 1988): 223–244.

Tate, Alison. "The Master Narrative of Modernism: Discourses of Gender and Class in *The Waste Land*." *Literature and History* 14 (Autumn 1988):160–171.

Tate, Allen, ed. *T. S. Eliot: The Man and His Work*. New York: Delta, 1966.

Trosman, Harry. "T. S. Eliot and *The Waste Land*: Psychopathological Antecedents and Transformations." *Archives of General Psychiatry* 30 (May 1974): 709–717.

Unger, Leonard. *T. S. Eliot: Moments and Patterns*. Minneapolis: University of Minnesota Press, 1956.

Uroff, Margaret Dickie. "*The Waste Land*: Metatext." *Centennial Review* 24 (1980): 148–166.

Vendler, Helen. "T. S. Eliot" in *Part of Nature, Part of Us*. Cambridge, MA: Harvard University Press, 1980.

Williamson, George. *A Reader's Guide to T. S. Eliot*. New York: Noonday Press, 1953.

Acknowledgments

"The Waste Land" by Hugh Kenner from *The Invisible Poet: T. S. Eliot*: 125–56. © 1959 by Hugh Kenner. Reprinted by permission.

"T. S. Eliot and the Carthaginian Peace" by Eleanor Cook from *English Literary History* 46 (1979): 341–55. © 1979 by The Johns Hopkins University Press. Reprinted with permission of The Johns Hopkins University Press.

"Personal Mood Transmuted into Epic" by James E. Miller from *The American Quest for a Supreme Fiction: Whitman's Legacy in the Personal Epic*: 101–25. © 1979 by the University of Chicago. Reprinted by permission.

"Discovering the Corpus" by Gregory S. Jay from *T. S. Eliot and the Poetics of Literary History*: 137–55. © 1983 by Louisiana State University Press. Reprinted by permission.

"Eliot, Russell, and Whitman: Realism, Politics, and Literary Persona in *The Waste Land*" by Cleo McNelly Kearns from *The Waste Land*, ed. Harold Bloom. © 1986 by Cleo McNelly Kearns. Reprinted by permission.

"Problems About Texts" by Louis Menand from *Discovering Modernism: T. S. Eliot and His Context*: 75–94. © 1987 by Oxford University Press, Inc. Reprinted by permission.

"*The Waste Land*: Beyond the Frontier" by James Longenbach from *Modernist Poetics of History: Pound, Eliot, and the Sense of the Past*: 200–37. © 1987 by Princeton University Press. Reprinted by permission of Princeton University Press.

"*The Waste Land*: T. S. Eliot's and Ezra Pound's Collaboration on Hysteria" by Wayne Koestenbaum from *Twentieth Century Literature* 34, no. 2 (Summer 1988): 113–39. © 1988 by Hofstra University. Reprinted by permission.

"Being Between Two Lives: Reading *The Waste Land*" by Eric W. Sigg from *The American T. S. Eliot: A Study of the Early Writings*: 185–218. © 1989 by Cambridge University Press. Reprinted with permission of Cambridge University Press.

"Disciplining *The Waste Land*, or How to Lead Critics into Temptation" by Jo Ellen Green Kaiser. From *Twentieth Century Literature* vol. 44, no. 1 (Spring 1998), pp. 82–99. © 1998 by Hofstra University. Reprinted by permission.

Every effort has been made to contact the owners of copyrighted material and secure copyright permission. Articles appearing in this volume generally appear much as they did in their original publication with few or no editorial changes. Those interested in locating the original source will find bibliographic information in the bibliography and acknowledgments sections of this volume.

Index